William Ross, Philadelphia Maritime Exchange

The Commercial Manual of Philadelphia

Issued under the auspices of the Maritime Exchange

William Ross, Philadelphia Maritime Exchange

The Commercial Manual of Philadelphia
Issued under the auspices of the Maritime Exchange

ISBN/EAN: 9783337117832

Printed in Europe, USA, Canada, Australia, Japan

Cover: Foto ©Suzi / pixelio.de

More available books at **www.hansebooks.com**

THE

COMMERCIAL MANUAL

OF

PHILADELPHIA,

ISSUED

UNDER THE AUSPICES OF THE MARITIME EXCHANGE.

EDITED BY WILLIAM ROSS.

PUBLISHED BY

BURK & McFETRIDGE, 306 AND 308 CHESTNUT ST.

PHILADELPHIA.

1886.

Press of Burk & McFetridge,
306-308 Chestnut St.

INTRODUCTION.

Since the publication of the first Shipping Manual of Philadelphia, six years ago, many changes in the laws, regulations, customs, forms, etc., have occurred, which have rendered it unreliable; and as it is likely to mislead those who require a correct reference-book of that character, and being fully aware of the importance to the shipping community of a Manual that would be of assistance and value to the rapidly increasing interests of the commercial public of this city, the undersigned has written and compiled this volume, which also embodies many features relating to some of the most prominent and extensive branches of industry of a commercial character established here, and which are powerful factors in promoting the general prosperity of the city.

As it was not considered absolutely necessary to confine the entire work to the customs and laws of one port only, it also embraces many matters that are of equal importance and value to the various maritime interests of the country, thus increasing its efficiency by extending the scope of its original limit, and at the same time giving a full and concise exposition of the subject-matter which was formerly the prime object of the first publication in 1880. This innovation will be found of special advantage to importers, exporters, ship owners, ship brokers and ship masters everywhere, being particularly adapted to the requirements of each. Much of the data which is the foundation of some of the subject matter under review, also many of the abstracts from Admiralty law, stowage, etc., have been obtained from the highest and best authorities, and may be confidently relied upon.

The Commercial Manual of Philadelphia is therefore offered in its present form, trusting that it will receive the indorsement of all those for whom it is issued, and to whom it is hereby respectfully dedicated.

Philadelphia, April, 1886.

WILLIAM ROSS, *Editor,*
Late Editor of the Maritime Manual.

BURK & McFETRIDGE,
Publishers.

CONTENTS.

1829.   CHARTER PERPETUAL.   1886.

Franklin Fire Insurance Company

OF PHILADELPHIA.

CAPITAL	$400,000 00
Insurance Reserve	1,779,731 25
Unpaid Losses and Dividends	38,134 22
Net Surplus	912,390 50
TOTAL ASSETS (January 1, 1886)	$3,130,255 97

OFFICERS.

JAS. W. McALLISTER, President.   *EZRA T. CRESSON, Secretary.*
FRANCIS F. STEEL, Vice-President.   *SAMUEL W. KAY, Assist. Secy.*

DIRECTORS.

JAS. W. McALLISTER,   JOHN WRIGHT,
ALFRED G. BAKER,   ALFRED FITLER,   GEORGE A. HEYL,   CHARLES M. SWAIN,
ISAAC LEA,   FRANCIS P. STEEL,   GEO. FALES BAKER,   CHARLES W. POTTS.

No. 421 WALNUT STREET.

UNITED STATES BRANCH

OF THE

LIVERPOOL AND LONDON AND GLOBE

INSURANCE COMPANY.

JANUARY 1, 1886.

Assets held in the United States		$5,924,010 83
All Liabilities		3,334,907 64
SURPLUS		2,589,103 19

INCOME IN 1885.

From premium receipts	$3,553,506 36	
From other sources	222,078 39	
Total		$3,775,584 75

EXPENDITURES.

Net amount paid for losses	$2,035,133 31	
Commissions, salaries and all other charges	804,270 16	
Amount paid for Taxes	86,374 65	
All other payments and expenditures	194,254 86	$3,120,032 98
Losses paid in the United States since organization		$37,468,135 57

J. E. PULSFORD, Resident Manager, N.Y. | Deputy Manager, HENRY W. EATON.
                                         Assist. Dep. Manager, GEO. W. HOYT.

Philadelphia Office { ATWOOD SMITH, GENERAL AGENT. } 333-337 Walnut St.

PHILADELPHIA AS A SHIPPING PORT.

Early in the history of the United States, Philadelphia occupied the first place as a commercial depot. The first shipment of American cotton goods to China was made from this port, and its trade with the East Indies was large and exceedingly profitable. Although at a somewhat later period there appears to have been a decline in the shipping trade, owing to causes of a general character which depressed business everywhere, considerable activity again sprung up about the year 1820, and from that time to the present day a steady growth has been manifested in all the branches of foreign trade, principally in the shipment of western cereals, breadstuffs, petroleum and coal, but including also the products of Philadelphia manufactories, which now bear an important part in meeting the demands of foreign countries as well as supplying the necessities of our own. The smallest value of the exports for one calendar year within the past sixty-five years was in 1843, which amounted to $2,354,948, and the largest value was $59,539,450 in 1876. As compared with the value of imports during the same period, goods to the amount of $3,760,630 came into this port in 1843, and $38,933,832 in 1880, and during the past ten years the total value of exports was $426,083,526, and imports, $284,575,745. From this it will easily be seen that Philadelphia holds an important position as a shipping port, and although one hundred miles from the sea, its comparatively greater distance from the principal foreign markets cannot be considered to its detriment in the least degree as compared with the geographical position of any other port, as its proximity to the West is fully as advantageous, and the navigation of the Delaware River easy, safe and with no special features of an objectionable nature. "Ice in the winter season" has always been a pet scarecrow regularly set up by jealous competitors for the tonnage of the world, to be knocked down by the three powerful city ice boats and the hundreds of tow boats which continually pass up and down the river in the dead of winter. With the means now employed to keep the river clear during the coldest days of the winter months— which, by the way, are few in number—the danger to navigation has been reduced to a minimum, and does not exceed that of any other northern port, and is even less than that of many ports claiming an open channel at all seasons. Forty-three lights at different points on the river act as aids to navigation, and regular navigators, whether by steam or sail, would never call into requisition the services of pilots if the existing laws did not make it compulsory.

The facilities for loading cargoes cannot be excelled. Steamers of the largest carrying capacity are loaded with grain at the elevators with surprising quickness. Ships are daily dispatched from the petroleum wharves with full cargoes for all parts of the world. American clippers may be seen at any time taking in general cargoes for San Francisco and the Pacific slope, while smaller vessels by the dozens are loading coal, cooperage, lumber and other merchandise for South America, West Indies and coastwise ports. Looking at the facilities which are offered for the transportation of western products to this port as a point for trans-Atlantic shipment, it is particularly noticeable that no port on the Atlantic coast possesses better advantages, as the railroad lines stretch out direct to all portions of the far West and bring merchandise of all descriptions to alongside vessels at tide water without breaking bulk; wharf and storage accommodations are complete; stevedores and laborers well skilled in their respective callings, are plentiful; a water front extending from Port Richmond on the Delaware, to Chestnut street wharf on the Schuylkill, with sufficient depth of water to float the largest ships offers excellent opportunities; and with the addition of a few more liberal minded and energetic shipping merchants with capital commensurate with the value of the foreign trade, the commerce of Philadelphia will doubtless increase beyond the most sanguine expectations of the shipping public of the present day.

The East India business is being revived, and the Calcutta and Bombay trade formerly so profitable, will probably again soon show good results. The imports from the British East Indies at this port during 1885 amounted to $230,113, and from the Philippine Islands $75,450.

Considerable interest is also manifested in the South American trade, and the importation of merchandise from the River Platte is opening a business which should continue to increase with the amount of energy displayed in working it to a successful issue. In connection with this project, it is generally conceded that so long as raw wool does not enter this country on as favorable terms as it does European countries, it is an obstacle to the sale of our manufactures in that portion of South America, and Europe consequently almost monopolizes the trade. Notwithstanding this, the large importation of the products of the La Plata States shows that successful efforts are being made to increase this trade, and the results must necessarily be beneficial to this port. Prosperity follows fast the efforts of the industries there located, and the purchasing capabilities of the people are thereby rapidly increasing, thus making them desirable customers for the products of our Philadelphia manufactories.

The desire for establishing new trading posts and opening commercial relations with ports heretofore neglected, is being shown by all the leading industrial nations, and although the business men and capitalists of this country are not making such extensive and wide-spread efforts as some of the European countries which are trying to build up a large business with the people of the interior of Africa, contesting the future trade of Indo-China, and extending railroads far into Burmah and Siam and other foreign lands effectually protected by miasma and half-civilized tribes, a more conservative view of new opportunities is being taken by the merchants, manufacturers and capitalists of this city which will probably in the near future show more satisfactory results, even if the proverbial element of Quakerdom tends, for the time being, to retard their movements. It is possible, however, that the American capital now being sent to China with the view of securing a share of the new concessions allowed foreigners, will result in the introduction of Philadelphia manufactured goods into the interior of that country by way of the projected railroad system now being perfected. Race prejudices and customs peculiar to the Orient, are not entirely impervious to the improvements and inventions of the present day, and in the radical changes going on in that strange country, Philadelphia enterprise will doubtless find an open market that will give employment to at least a portion of our merchant marine.

In the several articles relating to the Grain, Petroleum, Coal and other trades elsewhere presented in this volume, will be found detailed accounts of the extent of these several business enterprises, the facilities provided for successfully carrying them on, and the evidence of opportunities for even a larger volume of trade than is at present existing; but there are many other points which should be carefully considered. The inducements offered to shipping are valuable features which tend to increase the importance of Philadelphia as a shipping port. They consist in part of the dry-dock facilities; the excellent tow-boat system; the established connections of the Maritime Exchange with communicating points on the river and at Delaware Breakwater; the immense river front and wharf accommodations; the experienced corps of intelligent master stevedores; the comparative cheapness of all port charges; the quick dispatch at the grain elevators; the facilities for providing bunker coal to steamers at almost first cost; the opportunities for making repairs of any kind to hull, engines and boilers, and replenishing spars, rigging, sails, and all the necessary appointments of sail and steam tonnage; the prompt attention to the wants and requirements of the masters from all interested in their needs; and many other matters of a minor nature, but which take their proper place in making up the advantages which the port offers and affords to the entire maritime tonnage of the world.

There is no better dry-dock in the country than that belonging to William Cramp & Sons Company, of Philadelphia. It is known as "The William Cramp & Sons Ship and Engine Building

Company." They have two establishments, both on the Delaware river. At one of these, which has a frontage of 230 feet, and side line of 620 feet, is a machine and blacksmith shop, and marine railway capable of taking out vessels of 2000 tons register. There they have one of the largest basin-docks in the United States. The length is 462 feet, and can accommodate vessels 450 feet in length on a draft of 20 feet. The width is 111 feet. It has four centrifugal pumps, each having a lifting capacity of 30,000 gallons of water a minute, making an aggregate pumping capacity of 120,000 gallons a minute. This basin can be entirely freed of water in 45 minutes. The cost of this dock was $500,000.

The establishment at the foot of Norris street has a frontage of 750 feet, and is 700 feet in length. It is devoted to new work, such as iron and wooden hulls of vessels, and marine engines and boilers. Everything there is of the most improved pattern. A force of 2000 men is almost constantly kept employed by this company. It was founded in 1830, and for about thirty years was engaged in building wooden ships and steamboats. The famous iron-clad steam frigate New Ironsides, and many other iron-clad vessels were built there for the Government when its own yards were inadequate to turn out such work. Since the civil war they have been continually engaged in building iron steamships for the foreign and coastwise trades, and have furnished many extremely fine specimens. The four steamships of the American Line were built at this yard, also a number of iron screw steam colliers for the Philadelphia and Reading Coal and Iron Co., each of which is capable of carrying 1600 tons dead weight.

The sectional floating dry-docks of A. S. Simpson & Bro. at the foot of Christian street, have recently been improved and enlarged, which enables this firm to accommodate vessels of almost any size. These docks have been an established institution for many years, and are well known, not only along the Atlantic coast and among the Provinces, but in many parts of Europe, for the excellent and superior work turned out by the Simpsons. For hauling out, sheathing, re-sheathing, caulking and repairing vessels' bottoms, they are second to none, are extremely expeditious, employ only first-class workmen, and are moderate in their charges.

A. F. Kappella & Co., ship builders, have a yard at Petty's Island, opposite Port Richmond. They have a wharf frontage of 500 feet square on the Delaware river, with a depth of water of 20 feet; also a marine railway, capacity 500 tons, with saw mill, joiner and blacksmith shops, and every facility for building and repairing vessels.

There are many other first-class establishments, yards and docks for the building and repairing of vessels of all kinds, well located, easily accessible, and well patronized.

Capacious warehouses, bonded and free, are located near the water front, and afford safe storage for all classes of goods, both imported and domestic. The warehouses of Fitzpatrick & Pemberton are the largest and most complete, and are so built as to afford every possible accommodation, with the smallest minimum of risk, and with but light expense of handling and carting the goods. This is an important consideration to the importer.

The Philadelphia Warehouse Co. are always in position to make advances on any staple articles of commercial value stored in any Philadelphia warehouse.

The Philadelphia Transportation and Lighterage Co. have added largely to their facilities for transporting and forwarding goods of all kinds. Vessels requiring a part or whole of cargo to be removed into lighters and held therein, or carried to other points within the harbor precincts, are promptly looked after, and in case of bonded goods requiring transportation, this company's experience in such matters leaves but little to be attended to by the importer. They are the successors of the old house of Robert Patterson & Son, so long connected with this special branch of maritime business at this port, the same management being retained.

Lines of steamers connect the city with Liverpool, Antwerp, Glasgow, London, and other important European commercial centres, and also many seaboard ports of the United States.

A regular monthly line to San Francisco, composed of fast-sailing clipper ships, was established at this port a number of years ago, by Sutton & Co., the pioneer California shipping house of New York; and as shippers to the Pacific States are well aware of the advantages to them of shipping by the Sutton Line, either from Philadelphia or New York, all of the freight room is invariably taken up by the time the ships are placed in berth. The fact that shipments from the West, of agricultural implements, glass and stoneware, and other goods, are delivered by rail, by the Pennsylvania Railroad, directly alongside the ships here, and without re-handling and extra expense, makes this line especially desirable by Western shippers.

Girard Point on the Schuylkill is the seat of grain and provision shipments; Thurlow on the Delaware, and Point Breeze and Gibson's Point on the Schuylkill are the principal shipping points of petroleum; and at Port Richmond and Greenwich on the Delaware are found the loading piers of all the coal brought direct from the mines to Philadelphia.

The Girard Point Storage Co. have two grain elevators at Girard Point, where is stored grain coming over the Pennsylvania Railroad, and from which point it is delivered to steamers and other vessels, mostly for foreign markets. The capacity of Elevator " A " is 800,000 bushels, and of Elevator " B," 1,200,000 bushels. There is an elevator at Washington street wharf with a capacity of about 500,000 bushels, connected with the P. R. R., also used for the export trade. There is also an elevator at Port Richmond, at the terminal point of the Philadelphia and Reading Railroad, with a storage capacity of about 800,000 bushels, used for the export trade. For the local trade a large grain warehouse at West Philadelphia receives grain over the Pennsylvania Railroad, and an elevator on Twentieth street distributes from the cars of the Reading Railroad. The accommodations at the present time for the export trade are much beyond the requirements of shippers, this business having largely fallen off at this port during the past two or three years.

That a correct idea may be formed of the extent and value of the commerce of Philadelphia, abstracts from the official report of the business of the port for the year 1885 are herein presented. The total value of imports was $33,365,242, an increase of

$1,374,933 over 1884, and that of exports $37,281,739, an increase of $390,134 over the figures of the year preceding. The receipts of duties on imports were $13,801,190.61, and from other sources $114,363.05, making a total of $13,915,553.66, which was an increase of $1,385,101.80 over the receipts for 1884. The increase in collections is noteworthy from the fact that there were 347 less entries made during 1885 than in 1884, the total number for 1885 being 12,879. Over one-quarter of the business of the port, in the matter of importations, is represented by two items alone, sugar and molasses. The total value of these imports is $9,621,849, while the value of the entire imports is $33,365,242.

The principal items of imports, free of duty, and the values of the same, are as follows :—

Cinchona barks,	$761,503	Chemicals,	$260,912
Logwood,	184,891	Bananas,	103,638
Chloride of lime,	121,206	Raw goat-skins,	249,010
Licorice root,	120,124	Raw hides,	125,835
Sulphate of quinia,	176,970	Waste paper,	133,428
Nitrate of soda,	176,578	Silk waste,	111,951
Crude sulphur,	224,379	Bones,	202,053

The principal items of imports, subject to duty, and their value, are as follows :—

Art works,	$153,473	Wine in casks,	$101,530
Buttons,	151,387	Raw hemp,	239,659
182,635 lbs. of opium,		Burlaps,	403,882
valued at	388,223	Linens,	323,323
Soda ash,	639,104	Lemons,	190,896
Soda caustic,	205,826	Oranges,	268,345
Chemicals,	308,810	Prunes,	139,531
Colored cotton,	117,923	Raisins,	107,730
Cotton laces,	308,673	Hats, and material for	
Knit goods,	404,732	the same,	159,741
Pig iron,	400,037	Iron ore,	512,780
1,203,662 lbs. of bar iron,		Linseed,	420,632
valued at	21,560	16,187,933 gallons of	
4,627,312 lbs. of steel		molasses, valued at	1,884,328
ingots, valued at	52,797	16,586,282 lbs. of beet	
96,599,591 lbs. of tin		sugar, valued at	365,225
plates, valued at	3,057,153	255,059,957 lbs. of sugar	
Precious stones,	170,209	cane, valued at	7,372,296

Morocco, . .	235,612	339,573 lbs. of leaf to-	
Salt, ...	181,502	bacco, valued at . .	115,954
Cigars, ...	137,333	Ready-made clothing, .	106,031
Champagne, ...	81,293	Woolen cloths, . . .	467,531
Raw clothing wools, .	225,807	Dress goods, . . .	444,217
Raw combing wools, .	191,914	Yarns, ...	304,934
Raw carpet wools, . .	1,209,742	All other woolens,	948,895

In addition to these entries, goods valued at $3,010,287 were entered for immediate transportation in bond. The value of the imports by foreign vessels was $24,120,955, and by American vessels $9,244,287.

Petroleum shows a greater value than any other article of merchandise exported. Flour is next in value, or about one-third of that of petroleum, while wheat, corn and cotton follow successively, as may be seen by the following list of articles exported:—

Cattle, ...	$562,070	Manufactured tobacco, .	$121,382
Indian corn, ...	3,190,077	Lumber, ...	40,591
Corn meal, ...	53,515	Unmanufactured cotton,	2,676,101
Oats, ...	111,784	Hair, and manufactures	
Oatmeal, ...	60,373	of the same, . . .	75,436
Wheat, ...	3,218,198	Hides and skins, . . .	51,564
Wheat flour, ...	3,337,463	Hops, ...	238,950
Coal, anthracite, . . .	54,880	Lead, ...	11,047
Coal, bituminous, . .	198,910	Leather, patent or enam-	
Oil cake, ...	470,815	eled, ...	97,300
Crude mineral oils, . .	2,390,439	Salted or pickled beef, .	306,931
Naphtha, ...	373,836	Tallow, ...	261,996
Illuminating oil, . . .	9,288,128	Bacon, ...	2,618,817
Lubricating oil, . . .	64,454	Hams, ...	966,720
Residuum, ...	79,848	Pork, ...	24,950
Paraffine and paraffine		Lard, ...	791,712
wax, ...	164,036	Butter, ...	23,590
Canned beef, ...	232,471	Cheese, ...	97,519
Fresh beef, ...	1,002,430	Rags, ...	16,015
Seeds, ...	95,386	Hoops, ...	96,256
Soap, ...	53,641	Shooks, ...	96,210
Molasses and syrup, . .	484,397	Staves and headings, .	153,321
Refined sugar, . .	505,295	Empty hogsheads and	
Leaf tobacco, ...	1,685,201	barrels, ...	148,717

Regarding the nationality of the tonnage employed to carry these products to foreign markets, it is a notable fact that only 11 per cent. of the values was carried by American vessels.

Of the 22,747 immigrants landed at the port during the year, 7,683 were from England, 5,470 from Ireland, 2,367 from Germany, 1,475 from Scotland, 1,213 from Norway, 2,583 from Sweden.

The following list shows the values of goods exported to the several foreign countries, and it can be easily seen that the trade with some of them might be largely increased, if efforts were made in that direction. Many of the products of Philadelphia's manufacturing industries would find a ready market in foreign cities if agencies were established, and the value and utility of the goods properly represented.

England,	$17,091,958	British East Indies,	$133,115
Scotland,	3,437,003	Denmark,	128,456
Germany,	2,441,207	Dutch East Indies,	107,168
Belgium,	2,416,482	Sweden,	104,084
Ireland,	2,306,404	Greece,	89,364
Italy,	1,911,739	British Guiana,	82,452
France,	1,472,453	China,	77,996
Austria,	1,261,674	Norway,	45,269
Portugal,	978,934	Turkey,	30,669
Japan,	907,826	Danish West Indies,	26,306
Netherlands,	690,694	U. S. of Colombia,	21,039
Cuba,	671,030	Brazil,	14,686
Spain,	328,260	Nova Scotia,	10,181
British West Indies,	232,537	Venezuela,	1,900
Gibraltar,	183,952	British Possess'ns, add'l,	57,368

The following table gives the names of the several countries from which goods were imported, together with the value of such imports, and the amounts upon which duties were paid :—

	Free of Duty.	Subject to Duty.
Argentine Republic,	$129,466	$100,897
Austria,	242,868	24,470
Belgium,	301,146	969,602
Brazil,	....	424,265
Denmark,	12,331	11,435
Greenland,	110,750	....
Amount carried forward,	$796,561	$1,530,669

	Free of Duty.	Subject to Duty.
Amount brought forward, . .	$796,561	$1,530,669
French West Indies, ...	....	102,859
France, ...	347,129	1,455,245
Germany, ...	692,960	1,495,855
England, ...	2,227,764	10,906,834
Scotland, ...	22,604	974,451
Ireland, ...	....	45,480
Nova Scotia, ...	11,165	32,129
British West Indies, ...	172,725	734,631
British East Indies, ...	26,608	203,505
British Possessions in Africa, . .	140,490	29,557
Hayti, ...	146,962	152
Italy, ...	329,697	639,652
Netherlands, ...	114,803	146,083
Peru, ...	63,558	....
Portugal, ...	70,857	2,683
Spain, ...	6,210	534,580
Cuba, ...	61,287	7,972,687
Porto Rico, ...	....	273,245
Philippine Islands, ...	....	75,450
Sweden and Norway, ...	29,255	9,599
Switzerland, ...	2,642	90,447
Turkey in Europe, ...	....	283,289
Turkey in Asia, ...	121,534	141,584
Uruguay, ...	51,653	....
Venezuela, ...	2,628	....
Greece, ...	....	2,316
Mexico, ...	9,702	....
Hong Kong, ...	109	75
Japan, ...	527	3,743
Chili, ...	113,518	....
Cape Verde Islands, ...	....	88,699
China, ...	....	6
Dutch East Indies, ...	....	2,872
Arabia, ...	13,574	....
Total, ...	$5,586,797	$27,778,445

When the customs receipts and expenses of this port are compared with those of other prominent ports, it will be found that the cost of collecting duties here is comparatively small. At Boston it cost $699,342 last year to collect $19,610,577. In Philadelphia the cost of collecting $13,801,190 was $428,336.

In San Francisco the Customs officials required $422,808 out of $6,743,800. At Baltimore, where only $2,081,766 were collected, the amount necessary to leave behind was $300,911.

In comparison with the total value of the foreign commerce of the United States, Philadelphia makes a remarkably good showing. The value of exports from the United States for the fiscal year of 1885 was $742,000,000; of imports, $577,000,000; and of the in-transit and transhipment trade $68,000,000. This shows a falling off in the foreign trade of about $94,000,000, and at the same time there was a decline of $32,000,000 in the exports of gold. The decrease occurred mainly in the values of imports of sugar and molasses, silks, wool, and manufactures of silk and wool, and iron and steel and their manufactures. Great Britain not only takes about 60 per cent. of our agricultural and unmanufactured products, but also a larger share, amounting to 27 per cent., of our manufactures, than do Central America, the West Indies and South America combined. The total amount of duties collected on merchandise approximated $190,000,000 in 1884, but fell to $178,000,000 in 1885. Twenty-nine per cent. of this amount was collected on sugar and molasses, in which articles Philadelphia has largely dealt.

In order to show the extent of the trade of the United States with South America, Central America, the West India Islands, &c., during the year ended June 30, 1885, and the small proportion of this trade which Philadelphia has secured, and as an incentive for our merchants to make efforts to secure a larger share, the following table is inserted herein:—

Countries.	Imports.	Exports.
Brazil,	$45,263,660	$7,317,293
Venezuela,	6,309,580	3,043,609
Argentine Republic,	4,328,510	4,676,501
U. S. of Colombia,	2,342,077	5,583,369
Uruguay,	2,734,617	1,682,443
Chili,	604,525	2,211,007
Peru,	1,764,890	742,105
British Guiana,	921,354	1,640,657
Other South American countries,	1,020,743	538,855
Total, South America,	$65,289,956	$27,435,839

Countries.	Imports.	Exports.
Cuba and Porto Rico, ...	$48,410,356	$10,575,365
British West Indies, ...	10,363,381	7,210,879
Central America, ...	6,409,015	2,762,531
Hayti, ...	2,471,436	3,307,307
San Domingo, ...	1,461,419	986,701
Other West India Islands, . .	1,870,486	2,671,974
Mexico, ...	9,267,021	8,340,784
British Honduras, ...	218,360	369,753
Total West Indies, Central America and Mexico, . . .	$80,471,474	$36,225,294

Referring again to the geographical position of this city, and to show how thoroughly it is connected by navigable waters, and by lines of railroad with the Western grain fields, the oil and coal regions, and the Southern cotton States, and how perfect the arrangements are to satisfy all of the requirements of our merchants to insure superior advantages in the consummation of a successful competitive export trade, it is well to look at the established lines of communication by sea and land, with all the details of the same, their peculiar advantages of access with freight and distribution of merchandise, the numerous railroad branches leading out into every section of the city, where goods can be delivered and received at small cost to the manufacturer and merchant, either in the foreign or domestic trade; the close connection with other Lnes of railroads to all points inland and on the seaboard, and the easy approach to the discharging piers contiguous to the Government and private warehouses. In addition to the direct lines of railroads to the South there is the Ocean Steamship Company, of Savannah, which has a line of passenger and freight steamships to Savannah, at which port transhipments may be made at exceedingly light expense, to all points further south or inland, as desired; Clyde's Coastwise and West Indies Steam Lines to Boston, Providence, Fall River, New York, Washington, Charleston, Alexandria, and Havana; the Baltimore and Philadelphia Steamboat Daily Line, via Chesapeake and Delaware Canal, for freight and passengers; the Boston and Philadelphia Steamship Company's Line, of which the well-known firm of Henry Winsor

& Co. are agents, to Providence and Boston; the Lehigh Transportation Line, for forwarding freight on Lehigh and Delaware Canal, Union and Juniata Tidewater, and Pennsylvania Canal; the Philadelphia and Wilmington Steam Packets, for passengers and freight; the several packet lines to points above Philadelphia on the Delaware; etc., etc., etc.

The Pennsylvania Railroad system is, however, the principal source of transportation for all kinds of heavy and light merchandise for distribution or consumption at Philadelphia. The immense business transacted by this company is almost beyond the conception of the ordinary mind of man, and the question of how it is all managed with such little complication and confusion, is a puzzle to even the theorists. The managers of such an enormous conglomeration of freight and passenger traffic must be men especially fitted for such work, by practical experience and natural intuition. Philadelphia, as the great manufacturing and productive centre of the Union, is largely dependent upon the resources of this company for a continuance of its immense business relations with the rest of the world. It is the great artery which supplies the life-blood of trade to its numerous industries. Its lines of communication reach almost everywhere, and its hundreds of branches and sidings that are pushed into every quarter of the city, where the sound of the hammer and the forge is heard, and the noiseless shuttle of the weaver is accumulating the textile fabrics of the industrious manufacturer, gather the products of the mill, the work shop, the factory, and the forge, and carry them away to meet the wants of the great nation of consumers.

The total number of tons freight moved over the main line and branches of the Pennsylvania Railroad Co. during the year 1885 was 24,047,028, exclusive of 1,168,233 tons of fuel and material for the company's use. 2,257,180 tons were through freight, and 21,789 848 tons were local freight. This was an increase of 432,411 tons in through freight, and 1,030,792 tons in local freight.

Among the individual sidings connected with this road, and where tracks have been laid by the company to accommodate the business of the merchants of this city, are eleven sidings on the Kensington branch of the New York division, and six on the Connecting Railway. On the River Front Railroad are twelve sidings connected with the establishments of Wm. Cramp & Sons, I. P. Morris Co., the P. & R. R. R. pier, and coal, machinery, and rolling mills yards. On the Delaware extension are forty-two sidings, giving facilities for the transportation of goods from petroleum refineries, fertilizing works, salt manufactories, coal, wood and lumber yards, sugar and molasses refineries, storage warehouses, etc., etc. The Washington avenue track (Southwark R. R.) leads into the iron works, chemical works, coal and lumber yards, iron foundries, flour mills, ice depots, etc., of seventy-eight firms and companies; and on the Schuylkill river branch and Junction Railroad are seven sidings, including the branch to the extensive car works of W. C. Allison & Sons. Eighteen firms on the east side of Schuylkill river, between Chestnut street and South street bridges, have railroad connections, including several wholesale dealers and importers of marble, and ice and lumber companies who receive their stocks mostly by coastwise vessels, etc. On the east side, and below South street, are the wharves of the Atlantic Refining Co., at Point Breeze; and the Girard Point Elevators, at Girard Point. These alone represent the export trade of Philadelphia to the extent of millions annually, and their close connection with this road is extremely valuable to them. In addition to these are the chemical works of Harrison Bros. & Co., at Gray's Ferry, and a number of coal and ice companies. In all there are twenty-three sidings in this district. On the west side are eight sidings, all having water communications.

A branch line runs up Delaware avenue, connecting with all of the steamship lines, ferries, railroad stations, river steamers, salt works, ice companies, coal and lumber yards, marine railways, iron works, rolling mills, ship yards, storage warehouses, machine works, produce markets, sugar refineries, wood wharves, California packets, and thousands of business establishments, wholesale and retail dealers, commission merchants, oil works, the coal piers at Greenwich Point where colliers are loaded by Donaldson &

Thomas, Berwind, White & Co., the Gas Coal Companies and many other wholesale dealers, etc., etc.

Freight is received at the following stations:—Fifteenth and and Market streets, Thirtieth and Market streets, Dock street, Washington avenue wharf, Reed street wharf, Front and Prime streets, Old Navy Yard, Walnut street wharf, Kensington Station, Broad and Carpenter streets, Southwark Station, Shackamaxon Station, Thirty-first and Chestnut streets.

The fast freight lines connected with the Pennsylvania Railroad Co. consist of the EMPIRE LINE, UNION LINE, ANCHOR LINE (rail and lake), PENNSYLVANIA R. R. FAST LOCAL FREIGHT.

The fast freight lines in connection with the Philadelphia, Wilmington and Baltimore Railroad Co. are the VIRGINIA AND TENNESSEE AIR LINE, SEABOARD AIR LINE, ATLANTIC COAST LINE, CANTON INSIDE LINE, CONTINENTAL FAST FREIGHT LINE, and the PENNSYLVANIA AIR LINE TO RICHMOND.

Cranes and derricks for handling heavy goods by the Pennsylvania Railroad Co. are provided as follows:—

Ten-ton crane at Kensington.

Twenty-ton derrick at Thirtieth and Market streets.

Ten-ton crane at Old Navy Yard, for cars.

Fifteen-ton crane on pier 56, Old Navy Yard, for vessels.

Eight-ton crane at Broad and Carpenter streets.

Five-ton crane at Southwark freight station, foot of Washington avenue.

Ten-ton crane at Shackamaxon freight station.

Ten-ton crane at Market street yard.

The Philadelphia and Reading Railroad, which extends throughout the interior of Pennsylvania, and has direct lines to all points in the Lehigh and Schuylkill Valleys and the great anthracite coal fields of Pennsylvania, besides connections with other lines running north and west, is another valuable source of supply which the shipping merchants of Philadelphia possess. This Company have freight stations handily located in different sections of the city, and branches extending in many directions to accommodate all classes of trade and every line of manufactures. Its coal piers at Port Richmond comprise the terminal tide-water point of the P. and R. Coal and Iron Co., from which is shipped the products of this Company's immense coal fields. This road also has freight wharves at Port Richmond and at Willow street on the Delaware, connected by rail with the main line.

It is stated that still another shipping point is to be established shortly on the Delaware front, which will be the outlet of a large productive area not heretofore reached by the Philadelphia shippers.

Taking in the aggregate the immense resources of Philadelphia, based upon a capital of nearly $300,000,000—invested in the department of manufactures, the annual product of which approximates in value the sum of $600,000,000, the textile industries alone employing about 80,000 persons in the manufacture of carpets, hosiery, worsted and woolen yarns, silk and mixed goods, cotton, woolen and mixed fabrics; and the other leading manufactures, viz.: iron and steel, producing $35,000,000; machinery, $10,000,000; refined sugar, $20,000,000; house-building materials, $12,000,000; boots and shoes, chemicals, ale and beer, $15,000,000; hardware and tools, furniture, gold and silverware, etc., $10,000,000 each, etc., and with opportunities for direct communication with all parts of the world, there is nothing to impede its progress or to prevent it from becoming equal in importance as an exporting centre, to any other American port. The means to make it so are in the hands and at the doors of its own merchants and manufacturers.

When the revival of the shipping industry of Philadelphia is becoming such a prominent subject of discussion, it is well to look thoroughly at all the points which go to make up the grand basis upon which to further build and extend the foreign trade of the port. Railroad connections are the most important matters to consider. In this respect, Philadelphia is well supplied, as may easily be seen by the above statement of the facilities given to our merchants and shippers. The matter of railroad rates

3

becomes a subject which requires the co-operation of the Railroad
Companies and their finest calculations to enable the exporters
to successfully compete with the shippers of staple products from
other seaboard cities. The principal bone of contention at the
present moment, if not the only one, is the railroad rate on grain
from the West. If this can be harmonized so as to allow the
grain export trade to be resumed, there would be nothing to
prevent a general revival of the shipping business of the port.
This "bone" has been severely handled during the past three
years, but in view of possible better days soon to dawn, a general
apathy has succeeded the excitement of the fight ; and the eyes
of our grain merchants are wistfully turned to the South to catch
a glimpse of the iron horse with the long train which they are
prayerfully hoping will bring them relief. But the business of
Central America, Mexico, Brazil, the Argentine Republic, and
the West Coast of South America should not be lost sight of.
It is still as extensive and valuable as ever, but other countries
are taking the advantage of it to our detriment, more especially
in the trade of the West Coast. In former years a line of sailing
packets was established between Philadelphia and Valparaiso and
other ports on the Pacific. It failed to receive the support it
required, as our merchants and manufacturers did not make the
necessary exertion to introduce their goods in those markets.
Competition in prices would favor us, while tonnage for freighting
can always be obtained here as cheap as at any other port.

The Philadelphia Record.

SWORN AVERAGE "DAILY" CIRCULATION FOR FEBRUARY 1886,

106,958 COPIES.

SUNDAY ISSUE, 34,338 COPIES.

A Successful Advertiser.

"Steady and intelligent advertising pays a greater per cent. of profit than is realized from any other kind of expenditure."—*Frank Siddall, Philadelphia.*

An Authority on the Science of Advertising.

"When business men come to look on the cost of steady Newspaper advertising as an investment, sure to pay as well as any other, and not unlikely to be exceedingly profitable, they will use it more systematically than heretofore, and regard it as a necessary item of expense."—*J. H. Bates, New York.*

Facts for Thoughtful and Progressive Business Men to Digest

THE CIRCULATION OF THE PHILADELPHIA RECORD,

March 1, 1878 was 37,380 Copies.	March 1, 1882 was 84,814 Copies,
" 1879 " 50,131 "	" 1883 " 96,802 "
" 1880 " 58,920 "	" 1884 " 103,619 "
" 1881 " 68,240 "	" 1885 " 100,702 "

March 1, 1886 was 106,920 Copies.

Breadth, Boldness & Precision in Advertising Mean Success

Estimates cheerfully given and sample copies furnished on application to

THE PHILADELPHIA RECORD,

917-919 Chestnut Street, **Philadelphia, Pa.**

INCORPORATED 1835.

Office of DELAWARE MUTUAL SAFETY INSURANCE CO., Philadelphia.

November 11th, 1885.

The following Statement of the affairs of the Company is published in conformity with a provision of its Charter:

PREMIUMS RECEIVED from Nov. 1, 1884, to Oct. 31, 1885.

On Marine and Inland Risks	$319,518 10	
On Fire Risks	98,438 90	$417,957 00
Premiums on Policies not marked off, November 1, 1884		289,831 09
		$707,788 09

PREMIUMS MARKED OFF as earned from Nov. 1, 1884, to Oct. 31, 1885.

On Marine and Inland Risks	$332,871 34	
On Fire Risks	101,827 77	$434,699 11
Interest during same period—Salvages, etc		73,047 18
		$507,746 29

LOSSES, EXPENSES, etc., during the year as above.

Marine and Inland Navigation Losses	$149,885 49	
Fire Losses	37,205 85	
Return Premiums	21,724 52	
Re-Insurances	21,926 07	
Agency Charges, Advertising, Printing, etc	44,389 86	
Taxes—State and Municipal Taxes for the Year	13,741 58	
Expenses	34,065 33	$322,938 70
		$184,807 59

Assets of the Company, Nov. 1, 1885.

$237,400 00	State of Pennsylvania Five Per Cent. Loan	$282,506 00
212,000 00	State of New Jersey Six Per Cent. Loans, 1887 to 1902	243,800 00
85,000 00	City of Philadelphia Six Per Cent. Loans (Exempt from Tax)	113,050 00
100,000 00	City of Boston Six Per Cent. Loans	124,000 00
100,000 00	City of St. Louis Six Per Cent. Loans	114,000 00
50,000 00	City of Cincinnati Municipal, Seven Per Cent. Loans	57,000 00
25,000 00	City of Columbus, O., Six Per Cent. Loans	27,750 00
36,500 00	State of Tennessee Compromise Bonds	22,265 00
30,000 00	Philada., Wilmington & Baltimore Railroad Co. Trust Certificates, 4%	29,700 00
25,000 00	Pennsylvania Railroad Company, 500 Shares Stock	27,750 00
40,000 00	American Steamship Co. Six Per Cent. Bonds (Penn. R. R. guarantee)	42,600 00
120,200 00	Loans on Bond and Mortgage, First Liens on City Properties	120,200 00
$1,061,100 00	Par . . . . . . Cost, $1,078,852 00 . . . . Market Value, $1,204,621 00	
	Real Estate at Philadelphia and Pittsburgh	140,000 00
	Bills Receivable for Insurances made	94,724 10
	Balances Due at Agencies — Premiums on Marine Policies — Accrued Interest and other debts due the Company	61,429 50
	Stock and Scrip, etc., of Sundry Corporations, estimated value	3,473 00
	Cash—On deposit in Banks $200,562 60	
	In Office 639 72	$201,202 32
		$1,704,455 92

DIRECTORS.

THE GRAIN TRADE.

There is no longer any question as to the competition of India, Egypt, Australia and other countries in the European wheat markets. The wheat productions of these countries are continually increasing, and the producers and shippers of the United States are awakening to the realization of this fact, and also that some radical change in the treatment of this important branch of industry should be made at an early day. Just how it should be done, and what measures are necessary to adopt to retain this trade as heretofore, will command the skill of the most shrewd agriculturist, and the most profound ability of the experienced financier. During the past eighteen months, ending in January last, prices of wheat have ranged lower than at any time during the past twenty years, and yet the demand from the leading markets of Europe has been steadily declining, it being a fact that we have been regularly undersold, and a large surplus is consequently left on our hands. The export shipments of 1885 show a falling off of at least 35 per cent. at Philadelphia and New York, and nearly 70 per cent. at Baltimore. In connection with this, however, it is quite encouraging to know that the corn trade is much more satisfactory. It has increased in Philadelphia fully 200 per cent. over 1884, and possibly its importance may be this year still further enhanced by increased railroad facilities.

The shipments of wheat from the port of Philadelphia during the past ten years were as follows:—

Exports of Wheat during 1876, ... 2,989,704 bushels.
"   "   "   "   1877, ... 2,346,857   "
"   "   "   "   1878, ... 8,923,708   "
"   "   "   "   1879, ... 17,673,542 "
"   "   "   "   1880, ... 12,256,136 "
"   "   "   "   1881, ... 8,883,303   "
"   "   "   "   1882, ... 5,804,943   "
"   "   "   "   1883, ... 4,310,536   "
"   "   "   "   1884, ... 5,200,125   "
"   "   "   "   1885, ... 3,377,091   "

The shipments of corn during the same period were as follows:—

Exports of Corn during 1876, ... 16,790,691 bushels.
"   "   "   "   1877, ... 10,271,443   "
"   "   "   "   1878, ... 19,595,096   "
"   "   "   "   1879, ... 13,886,950   "
"   "   "   "   1880, ... 18,302,127   "
"   "   "   "   1881, ... 6,756,603   "
"   "   "   "   1882, ... 839,706   "
"   "   "   "   1883, ... 5,482,217   "
"   "   "   "   1884, ... 2,268,767   "
"   "   "   "   1885, ... 6,088,330   "

The fact that the price of wheat in Great Britain during 1885 was lower than in any other year of the entire period of 110 years since average market prices were recorded, and that at the same time the unsold stock of wheat in this country has been larger than in any previous year, gives peculiar interest to the inquiry as to the reasons for such a state of affairs. As long as such a fact exists, the tendency for low prices here will continue. It must be conceded that the competition above referred to is the chief cause of the extremely low prices in Great Britain, while the production in this country continues to increase, thus preventing any advance in prices beyond a temporary local improvement. A review of the course of agricultural production during fifteen years shows an estimated increase in corn of 37,000,000 acres, or 80 per cent.; in wheat, of 20,000,000 acres, or 108 per cent.; in oats, of 13,000,000 acres, or 142 per cent.; in all cereals taken together, 67,000,000 acres, or 97 per cent. The enlargement of wheat area was extraordinary during the period of partial failure of the crops of Western Europe; the extension of the breadth in corn was aided by the rise of the foreign trade in beeves and fresh meats, etc.; and the cultivation of oats has received special impetus from the seeding of rust-proof varieties in the South, and from the necessity of less heating feed for horses than a too exclusive corn ration. The average estimated product of the principal food crops of the last five years is compared with the average of the ten years preceding, from 1860 to 1879, inclusive, showing an enormous annual increase in the aggregate as well as per acre.

But the fact must not be overlooked that other countries are every year adding to their acreage, and the aggregate in a similar comparison shows a large increase in products, which prevents the grain merchants of this country from reaping any special benefit from large advances in the prices, which a more exclusive state of production would allow.

The reports of the Agricultural Bureau form indisputably the best evidence that is anywhere obtainable regarding the actual yield of wheat in this country. The proportion of the quantity required for consumption may be seen in the following, as reported by the Bureau :—

	Total export, and used for seed. Bushels.	*Remaining for consumption.* Bushels.
1877,	92,267,365	197,089,535
1878,	135,007,829	229,186,317
1879,	196,980,778	223,141,622
1880,	233,629,776	225,849,729
1881,	239,066,622	259,483,246
1882,	173,626,601	206,653,489
1883,	200,338,685	303,846,785
1884,	166,871,067	254,215,093
1885,	183,878,748	328,885,152

The precise consumption of wheat cannot be ascertained, as it is impossible to determine the quantity of flour carried over from one year to another by the multitude of dealers, and the quantity of wheat remaining, either in the hands of dealers or farmers; but as the population is continually increasing, of course the consumption keeps at an equal ratio as a general consequence. Taking the aggregate yield for the past fifteen years, and the net quantity exported and used for seed, the difference shows, as near as it is possible to figure, that the consumption per capita has been 4.435 bushels yearly. When the cheapness of wheat (which in part counteracted the effect of industrial depression) is considered, it is possible that the total quantity may reach this year 4.6 bushels per capita. If the consumption from July 1st, 1882, to July 1st, 1885, averaged 4.5 bushels per capita yearly, which is very likely, the surplus unconsumed and unsold July 1st, 1885, must have aggregated at least 130,000,000 bushels.

The wheat growers on the Pacific coast are equally interested
in the question of prices and the export of their products with
those east of the Rocky Mountains, and shipments from San
Francisco have been considerably less than those of the preceding
year. The receipts at that port during July and August were
nearly 1,675,000 bushels less than during the same two months
of 1884, which had a tendency to strengthen the pretentions of
holders; and although freights declined to 30 shillings per ton to
Cork for orders, the same reasons that prevented shipments from
the Atlantic ports resulted in but few operations of any importance in that direction, the difference, in comparison with the
shipments of July and August, 1884, being at least 1,000,000
centals. Although the California crop was considerably less this
year, the large quantity carried over from last year's crop, with
the new, would enable the shippers to export about as large a
quantity in 1885-'86 as in 1884-'85, in case the prices asked and
offered could be harmonized. At least 500,000 more acres have
been seeded to wheat this year than there were last year, making
an aggregate of 3,300,000 acres, furnishing a yield of 66,000,000
bushels, equal to about 2,000,000 short tons. In addition to this
there will probably be a yield of 20,000,000 bushels of barley.
The acreage of land adapted to wheat culture in the States on the
Pacific is estimated at 100,000,000 acres, distributed as follows :—
California, 25,000,000 ; Oregon, 18,000,000 ; Colorado and Idaho,
10,000,000 each ; Montana, Utah, Wyoming, 7,000,000 each, the
great bulk of which yet lies untouched.

It is always impossible to predict what the prices of grain will
be, even with war clouds hanging over the whole of Europe, and
short crops reported everywhere ; but it is always well to keep a
weather-eye on the prospects of crops in other countries as well
as in our own. In Southern Russia, where the wheat crop
suffered severely from drouth in June and July last, the yield is
much larger than expected, although less than the preceding year.
Hungary's wheat crop amounted to 114,000,000 bushels, raised
on 7,940,000 acres. The Russian crop of winter and spring
wheat was 48,000,000 bushels, and oats 200,000,000 bushels,
below an average ; but rye shows an increase of 80,000,000

bushels. Germany shows an average yield; and although there was a falling off in France, as compared with last year, the yield was an average one. Spain is not an important wheat-growing country. Its production was below the average. Great Britain had a smaller yield than last year, but a fairly good crop in quantity and quality. India showed a considerable excess. In South Australia the wheat crop amounted to about 10,000,000 bushels, a falling off of nearly 5,000,000 bushels.

That a correct idea may be formed of the actual consumption of grain in making distilled spirits in this country, showing that the demand for such purposes has no relative effect on the prices, the following is inserted :—

Articles.	1878.	1879.	1880.	1881.	1882.	1883.	1884.
	Bushels.	Bushels.	Bushels.	Bushels.	Bushels.	Bushels.	Bushels.
Malt,	1,047,886	1,334,897	1,830,562	2,455,184	2,192,719	1,478,271	1,633,914
Wheat,	3,947	6,473	5,103	180,886	301,241	291,365	114,475
Barley,	55,612	53,097	19,832	124,795	50,675	73,380	199,656
Rye,	2,156,812	2,838,933	3,623,051	4,630,800	4,228,649	7,978,473	2,867,603
Corn,	11,074,366	13,085,745	17,649,760	23,109,114	20,051,239	13,428,469	13,746,905
Oats,	84,231	141,112	140,982	177,855	168,486	127,583	124,165
Mill feed,	277,607	372,393	526,362	612,736	452,339	249,340	241,073
Other materials,	71	2,265	211,134	505	13,754	22,203	591
Total,	14,680,552	18,735,814	24,006,359	31,291,175	27,459,695	18,644,787	18,927,982

A considerable quantity of barley is consumed in the manufacture of fermented liquors which is not officially estimated.

The scheme of diverting the grain export trade from the Atlantic ports to New Orleans by way of the Mississippi river, has had no appreciable effect thus far. Its inefficiency is demonstated by the large falling off in the grain exports from that port; the shipments of last year being nearly 7,000,000 bushels less than the preceding year, while the ratio of the decline in shipments from the Atlantic ports is comparatively insignificant.

It appears from the statement which has been prepared, giving the elevator and storage capacity of the West and Northwest, that the elevator capacity of Minneapolis is 9,834,000 bushels; that of Duluth, 9,460,000, and of St. Paul, 1,500,000, making the total capacity of the three terminal points, 20,794,000. The capacity in Minnesota and Dakota, at all points outside of these three places, is 33,594,400, making a grand total capacity of

54,388,400. This is divided among 1,513 elevators and flat warehouses. The Manitoba roads lead in the number of elevators and capacity, which is 11,481,000 bushels; the Milwaukee road has 8,322,500; the Chicago and Northwestern, 5,581,500; the Northern Pacific, 4,859,200, and the Minneapolis and St. Louis, 2,206,200. These are the only roads whose individual capacity exceeds 2,000,000. The cost of the elevators comprising this vast system, is $10,000,000—invested permanently, and is entirely independent of the capital necessary to carry on the business which is handled by the system every year. This elevator system of the West, gives every necessary facility for the storage and handling of the harvested crops which have been sold by the producer, and provides prompt means for the shipment East, of any desired quantity. The private storehouses and granaries of the farmers and smaller purchases, are not taken into account; but they comprise in the aggregate room for the storage of millions of bushels, which are kept from the market an indefinite length of time.

The extent of territory in this country which can be utilized for the production of grain is almost incalculable, and comprises millions of acres which have never yet been upturned for any purpose; and although many years have passed away since it first occurred to some musical mind to set to verse and tune the satisfying fact that Uncle Sam was rich enough to give us all a farm, and millions of hardy and enterprising foreigners have came over to test the veracity of the author, the country has not yet been all farmed out, and the National Treasury is still replete. The gift of the farms, however, will probably always be doubtful, but the farms themselves are not so much so, as any one may discover who wants to take a trip across the Continent on foot, or by *easy* stage.

Our resources are exhaustless, and it is impossible to conceive that the time will ever come when the population will be sufficient to consume the entire yearly harvests of wheat and corn which this country is capable of producing.

As a terminal point for the tide-water delivery of grain, and with the facilities for handling and shipping it, Philadelphia should do a foreign grain business equal to that of any other American port. Instead of this, the shipments have been gradually declining in a greater ratio than those from her sister cities. Whatever remedy is necessary to counteract this should be applied at once. Railroad competition is urged by some as the only means to restore this trade, while many think that other measures should be adopted by the shipping merchants. At all events, it is not at all likely that the grain trade is forever lost to Philadelphia. It will doubtless return in good time, and renewed activity again gladden the hearts of all interested in its restoration.

SURVEYORS' RULES FOR LOADING GRAIN.

THE ASSOCIATION OF MARINE UNDERWRITERS.

Vessels loading Grain in Bags or Bulk on Voyage from Ports of the United States to Ports in Europe, will be required to conform to the following Rules, adopted by the Association of Marine Underwriters, at meeting of August 16th, 1881, to enable the Surveyor to issue the proper Certificate.

PUMP-WELL.

1. The Pump-well must be sufficiently large to admit of the passage of a man to the bottom of the hold, and room to work conveniently when there, say not less than four feet fore and aft, and five feet athwartships (reference, however, must be had to the size of the keelson and assistant keelsons), and must be grain-tight and ceiled if required.

2. Access to the Pump-well must be had either by a man-hole through the upper deck, or by a clear passage-way between decks from the after hatch. In no case must it be from the main hatch.

GRAIN IN BAGS.

DUNNAGE.

3. Vessels being loaded with Grain in Bags should be dunnaged twelve (12) inches on the floor, fifteen (15) inches on the bilges, and two (2) inches on the sides. If the vessel be very flat or sharp, the dunnage may be increased or diminished at the discretion of the Surveyor.

In between decks should be dunnaged two (2) inches from the sides.

4. The dunnage in the hold must be entirely covered with sails, or approved mats, so as to prevent any of the loose grain from running down on to the floor of the vessel, and thence to the Pump-well.   If sails are used, they must be of good quality and free from holes.

SHIFTING PLANKS.

5. Two-inch Shifting Planks (or equivalent), extending from the beams four feet downward, and between decks, from deck to deck, must be properly secured on each side of the stanchions in the hold, and between decks, to prevent the cargo from shifting, and care must be taken that the stanchions are well fastened at top and bottom, and properly shored.

6. Care must be taken that the bags are properly stowed, and that those stowed in the ground tier, as well as those that are next to the sides of the vessel, are in perfect order, and that the tiers are laid close and well filled.   When stowed on bulk or loose grain, must have boards under them laid fore and aft, and so placed that each bottom bag shall be supported by two (2) boards with athwartship bearing-boards sufficient to prevent the bags from settling into the bulk grain.

GRAIN IN BULK, AND IN BULK AND BAGS.

BINS.

7. Bulk or loose grain must be taken in bins prepared for that purpose.   Materials for bins must be of well-seasoned stock ;

unseasoned lumber must not be used where it will come in contact with the grain.

8. Rules first and second likewise apply to vessels being loaded with grain in bulk.

FLOOR OF BINS.

9. The Floor of the Bin must be laid on sleepers of scantling 2½ x 4 inches in size, sixteen inches apart from centre to centre, supported by studs of corresponding size, also sixteen inches from centre to centre.

It should be raised twelve inches over the floor of the vessel— in the bilge fifteen inches, and in vessels that are very flat or sharp, may be increased or diminished at the discretion of the Surveyor.

In no case should the floor of the bin be laid on loose dunnage.

The floor is considered as extending from the keelson to the turn of the bilge. It must be laid with two thicknesses of one-inch boards, so that they will break joints at the edges and ends, and care must be taken that it be perfectly tight. Vessels under 250 tons register may be permitted to have a single floor laid with one-inch boards placed edge and edge, and seams covered with battens 2 x 1 inch, or edges lapped one inch.

10. The studs for the forward and after bulkheads for vessels not exceeding fourteen feet depth of hold must be equal to 4 x 6 inches in size; for vessels of a greater depth than fourteen feet, they must be equal to 4 x 8 inches. They must be set twenty inches apart from centre to centre, firmly secured at the top and bottom, and properly braced and cleated in the ceiling to resist the pressure of the grain.

11. All air strakes and open seams must be closed, and the sides of the vessel above the turn of the bilge must be ceiled after the manner of clap-boarding reversed, and not furred when it can be avoided. When furring is used, the bilge ceiling must be made grain-tight at the sides. All lodging and bosom knees not fitting tight to deck must be cleated around the face of the knee.

SHIFTING PLANKS.

12. Shifting Planks, two inches thick (in vessels under 250 tons register, one-inch boards with edges lapped or battened may be substituted), must extend from the keelson to the deck on each side of the stanchions, fitted tight under and. between the beams and carlines, and care must be taken that the stanchions are well secured at both ends, and not more than seven feet apart. Exceptions may be made in cases where permanent shifting planks are satisfactorily fitted.

MASTS AND WATER TANKS.

13. Masts and Water Tanks, either of wood or iron, must be properly cased to prevent damage from leakage ; and mast coats must be strong and tight.

14. Vessels being loaded with over 12,000 bushels of grain in bulk must have intermediate partitions of bulkheads. (Vessels loading grain in bulk in quantity exceeding one-half their registered tonnage, or in bins exceeding 12,000 bushels each, on voyages from Atlantic ports of the United States to ports in Europe, will be required to conform to the foregoing, and also to the following rules) :

15. Vessels carrying a full cargo in bulk are required to have, in addition to the forward and other end bulkheads, two trimming bulkheads (thus making a division of three compartments), to extend from the upper deck to the bottom of the vessel. Except where the between decks are laid aft, the after one may extend only to lower deck, and so placed that in loading, the middle compartment will be entirely filled, and the end ones left to trim the vessel. If the end compartments are not entirely filled, care must be taken that the cargo be properly secured to prevent shifting. The studs for the trimming bulkheads to be not less than 3 x 6 inches and. set 22 inches from the centres, and all studs to be firmly secured at top and bottom and properly braced and cleated.

16. Vessels carrying bulk and bags, should not carry the bulk higher than to admit of the stowage of one-quarter of the cargo,

or not less than five heights of bags over it (except the vessels be under 500 tons register, when the height may be regulated by the Surveyor), and will be required to have, in addition to end bulkheads, a forward trimming bulkhead, extending from the top of the bulk to the bottom of the vessel, as provided in case of vessels carrying full cargoes in bulk.

Vessels with two decks, having bulk in the hold as high as the lower deck, should have four strakes of 'tween deck-plank open on each side over the bulk.

When the hold is not filled to the deck, enough space must be left to stow sufficient cargo over it to properly secure it. But no double-deck vessel is permitted to carry bulk grain in 'tween decks, except in properly constructed feeders, and if amidships having centre shifting boards.

DRAFT OR FREE BOARD.

17. The grain must be well trimmed up between the beams, and the space between the beams completely filled.

The draft of water, or free-board, to be regulated by a scale approved by the Loading Committee.

Free-board shall be measured from top of deck at the side of the vessel to the water's edge at lowest point of sheer.

IRON SAILING VESSELS.

18. The foregoing rules are also to apply to Iron Sailing Vessels, excepting that in cases where the frames and inside of plaiting are in such condition as to warrant it, the side ceiling may be dispensed with; while that on the floor should be laid six inches high and raised in the bilges to nine inches, if required by the Surveyor.

IRON STEAMSHIPS.

1. All steamers with water ballast tanks will not be required to sheathe over the same, if the flooring is in good condition and grain-tight, and the water-courses in bilges properly covered.

2. Steamers without water ballast tanks, and with the floors planked with 2½ or 3-inch planks, the same being sound, dry,

and grain-tight, and not less than 18 inches above cementing, will not be required to sheathe over the same.

3. Steamers with a continuous hold forward will require a close bulkhead in the same, and also aft, if deemed necessary by the Surveyor.

4. Shifting boards to be the same as required for sailing vessels, and care to be taken that they are well shored, especially abreast of the large hatches.

5. No bulk grain to be carried in between decks, or (where a ship has more than two decks) between the two upper decks, unless in properly constructed feeders to feed the hold; feeders amidships to have centre shifting boards.

6. Steamers not having properly constructed feeders, will be required to leave sufficient space above the bulk, not less than four feet, to properly secure it with bags or other cargo; the bulk to be platformed as in section 7.

7. Steamers having one deck and beams, may carry bulk to such a height as will permit the stowage over it of not less than five heights of bags, stowed athwartships over boards laid fore and aft, and so placed that each bottom bag shall be supported by two boards with athwartships bearing-boards sufficient to prevent the bags from settling into the bulk grain.

8. Section 17 for sailing vessels is also applicable to steamers.

GENERAL REGULATIONS.

Owners and Masters of vessels intending to load grain are particularly requested to give early notice to the Surveyors at this office, when ready for ceiling, and also when ready to receive grain.

Any deviation required under peculiar circumstances, must receive the approval of the Loading Committee or Board of Surveyors at port of loading.

Vessels loaded in conformity to the foregoing rules, may have a certificate to that effect from the Surveyor appointed by the Association of Marine Underwriters, and the respective Insurance Companies composing said Association will be duly notified thereof.

THE PETROLEUM TRADE.

The oil regions of the United States are in the western part of Pennsylvania, and consist of a belt running diagonally north 22° east, south 22° west, extending north a few miles beyond the boundary line of the State into New York State, and south into the State of Ohio. Oil is also found to some extent in West Virginia. The oil belt is about 200 miles in length and 25 to 30 miles in width, and all throughout this area wells almost without number have been sunk. Some of them have yielded largely, others moderately, while many have shown very little, if any, results. The most important developments are found on the banks of the tributaries of the Allegheny river, and occasionally on the banks of the river itself where it many times crosses the oil belt in its tortuous course. Oil Creek, one of the tributaries, was early made famous by the quantities of oil gathered on its surface, and which was represented as containing curative powers for many diseases. It was called Seneca Oil, and was obtained by spreading blankets and other absorbing materials on the surface of the creek, pressing out the oil, and putting it into small bottles. In 1854 the pioneer oil company was formed, called the Pennsylvania Rock Oil Co., which developed what has since been known everywhere as petroleum. The first well was sunk in 1858, near Titusville, Pa., and oil was obtained at a depth of 69 feet, at the rate of 10 barrels per day. The lands throughout that section of the State were almost non-productive, undesirable, and difficult of access, and were owned principally by a hardy set of woodmen who felled the forests of timber abounding there, and afterward remained to till the soil and eke out a scanty living on the products, principally buckwheat and oats. As the marvellous stories of the wonderful discovery of a natural product which was to make everybody wealthy spread throughout that section, and advance agents of mythical companies tramped through the territory, the impecunious holders of stubble land looked upon their possessions as so much treasure, to be parted with only for fabulous prices. The conceit was adroitly extracted from many of them by the shrewd speculators; but still the prices received were extremely large in their estimation, and, with their mode of living, were sufficient to make them independent for many years.

The great expense of carrying the oil to a market, was a serious obstacle to the earlier operators. It was not until 1862, that a line of railway was built projecting into the oil regions. Other lines were subsequently constructed which established direct communication with the principal Eastern and Western markets, and enabled the oil to be moved to the seaboard at comparatively low figures. The feasibility of pipe lines having been demonstrated as early as 1865, this mode of delivering oil was carefully studied and perfected, until at the present time, the pipe line system is almost exclusively used, and the crude oil is thereby sent from the oil regions to Philadelphia, New York, Cleveland, Buffalo, Pittsburgh and other points, and there refined and disposed of as required; the reduction in the expense of transmission, no doubt, being thereby reduced to a minimum.

The length of the first pipe line constructed was 3,200 feet. Now the entire length of the combined lines is upward of 1,300 miles, while the length of the collecting lines in the oil region is estimated to be nearly 10,000 miles. The length of the pipe line to New York is about 300 miles, the pipes being 6 inches in diameter, laid three feet under the ground. There are 11 pumping stations, 28 miles apart, and the greatest elevation above tidewater is 2,490 feet. The length of the pipe line to Philadelphia is 280 miles, and the number of pumping stations is 6. The Baltimore line covers 70 miles of direct pumping through a 5-inch pipe. The Cleveland line is 100 miles long, with 4 pumping stations. The Buffalo line is 70 miles long, and has 2 stations; and the Pittsburgh line is 60 miles long, with 2 stations. A few years ago it would have been deemed utterly impracticable to force oil through hundreds of miles of pipe, over a very broken country, crossing two ranges of mountains and innumerable rivers and creeks. But it has been permanently established, and the lines are in constant use; an engineering feat worthy to be classed one of the wonders of the age. The average amount pumped through the New York line is about 30,000 barrels per day. Receiving tanks are located at the different pumping stations, 90 feet in diameter by 30 feet high, and the oil is pumped from tanks at one station to tanks at the next. Occasionally loops are laid around stations, and oil forced a distance of 110 miles with one pumping engine.

Nearly three-fourths of the oil produced in this country is found in the great oil field of McKean County, Pa.

The shipments of crude oil in barrels of 42 gallons each, from 1859 to 1868, were as follows :—

	Barrels.		Barrels.
1859,	1,700	1864,	1,842,061
1860,	423,240	1865,	2,100,132
1861,	1,650,133	1866,	3,010,921
1862,	3,101,571	1867,	2,893,210
1863,	3,242,951	1868,	3,482,510

In 1878, the shipments amounted to 13,750,090 barrels, while in 1883, they reached 21,967,636 barrels, and the total pipe deliveries from 1876 to 1884, were :—

	Barrels.		Barrels.
1876,	9,068,376	1880,	24,788,950
1877,	13,012,713	1881,	29,674,458
1878,	15,011,425	1882,	31,789,190
1879,	20,085,716	1883,	24,385,966

The difference between the pipe runs and the shipments, shows the accumulated stock stored in large iron tanks. It amounted in December, 1883, to 35,715,565 barrels. The total exports of crude petroleum, run from 1,112,476 gallons in 1861, to 656,363,869 gallons in 1883, and the total export of petroleum and its products from the United States, and its value were, in the years 1864 and 1883, as follows:—

1864, 23,210,369 gallons, valued at $10,872,542
1883, 505,931,622 " " " 45,367,357

The great decline in value is particularly noticeable, but this is necessary in view of the fact that Russia is making every effort possible to compete with us in the markets of Europe. The Russia oil is not as good an illuminant as the American, but as it costs less, which is an important matter to consumers who are obliged to study the strictest economy in their domestic affairs, its use will be likely to supersede to a great extent, that of the American refineries, unless the cost of production here can be cheapened. The cost of transportation to foreign markets can hardly be figured at less rates than those ruling at the present time. It is barely possible that shipments in bulk may be effected in vessels peculiarly built for that purpose, in which case the cost of freight could probably be somewhat reduced. The objectionable features of this method of shipment will probably deter ship-owners from trying the experiment, although the transportation facilities of Russia in this respect, are found safe and profitable on the Caspian. Carrying in tanks across the Atlantic is quite another matter, and the prospect of not being able to bring return cargoes, as well as the unfavorable consideration of under-writers, until it is demonstrated beyond question that to transport oil in bulk across the ocean involves no greater risk to vessel or cargo than exists with the present manner of doing it, are matters of such apparent importance that it will be difficult to induce any party to invest the necessary money for the construction of many tank vessels.

Russia has no less than 14,000 square miles of oil-producing land, but of this vast territory the field at Baku is the only one worked, and even this covers only the limited space of some three and one-half square miles. The output, however, is enormous, and is refined on the spot, the residue being used as fuel for steamers and railways. The steamboats used in transporting oil from the Baku oil fields are using it exclusively for fuel, with the most satisfactory results. A large British ocean steamer was fitted up a short time ago to burn petroleum; and from all accounts, the experiment was considered satisfactory, and at a cost of about one-sixth the price of coal, and the saving in storage-room and labor, besides the freedom from smoke and dirt which is such an objectionable feature of passenger steamships. The simplicity of the liquid fuel furnace, and the ease with which it is controlled, renders it a great favorite with engineers. In the case of the oil steamers, referred to above, the engineers simply turn on the flame at starting, and concern themselves no more about the furnaces beyond giving them an occasional look, until the destination is reached in two days' time. The annoyance to passengers in the process of coaling the vessel is avoided, which is also an important point to be considered. The Central Pacific Railroad Co. has recently introduced crude petroleum into nearly all its steamers, including the Oakland ferry-boats at San Francisco. The oil is obtained in the State, some of it at Ventura, and some from wells recently opened near Livermore on the line of the Western Pacific branch. The method of application is practically identical with the Russian, by a steam jet, and the results have been most satisfactory, particularly in the matter of economy.

What has already been done in this direction would seem to indicate that, at no very distant day, petroleum will come generally into use as fuel for raising steam, although it is a remarkable fact that neither the United States, which have long produced the most oil in the world, nor England, which has been the parent of a whole series of liquid-fuel inventions, should have reaped any benefits from these advantages, and that the question of successfully using oil furnaces should have been solved by the Russians. This can probably be explained by the fact that in the Caspian region very little timber can be obtained, and the poor quality of coal necessarily used, and its exorbitant price, prompted the perfecting of this system.

The export of oil to Asia for 1885 amounted to 10,518,634 cases, equal to ten times that number of gallons. Java, India and Rangoon Straits, &c., fell off in demand over 900,000 cases,

but China increased her demand by over 1,000,000 cases, and
Japan by over 600,000.

Notwithstanding the excessive depression in freights to all
points, and in all branches during the last year, which would
naturally drive steamers into almost any trade that offered a
market, this Asian petroleum business was, as usual, carried on
amost entirely by sailing vessels, the total shipments by steamers
amounting to only twelve. The total number of vessels employed
in this trade last year was 259, of which about one-third were
American.

Summary of shipments of cases of petroleum from the United
States to ports in the East Indies, Java, China, Japan, &c., in
1885 :—

Total shipments to Java,			1,699,383
"	"	" Rangoon Straits,	688,844
"	"	" China Seaports,	3,155,069
"	"	" India,	2,650,146
"	"	" Japan,	2,325,192
			10,518,634

Comparison between shipments for 1884 and 1885 :—

	1884.	1885.	Increase.	Decrease.
Java,	2,200,917	1,699,383		501,534
Rangoon Straits, &c.,	796,014	688,844		107,170
China Seaports,	1,860,315	3,155,069	1,294,756	
India,	3,035,946	2,650,146		385,800
Japan,	1,708,174	2,325,194	617,018	
	9,601,366	10,518,636		

Total increase, ... 917,270 cases.

The shipments for 1884 showed an increase over those of 1883
of 1,338,031, making a grand total increase during the past two
years of 2,255,301 cases. The quantity shipped to the above
named ports from Philadelphia, will be found in the following
list of shipments of petroleum from that port to foreign countries
during 1885, viz. :—

	Gallons.		Gallons.
Aarhus,	354,291	Leghorn,	3,341,720
Alicante,	1,021,500	Leith,	190,099
Amsterdam,	2,029,443	Limerick,	180,490
Ancona,	264,000	Lisbon,	1,853,867
Anjer,	844,590	Liverpool,	2,437,108
Antwerp,	13,631,968	London,	13,660,574
Bari,	443,580	Malta,	573,340
Barcelona	535,197	Marseilles,	305,830
Belfast,	311,126	Messina,	248,960
Bergen,	785,295	Nagasaki,	802,500
Bisceglia,	432,130	Nantes,	147,305
Blaye,	795,882	Naples,	518,500
Bremen,	9,152,069	Newcastle,	234,462
Bristol,	269,976	Norkoping,	133,110
Cagliari,	4,663,280	Oporto,	401,042
Calcutta,	486,000	Padang	330,040
Catania,	736,410	Palermo,	473,000
Chantenay,	85,544	Patras,	500,000
Civita Vecchia,	118,570	Penang,	237,000
Constantinople,	194,320	Portland, E.,	94,847
Copenhagen,	129,775	Pozzuoli,	394,203
Corfu,	273,210	Rotterdam,	6,259,580
Cork,	246,136	Rouen,	5,295,896
Dantzic,	1,244,887	Sables d'Olonnes,	429,998
Drontheim,	185,033	Salonica,	132,200
Dublin,	135,373	Santander,	1,031,034
Dunkirk,	2,712,148	Savona,	808,260
Elsinore,	523,992	Seville,	1,035,967
Falmouth,	96,090	Shanghai,	831,330
Fiume,	17,147,442	Singapore,	758,710
Flensborg,	407,639	Stettin,	3,726,464
Flushing,	426,648	St. Loubes,	1,881,321
Frederica,	132,048	Stralsund,	282,661
Gefle,	133,163	Svendborg,	85,977
Genoa,	5,018,190	Trieste,	675,295
Gibraltar,	1,956,820	Venice,	2,133,410
Granatello,	952,720	Volo,	143,600
Hamburg,	13,563,427	Waterford,	141,292
Havre,	4,138,093	Wesby,	138,529
Helsingsborg,	168,433	Yokohama,	690,910
Hiogo,	9,001,900	Other ports,	225,759
Hull,	626,211		
Konigsberg,	1,432,538	Total.	151,756,812
Landskrona,	153,538		

		Gallons.			Gallons.
Exported during	1885,	151,756,812	Exported during	1876,	65,881,610
"	"	1884, 119,268,919	"	"	1875, 64,104,300
"	"	1883, 79,500,430	"	"	1874, 74,154,689
"	"	1882, 85,931,595	"	"	1873, 86,843,013
"	"	1881, 110,956,807	"	"	1872, 56,306,063
"	"	1880, 54,673,946	"	"	1871, 55,901,590
"	"	1879, 89,243,110	"	"	1870, 49,889,737
"	"	1878, 75,308,720	"	"	1869, 83,145,155
"	"	1877, 49,166,960	"	"	1868, 40,505,620

It will be seen by this table that the Philadelphia shipments exceeded those of any other single year for the past eighteen years by 32,487,893 gallons, showing that this branch of our export trade has assumed gigantic proportions, and is so firmly established that nothing can apparently divert it into other channels. The capital invested in permanent plants for refining and shipping, makes this business one of the most important commercial industries of Philadelphia. It gives employment to a vast number of skilled workmen, intelligent officials, and an immense vessel tonnage. Ship-owners of all nations give this city the preference for loading oil, and vessels can always be obtained, especially if the cargoes are to be supplied by the Chester Oil Company, which ships one-third of all the oil exported from this port. The reasons why this Company is preferred are obvious, and can be easily explained. Their point of loading is eighteen miles further down the river than that of any other Company, thus avoiding the ice embargo at the Horse-shoe in the winter season ; they have two covered loading piers, 60 feet wide and 250 feet long, and one pier for ballast ; steam hoisters capable of working an aggregate of eight hatches at the same time ; eleven vessels can be simultaneously accommodated handily, five of which could be loaded to a depth of 24 feet, and six at 20 feet draft; there is no bar outside of the piers, thus allowing vessels to be easily and promptly handled, and with no risk of grounding when moving out ; the river is 1½ miles wide opposite the loading piers, giving vessels all the sea room required in coming in or going out ; the river is never frozen over at this point, and as the prevailing wind is westerly, the space in front is nearly always clear of ice which may be coming from up the river; the Company has an ice harbor, probably the only private one in the United States, where vessels can take safe refuge when required; it is a fact that vessels have left the government ice harbor at Marcus Hook and taken shelter in the Chester Oil Co's harbor; no vessel has ever been damaged at their wharves; vessels can often sail direct to their piers when arriving, without the assistance of tugs; the piers are connected with branches from the Pennsylvania Railroad and the Philadelphia and Reading Railroad; there is never any unnecessary detention loading, as the facilities for preparing and delivering cargoes are so perfect that vessels receive prompt despatch; the officers and employees are gentlemanly and accommodating, and are always ready to render any assistance that the captains may require; the rates of wharfage are uniform with those of other companies; communication with the loading piers from Philadelphia is handy and rapid, there being trains every hour on the P., W. & B. R. R.; the office of the Company in Philadelphia is but a very short distance from all the ship-brokers' offices, and information can be obtained there at any time regarding the loading or position of vessels, or any other facts which captains may be desirous of knowing, as telegraphic communication is established direct with the works at Thurlow; in fact, every possible convenience that necessity requires is so well provided, that a general satisfaction is at once manifested by the captains, ship-brokers, and all others interested, when it is learned that orders have been sent for vessels to report for cargo to the Chester Oil Co. The Tidewater Pipe Line has its terminal station at their works at Thurlow, and the tankage capacity is equal to 150,000 barrels. The Company is in every way provided with facilities for systematically conducting their immense business, which has been continually increasing since the Company was first organized. Every precaution is taken to prevent fire, and its spreading in case fire should break out in any of the tanks. Pipes and space are economized by the use of a most perfect arrangement of valves, and the escaping gases are secured and utilized as fuel for the furnaces. No better burning oil of any grade was ever put upon the market than the Student Oil, produced at this refinery. A home trade in this specialty has been established which will probably, in good time, supersede most of the other oils now used. It gives a powerful, clear light, easy for the eyes, and economical in its consumption. Its general popularity is specially marked, and its merits particularly noticeable.

By authority of the Chief Signal Officer, U. S. A., the United States Weather Signals are hoisted at the refinery of the Chester Oil Co. every day, at 7.30 A. M., the weather forecasts indicated by them cover a period of 24 hours. This is greatly appreciated by those who are interested in the movements of shipping, and all captains whose vessels are ready for sea, make their arrangements in accordance with the predictions.

The total shipments of petroleum, during the year 1885, from Philadelphia, New York, Baltimore and Boston, amounted to 6,985,637 barrels and 16,525,844 cases; of which amount there were shipped from Philadelphia 2,107,142 barrels, and 4,176,521 cases.

SURVEYORS' RULES FOR LOADING PETROLEUM.

PORT OF PHILADELPHIA.

Owners, Masters, or Agents of Vessels loading Petroleum and its Products at this Port are required to observe the following Rules in preparing and loading their Vessels, in order to obtain a certificate from the Surveyors appointed by the Board of Marine Underwriters :

1. VESSELS with *Cabin* or *Forecastle* entirely under deck, will not be permitted to load *Naphtha, Gasoline, Benzine,* or *Spirits of Petroleum,* under *Inspection.*

2. BALLAST must be of *Stone, Shingle,* or *Dross. All vessels* intended to load *Petroleum,* and before taking in any oil, must be sufficiently stiff to change berths in all kinds of weather, when *Tugs* can safely tow them. *Ballast* of any description must be

covered with boards, and the *Barrels* kept clear in the wings, or *where ballast is trimmed against them* by boards or planks.

3. STOWAGE.—*All Barrels* and *Cases* must be stowed in straight tiers, fore and aft ; in no case will it be permitted to stow with the sheer of the vessel (rounded off) ; *all breakages* must be made perfectly solid with ballast (cased in), or suitable dunnage-wood : *no hanging beds permitted under any circumstances ;* the barrels must be stowed bilge and contline, and every barrel properly bedded and well chocked. *In the ground tier, each barrel must rest on two soft wood beds of about two inches thickness, placed by the quarter hoops, leaving the bilge of the barrel about one inch free.* No barrel to be stowed athwartship without special permission from the inspector, and in no case will it be permitted, where the barrel is subject to any pressure.

4. SINGLE DECK WITH LOWER BEAMS.—Single-deck vessels with *Between Deck Beams*, not more than 8 feet apart from centre to centre, taking over six heights of Barrels, *must lay a temporary Between-Deck*, with 3-inch planks, not less than 9 inches in width, directly under the *Bilge* of the *Barrels*, fore and aft ; planks to be securely blocked from side to side ; if the beams are closer than 8 feet, then 2 or 2½-inch plank, laid close together on the beams, may be used, and to be secured from side to side. Where the beams are further apart than 8 feet, heavier material in proportion must be used, *all to be regulated by the Inspector.* A *Stanchion* well secured at both ends *must be under each Between-Deck-Beam.* Vessels with Between-Deck-Beams, if over 13 feet hold, loading Oil in cases, will also be required to lay a Between-Deck of planks as above.

5. VENTILATION.—*All vessels* loading *Barrels* or *Cases*, especially those containing *Crude Oil, Benzine, Gasoline, Naphtha,* or *Spirits of Petroleum, must be ventilated through all the hatches,* unless already fitted with suitable *Permanent Ventilators,* fore and aft, *to be approved by the Inspector.*

6. DRAFT OF WATER.—Single-deck vessels will not be allowed to load deeper than their depth of hold, and the draft of all vessels, loading cases or otherwise, must not be beyond a safe and seaworthy condition, *to be approved by the Inspector.*

THE COAL·TRADE.

The first mention that is found of the coal deposits of the United States, is in the records of the travels of Father L. Hennepin; in this work, printed in 1698, he mentions a cole-mine, at about where is the present city of Ottawa, Illinois. The explorer, La Salle, calls Hennepin some pretty hard names for his pretended discoveries, but there can be no question about the fact of coal existing at the point named. In 1750, the bituminous coal of the Richmond, Va., basin was used, and for many years it was the sole reliance of the Atlantic coast for blacksmith fuel, in fact until 1845. In 1768, anthracite coal was known and used in Pennsylvania, and by its use, the patriots of 1776 were enabled to forge the implements of warfare.

The output of the coal fields of the United States during 1885, amounted to nearly 107,000,000 tons. The principal seaport points of delivery for distribution, are Philadelphia, Baltimore, Perth Amboy, South Amboy, Hoboken, Port Johnson, Elizabeth-port, Weehauken, Rondout, Georgetown and Alexandria. The nearest port to the anthracite and bituminous coal regions of Pennsylvania is Philadelphia, with which it is connected by the Pennsylvania, Philadelphia and Reading, North Pennsylvania and Lehigh Valley Railroads. The anthracite coals are mostly delivered into vessels at the numerous wharves of the Phila. and Reading Railroad Co., at Port Richmond, and the bituminous and gas coals at the Pennsylvania Railroad Co's wharves at Greenwich. There is plenty of water at both points, and the only expense to vessels is for trimming the coal on board. The total output of anthracite coal in 1885 was about 31,500,000 tons, while the prospects for a decided increase of this quantity in 1886 are very flattering. It is computed that 12 per cent. of the anthracite production is taken by the iron furnaces, 26 per cent. is used to generate steam, and 62 per cent. goes to domestic consumers. The soft coal fields of Pennsylvania have never been so actively worked as they will be this year. Large tracts are being taken up and companies formed to operate them. Spurs and branches are being built from the Pennsylvania and the Baltimore and Ohio Railroads to lands underlaid with coal, and many more are in contemplation. There is a perfect network of railroads between the Susquehanna and Allegheny rivers, penetrating the productive fields of Jefferson and Clearfield Counties. The development of the Youghiogheny fields this year is expected to be extraordinary, and a line of railroad has been projected there which will give the Pennsylvania Railroad an outlet for these coals East and West. Owing to the superiority of the coal for domestic purposes, it is intended to take it as far West as Cincinnati and Chicago.

The Western and Southern coal fields are producing largely, considerably in excess of all former yields; but it is not likely that they will ever interfere with the Pennsylvania mines. The coal industry of Illinois is continually enlarging. The number of counties in that State producing coal is 49; the number of mines and openings of all kinds, 786; of employees of all kinds, 25,446; of tons of coal mined, 9,791,874; the average value per ton at the mines, $1.17; the number of kegs of powder used, 140,382. Over-production has reduced the price per ton 54 cents during the past three years. The coal resources of Illinois must have a salutary effect upon the several industries of the West dependent upon coal as a fuel, and this large production must materially affect the prices of many manufactured goods, as well as lessen the expense of this necessary article of domestic economy.

The coal used in the manufacture of coke in the United States last year came chiefly from four of the great coal basins of the country—the Appalachian, the Illinois, the Missouri and the El Moro, Colorado. By far the largest part was derived from the measures of the great Appalachian fields, only about 3 per cent.

of the total coming from the other basins. The Appalachian basin is the most important, though by no means the largest in area of the coal fields of America. Beginning near the northern boundary of Pennsylvania, it extends for a distance of over 750 miles in a southwesterly direction, following the western line of the Allegheny mountains, with a course nearly parallel to the Atlantic coast line, through Western Pennsylvania, West Virginia, Kentucky, Tennessee, Georgia and Alabama, to Tuscaloosa, Ala., where it ends. The average breadth of the field is from 80 to 90 miles, the area being fully 70,000 square miles, and broadest in Pennsylvania, Ohio and West Virginia, and somewhat contracted through Tennessee and Northern Alabama. In the northern part of this basin the coal is found in isolated patches, the chief of which are the Blossburg, McIntyre and Barclay. Between the eastern edge and the ocean other detached fields are found, such as the anthracite coal fields of Northeastern Pennsylvania, the Broad Top semi-bituminous coal field of Middle Pennsylvania, and the Cumberland coal basin of Maryland. These patches are all that have been left by the denuding agencies which have swept away, and been so destructive to, the measures in this belt of country.

The greatest development in the manufacture of coke is in the Connellsville region of Western Pennsylvania, a tract about 50 miles long by 3 miles wide. This coke is regarded as the typical coke of this country, as the Durham is in England, being the best in quality for blast-furnace fuel manufactured. Whitney & Kemmerer, of Philadelphia, are the exclusive agents for this coke, and their sales are very extensive. The number of establishments making coke in the United States is 255; the number of ovens in use is about 20,000; and the amount of coal used annually in its manufacture will approximate 8,000,000 tons, and is constantly increasing. The quantity produced last year was about 5,000,000 tons. It is a remarkable fact that coke is both bulky and low-priced, and in proportion to its weight is one of the lowest, if not the lowest, priced of any manufactured article. The nearest point of consumption to the Connellsville region (which produced more than 68 per cent. of all the coke made last year) was Pittsburgh, about 60 miles distant, while hundreds of thousands of tons are carried to points much further away; and, considering the obstacles in the way, such as having to haul it long distances to market, its comparatively low price, etc., the development of the manufacture of coke must be regarded as one of the most marked achievements in our industrial progress.

The most numerous class of consumers of anthracite coal are the housekeepers; and each housekeeper has a special quality (or name) of coal which is considered best adapted to the domestic requirements. The *name* of the coal has a great deal to do with its popularity, and although the output of a single mine may be christened with a sufficient number of names to satisfy all consumers from all sections, and red-ash and white-ash may be extracted from the same mine, the *name* must not be changed, or a most decided expression of dissatisfaction would be the result. It is like the boy's *hot* pies which he cries out, while they lie congealed into most frigid intensity under the stiffening effects of a winter " norther ;" but to cry out *cold* pies at such a time would ruin his business. It is the *name* of the pies, and not their *character* or *condition*, and while he sticks to the name his chances for continuing his sales are thereby extended. In some localities in the eastern States, any anthracite coal that burns freely with a flame is called the favorite Lyken's Valley; and no matter from which direction it comes, the name is enough to insure its sale. The original division of the Pennsylvania coals into anthracite, semi-anthracite, semi-bituminous, and bituminous, was one founded largely upon their geographical distribution, although the supposed basis was the chemical composition of the coals. These names will doubtless always be made use of by the coal trade, but they have no scientific value.

The following table is of interest, as showing the amount of the several classified anthracite coals produced in 1884, and the number of collieries :—

		Number of Collieries.	Production, Tons.
1.	Free-burning White Ash,	213	17,109,523
2.	Hard White Ash,	105	9,206,639
3.	Wyoming Red Ash,	14	1,727,965
4.	Lehigh Red Ash,	11	1,510,494
5.	Shamokin,	29	1,409,854
6.	Lyken's Valley Red Ash,	8	1,145,008
7.	Schuylkill Red Ash,	14	227,467
8.	Trevorton,	2	116,695
9.	Lorberry Red Ash,	4	101,836
10.	Bernici White Ash,	1	86,018
	Total,	401	32,641,499

The following characteristics of the different varieties of anthracite coal are considered applicable to all mined in the different fields:—

Hard White Ash.—It is in great request for blast-furnace and locomotive purposes, having, to an unusual degree, the qualities of resisting change of form under high heat and pressure, and owing to its high percentage of carbon, it is valuable for producing steam; but for domestic use on a small scale, and for open grate fires, it does not ignite readily enough to be a favorite.

Free-burning White Ash.—The distinction between it and the hard-burning white-ash coal is, that under such a fire as is ordinarily used for smelting metals or producing steam, the impurities melt or clinker, which is not the case with the harder coal. This practical test is not, however, a very exact one. Some of the anthracites can be clinkered with a strong draft and with a thick bed of fire, and would, by a person who used them under such circumstances, be classed as free-burning, while another, whose method of burning was more economical, would call them hard. Analysis shows that the free-burning white-ash coals are quite as rich in fixed carbon, and that they have even higher heating power, as tested by the amount of water evaporated, than the harder variety, but their limited range of usefulness, which is due to their clinkering, prevents their price rising as high as the hard white-ash coals.

Schuylkill Red Ash.—Is easily ignited, easy to keep burning, and where used in open grates, makes less floating dust than white-ash coal, because its ash is composed of larger particles, and on account of the oxide of iron, which constitutes its coloring matter, has greater specific gravity than the ash of the white.

Shamokin.—It follows in hardness, and in case of ignition, next after the free-burning white-ash coals, and is used still more especially for domestic purposes; its lower percentage of carbon making it ill-adapted for purposes requiring intense heat.

Lorberry Red Ash.—It burns with a little flame, and is much in request for domestic uses in the Eastern market.

Lyken's Valley Red Ash.—It burns with considerable flame, and is greatly liked in the Eastern market for open grates, other domestic uses, and for steam and heating purposes, wherever quick heat is required.

Trevorton or North Franklin White Ash.—The coal is pure, but its heating properties are rather low, and it is of so friable a nature that it does not stand transportion well.

Wyoming Red Ash.—Is similar in its general characteristics to the Schuylkill red ash.

Lehigh Red Ash.—Is very similar to the hard white ash produced from the same region, with the exception of the color of the ash, due to the presence of iron, the same as in the softer red ash from Schuylkill.

Of the above qualities, Donaldson & Thomas of Philadelphia are wholesale dealers in, and sell large quantities of the Schuylkill red ash, one of the most popular coals in the country; also the Schuylkill hard and free white ash, and Shamokin Wilkes-Barre, the latter having an extensive sale at Eastern ports, it being largely used there for domestic purposes. Its volume is equal to 41 cubic feet to the gross ton, and has a gray and red ash. Their bituminous coals for steam purposes are reaping "golden opinions" from all who use them, more especially from the engineers and owners of ocean steamships. They find them economical and possessing the merits which are so desirable and necessary in these days of low freights. The sales of this special mining (Moshannon Creek), are continually increasing, although no special effort has ever been made by Donaldson & Thomas to place these bituminous coals in the market, from which it is evident that they are sold strictly on their merits.

The Pennsylvania Railroad Company is the largest coal carrier in the United States, and their total business for the year 1885 was as follows:—

Anthracite,	4,625,672 tons.
Semi-Bituminous,	5,487,151 "
Gas Coal,	1,278,321 "
Coke,	2,649,686 "
Total net tons,	14,040,830

The carrying of anthracite coal from the mines to the several delivery points during 1884 was distributed among the railroad companies as follows:—

Philadelphia and Reading R. R. Co.,	11,163,920 tons,	38.85 per ct.
Lehigh Valley Railroad,	5,935,254 "	19.60 "
Delaware, Lack. and Western R. R.,	5,204,362 "	16.05 "
Del. and Hudson Canal Co.,	3,362,680 "	11.00 "
Pennsylvania R. R. Co.,	3,169,287 "	8.00 "
Pennsylvania Coal Co.,	1,397,946 "	5.00 "
Erie R. R. Co.,	484,844 "	1.50 "
	30,718,293 "	100.00 "

The destination of the coal for consumption was as follows:—

Middle States,	21,047,293 tons.
New England States,	5,300,000 "
Western States,	2,500,000 "
Southern States,	1,200,000 "
Canada,	600,000 "
Foreign Ports,	46,000 "
Pacific Coast,	25,000 "
	30,718,293 "

This production was obtained from the following districts:—

Wyoming, ... 15,677,753 tons.
Schuylkill, ... 9,478,314 "
Lehigh, ... 5,562,226 "

30,718,293 "

The total production of bituminous and anthracite coals during the years 1882, 1883 and 1884 was as follows:—

Production in 1882.

Bituminous, . . 58,347,518 tons. | Anthracite, . 29,120,096 tons.

Production in 1883.

Bituminous, . . 65,082,357 tons. | Anthracite, . . 31,793,027 tons.

Production in 1884.

Bituminous, . . 69,139,514 tons. | Anthracite, . . 30.718,293 tons.

The bituminous production by States was as follows:—

Pennsylvania,	25,000,000	New Mexico,	350,000
Illinois,	10,101,005	Virginia,	300,000
Ohio,	9,000,000	Washington Territory,	260,000
Iowa,	3,903,458	Utah,	250,000
West Virginia,	3,000,000	California,	200,000
Missouri,	2,500,000	Georgia,	200,000
Maryland,	2,469,051	Arkansas,	150,000
Indiana,	2,260,000	Michigan,	135,000
Alabama,	2,000,000	Texas,	125,000
Kentucky,	1,550,000	Oregon,	60,000
Colorado,	1,500,000	Dakota,	50,000
Tennessee,	1,200,000	Montana,	50,000
Wyoming Territory,	1,000,000	Idaho,	20,000
Indian Territory	400,000		

The total value at the mines of all coal produced in the United States in 1885, was $110,097,361, of which $64,639,841 was the value of the production of Pennsylvania.

Comparison of the area and production of the coal-producing countries of the world for 1885:—

	Square Miles.	Tons.
Great Britain, ...	11,900	163,737,327
United States, ...	192,000	99,851,807
Germany, ...	1,770	66,870,634
France, ...	2,086	21,270,553
Belgium, ...	510	18,177,754
Austria, ...	1,800	19,000,000
Russia, ...	30,000	4,000,000
India, ...	2,000	4,000,000
Australia, ...	24,840	2,521,457
Nova Scotia, ...	300	1,422,553
Spain, ...	3,501	900,000
Japan, ...	5,000	900,000

The Upper Lehigh, Sandy Run, Spring Brook, Florence, and other first-class Lehigh and Wyoming coals, whose names are so familiar to their numerous consumers, retain their popularity, as the increasing sales testify; those of the Wyoming coals amounting from 2,941,817 tons in 1860, to 15,677,753 tons in 1884; while the Lehigh sales increased from 1,821,674 tons in 1860 to 5,562,226 tons in 1884. Whitney & Kemmerer, of Philadelphia, are the exclusive agents at tide-water for these coals. They are all of standard quality, and the agents have established for them a reputation which is valuable and permanent. They also handle large quantities of bituminous coal from the celebrated Cumberland (George's Creek) coal field, located at the western extremity of Maryland, the lines of transportation to the seaboard being the Baltimore and Ohio Railroad, the Chesapeake and Ohio Canal, and the Pennsylvania Railroad. This coal district has a very strong competitor in the Clearfield, which produces a quality of coal of equal excellence. Berwind, White & Co., of Philadelphia and New York, have the exclusive sale of the celebrated Eureka semi-bituminous coal mined in this region. It is used extensively by the ocean steamers, those of the regular passenger lines as well as the transient freight boats. It has also a justly earned distinction among many of the railroad companies on account of its being so well adapted to use on locomotives, while its merits are extolled by the many manufacturers who use it in their stationary engines. A considerable quantity is shipped to Cuba, a market having been established there for it a number of years since.

The average price of white-ash lump coal by the cargo, delivered on board vessels at Philadelphia, from 1880 to 1885, both included, was $4.50 per ton of 2,240 lbs. The year 1886 opened with a good demand from all quarters, but prices are much lower than the average above given. Coal is certainly very cheap, but the chances are favorable for an advance in prices of anthracite coal at an early day. The tonnage produced this year has been large, and it has gone very largely into consumption, but the profits accruing from the sales have the appearance of being gazed at through the big end of a telescope. In fact, the coal business at the present writing, seems to be in an active state of unsettlement, and needs reorganizing. Producers are bidding against each other, which demoralizes the trade and produces uneasiness. The grand result will probably be that a more united action will be developed, and protective combinations be organized which will put the trade into a more healthful state, even if prices should be advanced thereby.

THE SUGAR AND MOLASSES TRADE.

In the olden time sugar was considered a great luxury, and was very sparingly used. The youth of those far away days had but few opportunities, if any, to indulge in the pleasure of "lobbing" molasses when out of reach of the wharfinger's lath; but in later years this delectable enjoyment became a part and parcel of the occupation of the average school-boy between hours, and he invariably circumscribed his limit of territorial wanderings to an extent sufficient to take in the precincts of the molasses wharves. The writer of these dry lines, ruminating on the retrospect which covered the green and salad days of his lost youth, finds the long rows of hogsheads on Portland Pier just as he left them, with the long boards on top to cover the bungholes, which were left open apparently for his accommodation; the convenient stick ready for insertion; the spectacled gauger who conscientiously tallied the gallons on his sticky book with his sticky pencil; the argus-eyed wharfinger on the alert for sweet-toothed boys; the final surreptitious gathering of the delicious treacle, and the hasty departure with a soiled jacket.

"I remember the black wharves and the slips,
    And the sea tides tossing free;
And Spanish sailors with bearded lips,
And the beauty and mystery of the ships,
    And the magic of the sea."

But among the changes which Time brings around, the boy grows out of his taste for that particular method of obtaining his sweetness; the West India business gradually drifts away to other cities, and a new order of things springs up to satisfy the wants of the present generation; and it is now difficult to recognize in "the beautiful town that is seated by the sea," the brisk maritime port of our earlier experience.

During the fiscal year 1885, the purchases of sugar from foreign countries amounted to 1,358,937 net tons, or an average of about 48 pounds for each person in the United States. The price at the purchasing points has fallen to figures never before reached, as will be seen by the following table, showing the quantities and values of brown sugar imported into the United States during the year ended June 30, 1885, with the average cost per pound in each country :—

Countries.	Pounds.	Value.	Av. Cost per lb., Cts.
Cuba, ...	1,115,045,360	$30,442,097	2.72
Porto Rico, ...	159,799,898	4,200,883	2.62
Other Spanish Possessions, ...	179,503,732	4,307,438	2.40
Brazil, ...	329,294,506	6,834,096	2.10
British West Indies, including Guiana, .	316,389,399	7,806,622	2.47
Germany, ...	232,411,095	5,218,396	2.24
French West Indies, .	45,724,233	1,104,240	2.40
San Domingo, . . .	42,523,746	1,332,684	3.13
Belgium, ...	37,158,233	872,657	2.34
British Possessions in Africa, ...	18,280,959	384,814	2.10
British East Indies, . .	14,078,594	237,114	1.69
England, ...	10,313,301	241,199	2.39
Danish West Indies, .	10,048,008	250,862	2.49
Dutch East Indies, . .	7,721,862	247,254	3.20
Cent. American States,	6,987,514	254,095	3.63
Total, including other countries, ...	2,548,222,809	$64,320,862	2.52
From Hawaiian Islands	169,652,603	8,198,164	4.83

The importation from the Hawaiian Islands is exempt from duty under the provisions of the reciprocity treaty with that country. Of the imports of sugar subject to duty, no less than 57 per cent. came from the islands of Cuba, Porto Rico and other Spanish possessions. These islands and San Domingo, with small quantities from Central America and the East Indies, furnish the better qualities. A large quantity is credited to Germany, coming by way of Hamburg and Bremen from sugar producing countries ; a small quantity also came via England. The average cost of dutiable sugars is only 2½ cents per pound, while the imports under the Hawaiian reciprocity treaty average 4.83 cents. The original intention was to admit under the treaty very low grades of sugar, suitable only for refining purposes, but the quality has been vastly improved, and the price has therefore advanced to nearly double the average value of duty-paid sugar.

Considering the fact that $65,000,000 were paid in a single year to foreign countries for sugar, the matter of protection to our native sugar productions is worthy the attention of all legislators. The home production the past year reached 100,876 tons, a decrease from that of the previous year, of 34,567 tons. 47,259 tons were made from molasses, 25,900 tons of maple sugar were manufactured, and about 2,000 tons sugar were made from beet-root and sorghum.

During the last fiscal year the exports of refined sugar from this country far exceeded the production of raw sugar, but the production was less than a tenth of the quantity consumed by our own people.

The following table is substantially a continuation to the present date, of previous official publications:—

SUPPLY AND EXPORTS OF SUGAR, IN POUNDS.

Fiscal Years.	Imports.	Production.	Total Supply.	Exports.
1885,	2,717,884,653	225,962,240	2,943,846,893	258,159,657
1884,	2,756,416,896	287,712,230	3,044,129,126	85,532,916
1883,	2,137,667,865	303,066,258	2,440,734,123	30,550,506
1882,	1,990,152,374	159,874,950	2,150,027,324	19,436,376
1881,	1,946,745,205	272,982,899	2,219,728,104	31,980,791
1880,	1,829,291,684	198,962,278	2,028,253,962	40,640,206
1879,	1,834,365,836	239,478,753	2,073,844,589	82,741,564
1878,	1,537,451,934	147,101,941	1,684,553,875	50,109,065
1877,	1,654,556,831	190,672,570	1,845,229,401	42,872,675
1876,	1,493,977,472	163,418,070	1,657,395,542	67,730,198
1875,	1,797,509,990	134,504,691	1,932,014,681	35,350,785
1874,	1,701,297,869	103,241,119	1,804,538,988	29,442,750
1873,	1,568,304,592	125,346,493	1,693,651,085	34,010,402
1872,	1,509,185,674	146,906,125	1,656,091,799	16,598,822
1871,	1,277,473,653	168,878,592	1,446,352,245	14,203,714
1870,	1,196,773,569	99,452,940	1,296,226,509	22,760,904
1869,	1,247,833,480	95,051,225	1,342,884,655	20,995,911

The greater part of the increase has been in exports to Great Britain, which increased from 2,400 cwt. in January of 1884, to 197,779 cwt. in June, while in 1885 it rose from 62,000 in January to 483,000 in June. The aggregate for 12 months was 257,443,760 lbs., or substantially nine-tenths of our entire exports. Great Britain formerly imported more from Germany, France and Holland, than from the United States, but now the receipts are 2,298,605 cwt. from the United States, 1,277,092 from Holland, 977,097 from Germany, 494,935 from France, and only 290,321 from all other countries, for the calendar year 1885.

The following circular report of John F. Craig & Co., of Philadelphia, shows the comparative extent of the sugar and molasses trade at that port for the past four calendar years. The importations of sugar were mostly from Cuba; and those of molasses were entirely from the West India Islands.

SUGAR.

Receipts. January 1st to December 31st.	Hhds.	Boxes and Bags.	1885.	1884.	1883.	1882.
			Tons.	Tons.	Tons.	Tons.
From Cuba, ...	86,272	236,310	78,276	65,263	36,856	50,702
" English Islands, .	6,101	10,738	5,828	9,809	21,258	3,110
" French Islands, .	1,208		674	4,531	4,570	5,444
" Porto Rico, . . .	6,045	3,615	3,744	1,432	1,005	1,366
" Brazil, ...	4	107,645	8,653	8,125	3,846	4,338
" Phillippine Islands		65,519	1,755	9,795		
" German Beet, . .		56,088	6,260	1,936	1,493	
Total, ...	99,630	479,915	105,190	100,891	69,028	64,960

Stock of Sugar on hand January 1st, 1886, 4,018 hogsheads.

MOLASSES.

Receipts. January 1st to December 31st.	1885.	1884.	1883.	1882.
From Havana, hogsheads, ...	14,275	15,799	6,384	7,575
" Matanzas, "	18,989	9,551	19,684	24,452
" Cardenas, "	51,524	43,618	26,137	45,531
" Sagua, "	19,824	14,396	9,183	13,832
" Cienfuegos, "	2,063	2,049	2,242	4,068
" Trinidad, "	1,288	2,741	1,935	3,015
" Caibarien, "	2,357	1,955		688
" Manzanilla, "	1,259			
" Porto Rico, "	142	473		6,027
" Barbadoes, "	2,344	8	1,134	12,512
Total, hhds., ...	114,065	90,590	66,699	117,700

Molasses boiled, hhds.: 1885, 113,093; 1884, 92,173; 1883, 64,062.

Freights on sugar and molasses from Cuba have been quite uniform throughout the year. The number of American vessels engaged in this trade shows in the aggregate a large tonnage; and although freights have been confined to comparatively low figures, ruling generally at $3.00 per hhd. sugar and $2.00 per 110 gals. molasses, this business is preferred to the coastwise trade by the vessels adapted for it. Coal and cooperage can generally be obtained at Philadelphia at rates of freight sufficient to pay all port charges in Cuba. Out-and-back charters are not so much in order as formerly, the old West India traders preferring to take their chances on the market. The stevedore charges for loading and discharging have been reduced to a minimum; and as coal freights East or South can always be obtained, Philadelphia as a discharging port for sugar and molasses cargoes is generally preferred to other ports.

The West India business of this port is almost exclusively confined to the old firms of Isaac Hough & Co., S. & J. Welsh, Lawrence Johnson & Co., and E. F. Cabada & Co.; the latter having close connection with the sugar and molasses houses on the south side of Cuba; the others confining the most of their business to the north side. Shipments to the Windward Islands are chiefly made by Thomas Wattson & Son and John R. Rue, the former having extensive business connections at Port Spain, Island of Trinidad.

Philadelphia has three large sugar refineries and eight boiling establishments for making sugar from molasses, and the quality of sugars turned out is superior in every respect, which insures for it the highest market prices for export and domestic demands.

1886   1886
OFFICERS AND COMMITTEES
— OF THE —
Philadelphia Maritime Exchange.

PRESIDENT,
✓ WILLIAM BROCKIE.

VICE-PRESIDENT,
✓ PHILIP FITZPATRICK.

TREASURER,
GEORGE E. BARTOL.

SECRETARY,
EDWARD R. SHARWOOD.

DIRECTORS.

LARS WESTERGAARD,	F. A. CHURCHMAN,
DAVID S. STETSON,	NICHOLAS LENNIG,
JOHN H. CATHERWOOD,	JOHN F. CRAIG,
EDWARD W. BARKER,	S. B. MACDONNELL,
CHARLES GIBBONS, Jr.	FRANK L. NEALL,
THEODORE FROTHINGHAM,	JOSEPH E. MORSE,
ISAAC HOUGH,	WILLIAM J. LATTA,
WILLIAM A. PLATT,	SAMUEL T. KERR.

COMMITTEES OF THE BOARD OF DIRECTORS.

FINANCE.
ISAAC HOUGH,
JOHN H. CATHERWOOD,
JOHN F. CRAIG.

TELEGRAPH AND STATION.
THEO. FROTHINGHAM,
CHARLES GIBBONS, Jr.
NICHOLAS LENNIG,
FRANK L. NEALL,
WM. J. LATTA.

ROOM.
LARS WESTERGAARD,
NICHOLAS LENNIG,
SAMUEL T. KERR.

MEMBERSHIP.
JOHN H. CATHERWOOD,
D. S. STETSON,
JOHN F. CRAIG.

*METEOROLOGICAL AND AIDS
TO NAVIGATION.*
CHAS. GIBBONS, Jr.
JOSEPH E. MORSE,
WILLIAM A. PLATT.

PILOTAGE and NAVIGATION.
FRANK L. NEALL,
DAVID S. STETSON,
F. A. CHURCHMAN,
LARS WESTERGAARD,
THEO. FROTHINGHAM.

COMMERCIAL REPORTS.
EDWARD W. BARKER,
ISAAC HOUGH,
S. B. MACDONNELL.

EXECUTIVE.
WM. BROCKIE,
PHILIP FITZPATRICK,
LARS WESTERGAARD,
ISAAC HOUGH,
THEO. FROTHINGHAM,
CHAS. GIBBONS, Jr.
JOHN H. CATHERWOOD,
FRANK L. NEALL,
EDWARD W. BARKER.

*SOLICITOR OF PROTECTIVE
FUND.*
CHARLES GIBBONS, Jr.

PORT OF PHILADELPHIA.

HARBOR RULES AND REGULATIONS.

*Adopted by the Board of Wardens of the Port of Philadelphia,
March 5, 1883.*

For the information of Owners, Masters, and other having
command, care, or charge of Vessels within the Port or Harbor
of Philadelphia, the following rules and regulations are published:

VESSELS TO REPORT AT WARDENS' OFFICE.

1. All vessels arriving at the Port of Philadelphia must report
at the Wardens' office, rooms 11 and 13, Chamber of Commerce,
within twenty-four hours after arrival, and before leaving the port
must report their clearance. Penalty for neglecting to report
from $10 to $50.

ANCHORAGE.

2. Vessels must not anchor in the river Delaware below
Kaighn's Point, west of the buoy marking the main channel.

Vessels must not anchor above Kaighn's Point, except eastward
of Windmill Island, or in the east channel at Cooper's Point.

Vessels must in no case anchor where they will interfere with
the ferries.

Vessels must not anchor at Port Richmond, except by permission and under the direction of the Harbor Master.

Vessels must not anchor at any place in the channel of the
river Schuylkill, nor lie at any wharf in that river more than two
abreast, without the permission of the Harbor Master.

Vessels must not anchor on the range line of any range lights.

Vessels at anchor must exhibit, between sunset and sunrise, a
visible white signal light in the rigging, at least fifteen (15) feet
above the deck.

3. Vessels hauled into any wharf or dock, or alongside of other vessels lying at any wharf or dock, must be made fast to the shore with proper lines, with sufficient fenders between them and the inside vessels, and shall, when so ordered by the Harbor Master, have their jib-booms, sprit-sail-yards, main-booms, spankers, ring-tail booms, davits and bumpkins, if any, rigged in, their lower yards topped, and anchors either a cockbill or at the hawse-pipe, as most convenient.

4. When fasts of vessels extend across a dock so as to obstruct passing vessels, the captain or person in charge shall, when so ordered by the Harbor Master, cause the fasts to be slackened or cast off.

5. Vessels lying at the ends of piers, so as to obstruct the passage to the adjoining docks, must move when necessary to accommodate other vessels entering or leaving the docks.

6. Vessels lying alongside of a wharf, and not taking in or discharging cargo, must make way for and permit other vessels that want to load or unload cargo to come inside next to the wharf.

7. If the person in charge of any vessel refuses to move, the Harbor Master shall cause the same to be done at the cost and risk of the master, owner, or consignee.

8. No wharf shall be obstructed so as to prevent the loading or unloading of cargo, but reasonable facilities will at all times be allowed on application to the Harbor Master.

9. No tar, pitch, turpentine, or rosin shall be heated on a wharf or on board any vessel lying at a wharf.

10. Vessels that may increase their width by using ballast-logs, pontoons, or devices of the same nature, must move to accommodate other vessels, when so ordered by the Harbor Master, and shall pay the expenses of other vessels that may be required to move to allow a vessel with the above appliances to get in or out of docks.

11. Any master, captain, or whoever is in charge of a vessel, who shall refuse or neglect to comply with the directions of the Harbor Master, or whoever shall obstruct his authority, shall be fined in a sum not exceeding $100 for each and every offense.

(Act of February 4, 1846, P. L. 30.)

SECTION LXXV. That if any person or persons whoever shall, from and after the passage of this act, cast into the tide-way of the river Delaware, or into the river Schuylkill, from the lower falls thereof to its junction with the river Delaware, any ballast, cinders, ashes, or any heavy articles whatever, from any ship, vessel, steamboat or wharf, he or they so offending, for every such offence, shall forfeit and pay a sum not exceeding one hundred dollars, to be sued for and recovered with costs of suit, before any alderman of the city, or justice of the peace of the county of Philadelphia, or in any court of record in this State, in the same manner and for the same uses as directed by the thirty-sixth section of the Act of Assembly, entitled "An act to establish a Board of Port Wardens for the Port of Philadelphia," &c., passed twenty-ninth day of March, one thousand eight hundred and three: *Provided*, that the jurisdiction of the Board of Wardens of the Port of Philadelphia shall not extend on the river Delaware beyond the jurisdiction of the Collector of Customs for the district of Philadelphia, upon said river.

That it shall be the duty of the Harbor Master, and he is hereby required to enforce and superintend the execution of all laws of the Commonwealth, and of all by-laws, rules and regulations of the corporation of the city, or of the Wardens of the Port of Philadelphia, enacted, ordained, and declared, or hereafter to be ordained, enacted, and declared, for cleaning the docks and wharves of the Port of Philadelphia; for preventing all nuisances at the wharves and in the docks aforesaid, by burning or breaming any ships or vessels, or otherwise howsoever; *for regulating and stationing all ships or vessels in the stream of the river Delaware, or at the wharves within the boundaries of the City of Philadelphia;* for removing, from time to time, ships and vessels, in order to accommodate and make room for others, or for admitting the river craft to pass in and out of the docks, and for compelling the masters and captains of ships and vessels to accommodate each other, so that ships and vessels arriving from sea, shall, for a reasonable time, not exceeding six days, be entitled to berths next to the wharves, until they have landed their cargoes.

6

(Act 15th June, 1874, P. L. 390.)

SECTION CXLVII. *Be it enacted by the Senate and House of Representatives of the Commonwealth of Pennsylvania, in General Assembly met, and it is hereby enacted by the authority of the same,* That all vessels over seventy-five tons' burthen, shall, within twenty-four hours after their arrival at the Port of Philadelphia, report and register at the office of the Board of Wardens for the said port; and all proceedings for neglect to obey the harbor regulations, as at present existing, shall be held before any justice of the peace or alderman of the City of Philadelphia, and the proceedings for the enforcement of penalties, in all cases, shall be commenced by capias. All laws or parts of laws inconsistent with these laws are hereby repealed.

Every vessel arriving from, or bound to a foreign port, is bound by law to receive a pilot, except outward bound American vessels carrying their registered tonnage of coal.

Every master is bound to report immediately on arriving to the Wardens' office, under a penalty of $10, and incurs a like penalty if he does not record his clearance with them before departing.

No license shall be granted to any person to act as a pilot, unless he has served an apprenticeship of six years on board of a pilot boat.

The pilot of every vessel is obliged to inform the master of his having to report at the Wardens' office.

Every pilot detained by the master, owner or consignee, or by the ice, is entitled to $3 per day.

Every pilot, obliged by the ice, or stress of weather to proceed to another port, is entitled to his pilotage, and if there discharged, to eight cents a mile for every mile he has to travel home.

The masters of vessels shall give an account to the pilot when boarding of the draught of such vessels, and in case he shall misrepresent said draught, and give it as less than the actual draught, he shall forfeit and pay the sum of $25, to be sued for and recovered before any alderman of the City of Philadelphia, by the Master Warden, who shall pay the same over, when collected, to the Society for the Relief of Decayed Pilots, their Widows and Orphans; he having first deducted the expenses incurred in recovering the same.

Towage Rates Outward.

REVISED MARCH 10, 1884.

SQUARE-RIGGED VESSELS.

Towage from Philadelphia, Port Richmond, Gibson's Point, Point Breeze, South Chester Oil Works, and Grand Point down the Delaware River and I

If from West Philadelphia, twenty (20) per cent. of Point Breeze towage being rate additional.

If lying in stream opposite South Chester Oil Works, a deduction of ten (10) per cent. to be allowed.

STEAM TOWING

ON THE

Delaware River *AND* Bay *AND* Schuylkill

BY THE

TUGS GEO. W. PRIDE, Jr., ARGUS and IVANHOE,

and others, at shortest notice.

Tugs GEO. W. PRIDE, JR., ARGUS and IVANHOE are fitted complete with
Steam Pumps and all necessary materials to assist Vessels in
Distress; also engaged in Towing Vessels to and from
Philadelphia, New York, Boston, Baltimore,
and other Ports on the Atlantic Coast.

GEO. W. PRIDE & SON,

Office, 502 South Delaware Avenue,   Also Office, 119 Walnut Street,

RESIDENCE, 230 GERMAN ST.   GEO. W. PRIDE, Jr.

PHILADELPHIA.

Orders by Mail or Telegram promptly attended to.   Telephone No. 1758.

GEO. W. PRIDE & SON

STEAM

WRECKING TUGS

PHILADELPHIA

Every outward bound ship or vessel is bound to remain at the Capes twenty-four hours after its arrival, to give the pilot an opportunity to be taken out, under a penalty of $800.

CITY ICE BOATS.

The City of Philadelphia owns and operates three Ice Boats (side-wheel steamers) of power and equipment scarcely second to any in the world. Their office is to keep the channels of the Delaware and Schuylkill Rivers navigable in the severest winter weather, and the original intention was that they should be used solely for that purpose; but in times of emergency, when Tow Boats are not at hand, and navigation is rendered very difficult, if not impracticable, except in their wake, they accept tows at rates which, though apparently high, pay but a small portion of their operating expenses.

RATES OF TOWAGE.

SCALE OF DISTANCES.	MILES.	TONS.	TONS.	TONS.	TONS.	TONS.	TONS.
	U.S. Survey.	70 to 200, under 70 to be charged 70.	200 to 500.	500 to 800.	800 to 1,100.	1,100 to 1,300.	1,300 and upwards
PHILADELPHIA, TO OR FROM	Statute Miles.	Cents Per ton.	Cents Per ton	Cents Per ton	Cents Per ton.	Cents Per ton.	Cents Per ton.
Chester, ...	16½	18	16	14	13	12	11
Marcus Hook, ...	20	19	17	16	14	13	12
Grubb's Landing, ...	24	20	18	17	15	14	13
Wilmington Creek, ...	28½	22	21	19	17	15	14
New Castle, ...	33½	23	22	21	19	17	15
Delaware City, ...	40	27	25	22	21	20	19
Reedy Island Lighthouse, . .	46	29	27	25	22	21	20
Morris Liston's (half-way) .	52	31	28	26	24	22	21
Duck Creek Lighthouse, . . .	56½	32	30	28	25	23	22
Bombay Hook Point, ...	61	34	32	29	27	25	23
Buoy of Middle, ...	71	39	35	33	30	28	26
Ledge Light Boat, ...	77	41	38	35	32	30	28
Buoy on the 14 Feet Bank, . .	84	44	40	37	34	31	30
Brandywine Light Boat, . .	90	47	42	40	36	33	31
Buoy on the Brown, ...	94	48	44	42	37	34	33
Breakwater, ...	103	52	48	44	40	37	35
Light Boat on 5 Fathom Bank,	128						

NOTE.—Vessels using the Ice Boats' hawser shall pay ten per cent. in addition to the amount of their towage.

RATES OF PILOTAGE FOR DELAWARE RIVER AND BAY.

FEET.	STATE OF PENNSYLVANIA RATES. (Act of June 8, 1881.)				STATE OF DELAWARE RATES. (Act of April 5, 1881.)	
	INWARD. If spoken East of Five Fathom B nk Lightship, or North of Hereford Inlet Lighthouse, or South of Fenwick's Island Light.	INWARD. If spoken inside of Five Fathom Lightship and outside of line drawn from Cape May Light to Cape Henlopen Light.	INWARD. If not spoken until inside of line drawn from Cape May Light to Cape Henlopen Light.	OUTWARD.	INWARD.	OUTWARD.
12	$49 37	$44 88	$40 39	$36 00	$44 88	$44 88
12½	57 20	52 00	46 80	37 50	52 00	52 00
13	59 49	54 08	48 67	39 00	54 08	54 08
13½	61 78	56 16	50 54	40 50	56 16	56 16
14	64 06	58 24	52 42	42 00	58 21	58 22
14½	66 35	60 32	54 29	43 50	60 32	60 32
15	68 64	62 40	56 16	45 00	62 40	62 40
15½	70 93	64 48	58 03	46 50	69 75	69 75
16	73 22	66 56	59 90	48 00	72 00	72 00
16½	75 50	68 64	61 78	49 50	74 25	74 25
17	77 79	70 72	63 65	51 00	76 50	76 50
17½	80 08	72 80	65 52	52 50	78 75	78 75
18	82 37	74 88	67 39	54 00	81 00	81 00
18½	84 66	76 96	69 26	55 50	92 50	92 50
19	86 94	79 04	71 14	57 00	95 00	95 00
19½	89 23	81 12	73 01	58 50	97 50	97 50
20	91 52	83 20	74 88	60 00	100 00	100 00
20½	93 81	85 28	76 75	61 50	112 75	112 71
21	96 10	87 36	78 62	63 00	115 50	115 50
21½	98 38	89 44	80 50	64 50	118 25	118 25
22	100 67	91 52	82 37	66 00	121 00	121 00
22½	102 96	93 60	84 24	67 50	123 75	123 75
23	105 25	95 68	86 11	69 00	126 50	126 50
23½	107 54	97 76	87 98	70 50	129 25	129 25
24	109 82	99 84	89 86	72 00	132 00	132 00
24½	112 11	101 92	91 73	73 50	134 75	134 75
25	114 40	104 00	93 60	75 00	137 50	137 50
25½	116 69	106 08	95 47	76 50	140 25	140 25
26	118 98	108 16	97 34	78 00	143 00	143 00
26½	121 26	110 24	99 22	79 50	145 75	145 75
27	123 55	112 32	101 09	81 00	148 50	148 50

NOTE.—An extra rate of *Ten Dollars* is charged under the law of the *State of Delaware* for *Winter Pilotage*, between the first of November and the first of April.

WHARFAGE.

No charge is made by the Grain Elevator Companies, of Philadelphia, on either Steamships or Sailing Vessels, while loading grain alongside the elevators.

RATES FOR WHARFAGE AT PETROLEUM WHARVES, POINT BREEZE, PHILADELPHIA, AND AT CHESTER, PA.

APPROVED BY THE MARITIME EXCHANGE.

VESSELS' REGISTERED TONNAGE.	For Vessels lying at inside Berths, either idle or working, and while working a: outside Berths.	FOR VESSELS WHILE IDLE AT OUTSIDE BERTHS.	
		Second Tier.	Outside of Second Tier.
TONS.	PER DAY.	PER DAY.	PER DAY.
200 or under.	$2 75	$1 40	$1 05
300	3 25	1 65	1 20
400	3 75	1 90	. 1 40
500	4 50	2 25	1 70
600	5 00	2 50	1 90
700	5 25	2 65	1 95
800	5 50	2 75	2 05
900	6 00	3 00	2 25
1000	6 50	3 25	2 45
1100	6 75	3 40	2 55
1200	7 00	3 50	2 65
1300	7 50	3 75	2 80
1400	8 00	4 00	3 00
1500	8 50	4 25	3 20
1600	9 00	4 50	3 40
1700	9 25	4 65	3 45
1800	9 50	4 75	3 55
1900	9 75	4 90	3 65
2000	10 00	5 00	3 75

The reduced rates, as above, for vessels idle at outside berths, are to be allowed only when such berths are occupied by direction of the Wharf Superintendent or Harbor Master; otherwise, full rates will be charged, the same as for inside berths.

With the preceding exceptions, there is no fixed scale of wharfage rates in Philadelphia.

The charge to STEAMERS ranges from $8 to $25 per day, according to the location and facilities included.

The charge to SAILING VESSELS ranges from $4 to $8 per day, according to the views of the wharf-owner; but masters of vessels can usually arrange to pay only half-rates while vessel is neither loading nor discharging.

In case a vessel is not working, and the berth is required for another vessel, the Harbor Master is empowered to compel the vessel to move; and if necessary, he may employ a Tug for the purpose, at vessel's expense.

The following are the wharfage rates now in force at the Port Richmond (Philadelphia) freight wharves:—

Under 300	tons register,	.	$2.00 per day
300 to 500	" "	.	3.00 " "
Over 500 to 800	" "	.	4.00 " "
" 800	" "	.	½ ct. per ton
Maximum charge per day,	.	.	. $10.00

Full rates will be charged while vessels remain in dock, loaded or light.

After January 1st, 1886, no exception will be made on vessels carrying lumber, ties, or other material for use of Railroad Co.

FORMS OF CHARTER PARTIES.

FORM OF GRAIN CHARTER. (DIRECT PORT.)

This Charter Party, Made and concluded upon in the City of PHILADELPHIA, the . . . day of . . . in the year of our Lord, one thousand eight hundred and . . . , *Between* . . . Master and Agent for the owners of the . . . of . . . built . . . at . . . of . . . tons, or thereabouts, register measurement, now . . . . and guaranteed to class . . . at . . . of the first part, and . . . of the second part, *Witnesseth:* That the said party of the first part agrees on the freighting and chartering of the whole of the said vessel (with the exception of the deck, cabin, and necessary room for the crew and storage of provisions, sails and cables) for the cargo hereinafter mentioned, unto said party of the second part, for a voyage from PHILADELPHIA

TO . . . .
orders, on signing Bills of Lading, or as near thereto as she may safely get and always
lie afloat, on the terms following :—

The said Vessel shall be tight, staunch, strong, and in every way fitted for such a
voyage, and receive on board the merchandise hereinafter mentioned.

The said party of the second part doth engage to provide and furnish to the said
Vessel a full and complete cargo of WHEAT and INDIAN CORN, say as much as
she can reasonably stow and carry on the draft of water allowed by the Surveyors
appointed by the Philadelphia Board of Marine Underwriters, under whose inspection
the Vessel is to load, and guarantees to carry, under said inspection . . . quarters, ten
(10 %) per cent., more or less ; and, furthermore, it is hereby agreed, that the Vessel
shall prepare for Bulk and Bag Grain, at her expense, according to the rules and regulations of the Philadelphia Board of Marine Underwriters, and shall furnish from them
to Charterers a certificate of proper lading before clearing at the Custom House.

And it is furthermore agreed, that the party of the second part shall pay to the said
party of the first part, or his agent, for the use of the said Vessel during the voyage
aforesaid . . . ( ) shillings and . . . ( ) pence, if ordered to . . . . . .
. . . .
all per quarter of 480 pounds delivered ; freight payable in cash, on right delivery of
cargo ; if discharged in the United Kingdom, in British Sterling ; if discharged on the
Continent, as above, in cash, at the current rate of exchange for bankers' short-sight
bills on London, without discount or allowance ; and it is further agreed, that the
freight, as per Bills of Lading, shall be taken without deduction in payment of this
Charter, any deficiency to be paid here by the Charterers in cash, less insurance, and
any surplus over and above estimated Charter to be settled here before Vessel clears
at the Custom House by Captain's draft in Charterers' favor upon Consignees, payable
Ten days after arrival of Vessel at port of discharge. The Master to call at Broker's
office as requested to sign bills of lading as presented, without prejudice to this
Charter Party.

It is further agreed, that . . . ( ) running lay-days, to commence when the
Vessel is all ready and prepared to load Bulk Grain, and Surveyor's certificate thereof
given to Charterers, shall be allowed for loading the Vessel at Philadelphia, and discharging (days expended at Philadelphia to be endorsed on Bills of Lading or Charter
Party). And if the Vessel be longer detained, Charterers to pay demurrage at the rate
of . . . ( ) pounds, British Sterling, or its equivalent, per day, payable day by
day, to the party of the first part or authorized agent : *Provided*, such detention shall
happen by default of the said party of the second part or their agent. Vessel to employ
competent Stevedore, and to load at such elevator, elevators, wharf or wharves, as
may be designated by the Charterers, who are to pay the ordinary expense of towage
after the first move. Cargo to be delivered on board of vessel by elevator or otherwise, free of charge to the vessel, and to be received at port of discharge within reach
of Vessel's tackles. Lighterage, if any, at expense and risk of cargo. If more than
one kind of grain is shipped, all extra expense to be paid by Charterers. The Charterers' responsibility under this charter to cease upon shipment of the cargo, but the
Vessel to have a lien thereon for all freight, dead freight, demurrage and average.
Vessel is likewise to discharge in such dock or at such wharf as may be specified by

Consignees on arrival, provided not conflict ng with above te ms, and no extra detention or expense is thereby incurred by the Vessel. A commission of Five per cent. on the amount of this Ch ter is due and p yable by Vessel and owners, upon signing hereof, vessel lost or not lost, to . . ., and Vessel to be entered and cleared at Custom House by them, at port of loading, on customary terms.

Vessel to be free of Consignment Commission at port of discharge.

Funds for ordinary expenses of Vessel, if desired by Master, to be advanced by Charterers at Port of Loading, subject to commission and insurance only.

To the true and faithful performance of all and every of the foregoing agreements we, the said parties, do hereby bind ourselves, our heirs, executors, administrators, and assigns, each to the other, in the penal sum of estimated amount of frei ht.

In Witness Whereof, We have hereunto set our hands the day and year first above written.

SIGNED IN THE PRESENCE OF

FORM OF GRAIN CHARTER. (FOR ORDERS.)

This Charter Party, Made and concluded upon in the City of PHILADELPHIA, the . . . day of . . . in the year of our Lord one thousand eight hundred and . . . *Between* . . . Master and Agent for the owners of the . . . of . . . Built . . . at . . . of . . . tons, or thereabouts, re ister measurement, now . . . .

. . . . and guaranteed to class . . . at . . . of the first part, and . . . of the second part, *Witnesseth:* That the said party of the first part agrees on the freighting and chartering of the whole of the said vessel (with the exception of the deck, cabin, and necessary room for the crew and storage of provisions, sails and cables), for the cargo hereinafter mentioned, unto said party of the second part, for a voyage from PHIL-ADELPHIA TO QUEENSTOWN, FALMOUTH, OR PLYMOUTH FOR ORDERS (which are to be given within forty-eight (48) hours after arrival of vessel at port of call or lay-days to count), to discharge at a safe Port in the UNITED KINGDOM or on the CONTINENT between BORDEAUX and HAMBURG (both included), or as near thereto as she may safely get and always lie afloat, or to a direct Port within the above limits, if named before Vessel sails from PHILADEL-PHIA, on the terms following:—

The said Vessel shall be tight, staunch, strong, and in every way fitted for such a voyage, and receive on board the merchandise hereinafter mentioned.

The said party of the second part doth engage to provide and furnish to the said Vessel a full and complete cargo of WHEAT and INDIAN CORN, say as much as she can reasonably stow and carry on the draft of water allowed by the Surveyors appointed by the Philadelphia Board of Marine Underwriters, under whose inspection the Vessel is to load, and guarantees to carry, under said inspection, . . . quarters, ten (10 %) per cent., more or less; and, furthermore, it is hereby agreed, that the Vessel shall prepare for Bulk and Bag Grain, at her expense, according to the rules and regulations of the Philadelphia Board of Marine Underwriters, and shall furnish from them to Charterers a certificate of proper lading before clearing at the Custom House.

And it is furthermore agreed, that the party of the second part shall pay to the said party of the first part, or his agent, for the use of the said Vessel during the voyage aforesaid, if ordered from QUEENSTOWN, FALMOUTH, or PLYMOUTH to discharge at a Port in the UNITED KINGDOM, . . . ( ) shillings and . . . ( ) pence; if ordered from QUEENSTOWN, FALMOUTH, or PLYMOUTH to discharge at a Port on the CONTINENT, as above, ten per cent. additional on above-named freight; if ordered to a direct Port in the UNITED KINGDOM, . . . shillings . . . pence ( ); if ordered to a direct Port on the CONTINENT, as above, . . . shillings . . . pence ( ), ...

. . . .

all per quarter of 480 pounds delivered; freight payable, in cash, on right delivery of cargo; if discharged in the United Kingdom, in British Sterling; if discharged on the Continent, as above, in cash, at the current rate of exchange for bankers' short-sight bills on London, without discount or allowance; and it is further agreed, that the freight, as per Bills of Lading, shall be taken without deduction in payment of this Charter, any deficiency to be paid here by the Charterers in cash, less insurance, and any surplus over and above estimated Charter to be settled here before Vessel clears at the Custom House by Captain's draft in Charterers' favor upon Consignees, payable Ten days after arrival of Vessel at Port of discharge. The master to call at Broker's office as requested to sign bills of lading as presented, without prejudice to this Charter Party.

It is further agreed that . . . ( ) running lay-days, to commence when the Vessel is all ready and prepared to load Bulk Grain, and Surveyor's certificate thereof given to Charterers, shall be allowed for loading the Vessel at Philadelphia, waiting orders at port of call (after expiration of 48 hours, as above), and discharging (days expended at Philadelphia to be endorsed on bills of lading or Charter Party). And if the Vessel be longer detained Charterers to pay demurrage at the rate of . . . ( ) pounds British Sterling, or its equivalent, per day, payable day by day, to the party of the first part or authorized agent : *Provided*, such detention shall happen by default of the said party of the second part or their agent. Vessel to employ competent Stevedore, and to load at such Elevator, Elevators, wharf or wharves, as may be designated by the Charterers, who are to pay the ordinary expense of towage after the first move. Cargo to be delivered on board of Vessel by Elevator or otherwise, free of charge to the Vessel, and to be received at port of discharge within reach of Vessel's Tackles. Lighterage, if any, at expense and risk of cargo. If more than one kind of grain is shipped, all extra expense to be paid by Charterers. The Charterers' responsibility under this Charter to cease upon shipment of the cargo, but the Vessel to have a lien thereon for all freight, dead freight, demurrage, and average. Vessel is likewise to discharge in such dock or at such wharf as may be specified by Consignees on arrival, provided not conflicting with above terms, and no extra detention or expense is thereby incurred by the Vessel. A commission of Five per cent. on the amount of this Charter is due and payable by Vessel and owners upon signing hereof, Vessel lost or not lost, to . . . and Vessel to be entered and cleared at Custom House by them, at port of loading, on customary terms.

Vessel to be free of Consignment Commission at port of discharge.

Funds for ordinary expenses of Vessel, if desired by master, to be advanced by Charterers at Port of Loading, subject to commission and insurance only.

To the true and faithful performance of all and every of the foregoing agreements we, the said parties, do hereby bind our-elves, our heirs, executors, administrators, and assigns, each to the other, in the penal sum of estimated amount of freight.

In Witness Whereof, We have hereunto set our hands the day and year first above written.

SIGNED IN THE PRESENCE OF

FORM OF PETROLEUM CHARTER.

This Charter Party, made in the City of Philadelphia, the . . . day of . . . of the year one thousand eight hundred and . . . *Between* . . . Master and Agent for the Owners of the . . . of . . . of the burden of . . . tons, or thereabouts, register measurement, now lying in the harbor of . . . of the first part, and . . . of the second part.

Witnesseth, That the said party of the first part agree on the freighting and chartering of the whole of said vessel (with the exception of the deck, cabin and necessary room for the crew and storage of provisions, sails, and cables), unto the said party of the second part, for a voyage from Philadelphia to . . . .

. . . . or so near thereto as she may safely get, and always to lie afloat, on the terms following, viz. :

The said vessel shall be tight, staunch and strong, and in every way fitted for such a voyage, and receive on board during the voyage aforesaid, the merchandise hereinafter mentioned. The said party of the second part doth engage to provide and furnish to the said vessel a full and complete cargo of . . . " PETROLEUM," in the customary barrels and boxes of ten gallons each,

. . . . and to pay to the said party of the first part, or his agent, for the use of the said vessel during the voyage aforesaid, in manner following—that is to say : . . . Shillings, . . . Pence, British Sterling, ... all with 5 per cent. primage per forty (40) gallons, gross American gauge, all payable in cash, on right delivery, at the current short sight rate of Exchange on London, without discount or allowance, on each and every barrel or case, whether delivered full, part full, or empty.

It is agreed that . . . running lay days shall be allowed for loading the vessel at Philadelphia, commencing from the time the Captain gives written notice to charterers that his vessel is ready and prepared to receive cargo and customary dispatch for discharging cargo at port of discharge, all over to count as lay days, and for each and every day's detention by default of the said party of the second part, or their agent, demurrage at the rate of . . . Pounds, British Sterling, shall be paid, day by day, by the said party of the second part, or their agent, to the said party of the first part, or his agent.

It is also further understood and agreed, that the cargo or cargoes shall be received and delivered alongside of the vessel, within reach of her tackles. Lighterage, if any, at the expense and risk of the cargo.

The vessel is to haul to such loading berth as may be designated by charterers, at her own expense; if required to move thence, charterers to pay the towage. Vessel to load, if required, in the Schuylkill, where she can lie afloat; also under inspection as to stowage by authorized Inspectors appointed by the U. S. Petroleum Association, free of charge to vessel for such inspection.

Bills of lading to be signed as presented, without prejudice to this charter. Any difference to be settled before the vessel sails. If in favor of vessel, cash, at current rate of exchange, less insurance. If in favor of the party of the second part, by draft of Captain upon his consignees, payable ten days after the arrival of vessel at port of discharge.

The charterers' responsibility under this charter to cease upon shipment of the cargo, but the vessel to have a lien thereon for all freight, dead freight, demurrage or average.

A commission of five per cent. upon the gross amount of this charter (with accrued demurrage) payable by the vessel, is due upon the signing hereof.

To the true performance of all and every of the foregoing covenants and agreements, the said parties, each to the other, do hereby bind themselves, their heirs, executors, administrators and assigns (especially the said party of the first part, the said vessel, her freight, tackle and appurtenances; and the said party of the second part, the merchandise to be laden on board), each to the other, in the penal sum of . . . . , ESTIMATED AMOUNT OF THIS CHARTER.

In Witness Whereof, the parties have hereunto interchangeably set their hands and seals, the day and year above written.

SEALED AND DELIVERED }
IN THE PRESENCE OF   }

FORM OF LUMBER CHARTER.

George W. Bush & Sons' Lumber Company, Wilmington, Del.

This Charter Party, Made and concluded upon in the City of Philadelphia, this . . . day of . . . in the year of our Lord, one thousand eight hundred and . . . *Between* . . . of the good . . . of . . . of the burden of . . . tons, or thereabouts, register measurement, now lying in the harbor of . . . of the first part, and . . . of the second part; *Witnesseth,* That the said party of the first part agrees on the freighting and chartering of the whole of the said vessel, (with the exception of the cabin and necessary room for the crew and storage of provisions, sails and cables,) unto the said party of the second part, for a voyage from . . . .
. . . .
on the terms following : The said Vessel shall be tight, staunch, strong, and in every way fitted for such a voyage and receive on board during the voyage aforesaid the merchandise hereinafter mentioned. The said party of the second part doth engage

to provide and furnish to the said Vessel, a full and complete cargo, under and on deck, of PITCH PINE Boards ^{and} Re-sawed Lumber (optional with Charterers), . . . And pay to the said party of the first part, or . . . agent, for the use of the said Vessel during the voyage aforesaid, ($ . . .) . . . Do'lars per thousand (1000) superficial feet delivered, payable cash, without discount or commission, upon proper delivery of cargo . . . . It is agreed that the Vessel shall be loaded at the rate of fifteen thousand (15,000) feet per running lay day (Sundays excepted), at . . . commencing from the time the Captain reports himself ready and prepared to receive cargo, and to be discharged with customary despatch at port of discharge, and that for each and every day's detention by default of the said party of the second part or agent, . . . dollars per day, day by day, shall be paid by the said party of the second part or agent, to the said party of the first part or agent. The cargo or cargoes to be received and delivered alongside within reach of Vessel's tackles.

. . . . Vessel to haul to wharf designated by charterers or their agents to receive and discharge cargoes.

A commission of five per cent. upon the amount of this charter, (with the accrued demurrage), payable by the vessel and owners, due to . . . upon the signing thereof.

Charterers' responsibility to cease upon shipment of the cargo, but the vessel to have a lien thereon for all freight, deck freight, demurrage, or average.

To the true and faithful performance of this agreement, we, the said parties, do hereby bind ourselves, our heirs, executors, administrators, and assigns, each to the other, in the penal sum of ESTIMATED AMOUNT OF CHARTER.

In Witness Whereof, We have hereunto set our hands, the day and year first above written.

SIGNED IN THE PRESENCE OF

TIMBER AND DEAL CHARTER PARTY.

Adapted to South Atlantic and Gulf Ports of Loading.

SAUNDERS & ROSS,
   Ship Brokers,
MOBILE, ALABAMA.

It is this day mutually agreed between . . . of the good Ship or Vessel called the . . . of the Burthen of . . . tons Register, or thereabouts, now at . . . and . . . Charterers; That the said Ship, being tight, staunch and strong, and every way fitted for the voyage, shall, with all convenient speed, sail and proceed to . . . and there load from the Factors of the said Merchants, or Agents, at such safe anchorage ^{and} dock as they may direct (where the ship can lie afloat, giving notice three clear days before Cargo is required, after being at such anchorage or dock ready for Cargo), a full and complete Cargo, to consist of Square Pitch Pine . . . Timber ^{and} Deals, ^{and} Boards, at Merchants' option. Merchants to supply timber ^{and} Planks for Beam Fillings and Broken Stowage at their option; Deckload, if required by the Master, to be supplied at full freight.   No timber or deals to be cut without the written permission of the Shippers, and number of cuts (if any) to be inserted in the Bill of Lading.   The Cargo to be delivered alongside at Merchants' risk and expense, and to be received by the Master and secured by the Ship's dogs and chains when so delivered, and to be then at Ship's risk.   Should the Master order more Timber or Deals alongside than the Ship requires for loading, the expense of returning it to the Booms or Mills to be paid by the Ship.   The Ship to discharge each Lighter having Lumber for Cargo or Broken Stowage without unreasonable detention, and to give Charterers' Agent written notice three clear days before Beam-filling Broken Stowage is required; and being so loaded, shall therewith proceed to . . . any safe Port in the United Kingdom or between Gibraltar and Hamburg (both Ports inclusive), as ordered on signing Bills of Lading, and deliver the same on being paid Freight as follows :—

	£	s.	d.	
For Hewn Timber for Cargo,				℔ Load of 50 Cubic feet calliper measure, as customary at Port of discharge.
For Sawn,				℔ St. Petersburg Standard Hundred of 165 Cubic feet.
For Deals and Boards, ...				

For Timber and Deals used for Beam- }
fillings and Stowage.   } Two-thirds above rates.

Charterers to have the privilege of ordering Vessels to Queenstown or Falmouth for orders to be given within twenty-four hours after arrival at 1s. 6d. additional per load on Hewn or 5s. per Standard on Sawn Timber and Deals and Boards.   (The Act of God, restraints of Princes and Rulers, Public Enemies, Fire, Floods, Strikes, Combinations of any extraordinary occurrence beyond control of either party, and all and every other danger and Accident of the Seas, Rivers and Navigation of whatever nature and kind soever, during the said voyage, always mutually excepted).   Freight to be paid as follows :—One-third in Cash on arrival, and the remainder on right delivery of the Cargo, by a good and approved Bill, payable in London at Four Months' date following, or in Cash, less two per cent., at Merchant's option.   Freight upon Deals and Boards, to be paid upon intake measure of quantity delivered.   Cash for Ship's ordinary disbursements to be advanced at Port of Loading by Charterers at current rates of exchange, subject to cost of Insurance and two and one-half per cent. commission, for which amount Captain is to give his draft, and to endorse said advance on Bills of Lading, it being distinctly understood that the Charterers or their Agents shall in no way be responsible for the appropriation of such advance. Any advance abroad, with charges thereon, to be deducted from first payment of Freight.

In the computation of the days allowed for delivering the Cargo shall be excluded any time lost by reason of Drouth, Floods, Storms, or any extraordinary occurrence beyond the control of the Charterers.

Charterers' Stevedore to be employed for loading at customary rates . . . weather working days are to be allowed the Merchants (if the Ship is not sooner dispatched) in which to deliver the Cargo at Port of Loading, and the Cargo to be unloaded as customary at Port of Discharge, at such wharf or dock as the Charterers or their Agents may direct, and Ten Days on Demurrage, over and above the said lying days, at . . . Pounds per day. Vessel to be consigned to Charterers or their Agents at Port of Loading, paying them 2½ per cent. Commission on Gross Freight for doing Ship's business.

It is agreed that the Charterers shall not be responsible for any of the conditions of this Charter after the Cargo is delivered to the Ship. The Master or Owner to have a lien on Cargo for all Freight, Dead Freight and Demurrage. Penalty for non-performance of agreement, Estimated Freight.

It is understood that the Vessel insures at the regular rates on Cargo, or is chargeable with the difference. Captain is not permitted to take any Timber or Deals on board besides the Cargo, except on written permission of the Shippers.

The custom of each Port to be observed in all cases when not specially expressed, and if steam is required, vessel to be towed by Charterer's Tug-Boat . . . at customary rates. Charterers have privilege of taking Ship's ballast at customary rates.

Five per cent. Commission is due on signing this Charter to . . . .

DEMURRAGE AND LAY-DAYS SCALE.

Scale for Loading and Discharging Steamers with Full Cargoes of Grain.

When Capacity Guaranteed is

6,500 / 7,000	Qrs. 10% 12 days, Sundays excepted, £30 Demurrage.					
7,500 / 8,000	Qrs. 10% 13	"	"	"	£35	"
8,500 / 9,000	Qrs. 10% 14	"	"	"	£40	"
9,500 / 10,000	Qrs. 10% 15	"	"	"	£45	"
10,500 / 11,000	Qrs. 10% 16	"	"	"	£45	"
11,500 / 12,000	Qrs. 10% 17	"	"	"	£50	"
12,500 / 13,000	Qrs. 10% 18	"	"	"	£50	"
14,000	Qrs. 10% 19	"	"	"	£60	"

SCALE FOR SAILING VESSELS,

As approved by THE PHILADELPHIA MARITIME EXCHANGE on the 6th of June, 1882 ; and, in absence of any special agreement to the contrary, to be understood as governing all Grain and Petroleum charters made on Philadelphia account, or for Vessels to load at Philadelphia, to be known as the Philadelphia Demurrage and Lay-Day Scale, to take effect July 1st, 1882.

FOR SAILING VESSELS LOADING GRAIN FOR FOREIGN PORTS.

FOR VESSELS REGISTERING.	LAY-DAYS.
From 200 to 250 tons	21 days to load and discharge.
" 251 " 300 "	22 " " "
" 301 " 350 "	23 " " "
" 351 " 400 "	24 " " "
" 401 " 450 "	25 " " "
" 451 " 500 "	26 " " "
" 501 " 550 "	27 " " "
" 551 " 600 "	28 " " "
" 601 " 650 "	29 " " "
" 651 " 700 "	30 " " "
" 701 " 800 "	31 " " "
" 801 " 900 "	32 " " "
" 901 " 1000 "	33 " " "
" 1001 " 1100 "	34 " " "
" 1101 " 1200 "	35 " " "
" 1201 " 1300 "	36 " " "
" 1301 " 1400 "	37 " " "
" 1401 " 1500 "	38 " " "
" 1501 " 1600 "	39 " " "
" 1601 " 1700 "	40 " " "
" 1701 " 1800 "	40 " " "

FOR VESSELS LOADING PETROLEUM FOR FOREIGN PORTS.

LAY-DAYS.

Vessels of 2000 to 2500 bbls. capacity to have 10 lay-days.					
" 2501 " 3000 "		"		12	"
" 3001 " 4000 "		"		14	"
" 4001 " 5000 "		"		15	"
" 5001 " 6000 "		"		17	"
" 6001 " 7000 "		"		20	"
" 7001 " 8000 "		"		22	"
" 8001 " 9000 "		"		25	"

Customary despatch for discharging.

DEMURRAGE SCALE.

The demurrage on sea-going *Sailing* Vessels shall be as follows, viz. :

For Vessels of 200 tons or under, 12 cents per ton.

For Vessels over 200 tons, and not exceeding 500 tons, $24 for the first 200 tons, and 8 cents per ton for each ton additional.

For Vessels over 500 tons, and not exceeding 900 tons, for $48 the first 500 tons, and 6 cents per ton for each ton additional.

For Vessels over 900 tons, $72 for the first 900 tons, and 5 cents per ton for each ton additional.

CASE OIL CARGOES.

In absence of any fixed Scale of days, either at Philadelphia or New York, it has been customary to use the Barrel Oil Scale ; and taking Cases at five to the Barrel, on the present scale, makes an arrangement satisfactory alike to vessel and shipper.

SHIP BROKERS' COMMISSIONS.

The matter of commissions on Charters and Sales of vessel property is generally well understood by Ship Brokers, but it has been deemed advisable to insert under this head, for the information of all the patrons of this work who are not familiar with the customs of the business, a general outline of what constitutes the ship brokers' rights, whether he gets them or not. The proverbial modesty of the American broker is a serious barrier to his ever attaining great prominence among the wealthy men of the country, but he at least receives credit for his ability to see far more money in a charter than the ship-owner can possibly discover, and this gives him courage to continue in the business, hoping that some favoring breeze may blow into his sanctum an occasional general average case to help pay expenses. What with the usual return to the owners, the "divvies" among interested brother brokers, the captain's "hat," and concomitant tips in various shapes, the amount of commissions left to be divided among the several partners is infinitesimally small, and hardly worth struggling for. In fact, the broker's lot is not a happy one. All the responsibilities that naturally attend the various phases of the shipping business are piled upon his shoulders. He is severely criticised by the owners on all possible occasions, surfeited with cheering notices of derelictions of duty by the shippers, banqueted with opprobrious accusations by the captains, feasted with notifications of all kinds and descriptions bearing upon the payment of certain sums for mistakes made in the manifests and neglect to report this, that and the other, made to furnish bonds at Court when any are required, expected to fight all claims presented, and make the disbursements of the ship next to nothing, at the same time having no authority to make bargains, purchase outfits, or superintend expenditures.

7

In the days of big freights he was more independent, and the chances of retiring on a competency were hopeful and inspiring. Now, the loaf is a small one, and terribly cut up at that, while the responsibilities continue with methodical exactness. Classed among the legitimate merchants, he is active, intelligent, honest, courteous, hard worked, and poorly paid. The right to his commission depends entirely on the usage of trade. The law assumes that the parties assent to pay the broker the usual commission unless a special agreement has been made respecting his remuneration. But as the usage is only admitted in evidence to show the supposed intention of the parties, evidence of former transactions between the same parties may be given for the purpose of explaining their intention in the matter in question.

To entitle the broker to commission, he must first be either actually or constructively employed; secondly, he must introduce the parties to each other; and, lastly, the business must have been completed in consequence of such introduction; and if these conditions are complied with, the parties cannot by any arrangement among themselves defeat his right to his commission.

The principal cannot be liable unless there is either some express employment by him, or recognition and adoption of the services of the broker. If the principal recognizes and adopts the services of the broker, knowing that he is a broker, he is assumed also to agree to pay for the services, and he cannot afterwards repudiate his liability. Unless there is *some* agency established, there is no foundation for any contract between the parties. A jury must decide whether they are satisfied that, *with the assent of both* parties the plaintiff is the agent or middleman, by whose means the negotiation was commenced and made.

He must introduce the parties to each other, either personally or by name, or bring them into communication with each other, with the object of effecting the business. A mere introduction is not enough; the particulars of the business must be named to the parties, and the negotiation of the business must be the direct result of the introduction. If the broker communicates to the merchant what the ship-owner charges, and also communicates to the ship-owner what the merchant will give, and he names the ship and the parties, so as to identify the transaction, and a charter party be ultimately effected for that voyage, the broker is entitled to commission ; but if he does not mention the names, so as to identify the transaction, he does not get his commission, to the exclusion of another broker, who afterwards introduces the parties personally to each other.

The introduction he has made must be the foundation on which the business proceeds ; therefore, as a general rule, the first broker who introduces the two principals to each other is entitled to the commission ; but if, before the introduction by the broker, the ship has been pointed out by the merchant without that being the basis of any negotiations, that fact will not deprive a broker of his right to commission who afterwards brings the parties together for the purpose of effecting the business. Thus, in one case, a broker introduced a purchaser to the owner of a ship which was for sale ; but before that time another person, who was not a broker, had pointed out the same vessel lying in the dock to the same purchaser, and stated that she was for sale, but he did not know who was the owner. The broker, who afterwards introduced the parties personally to each other, was held entitled to his commission.

After the broker has introduced the parties to each other, they cannot evade payment of the commission, either by settling the terms or completing the business themselves, or by doing it through another broker. The question is whether the sale really proceeds in effect from the acts of the brokers, though they did not actually complete the contract.

To entitle the broker to his commission, it is necessary that the business should be completed ; if it is not completed he has no right to charge anything for his trouble. He is entitled to his commission as soon as a valid agreement, whether for sale or charter of the ship, has been entered into, and the amount of the commission depends upon the custom, unless some special agreement has been made. If there is no uniform usage, he is entitled to a reasonable remuneration for his services, which in case of dispute may have to be settled by a jury.

If the amount of the freight depends on a contingency, the broker cannot sue for his commission until that contingency is determined. So long, however, as the amount of the freight can be ascertained, he is entitled to his commission on that amount, although the ship may be lost and the freight never earned, or although no cargo may be supplied by the merchant. In one case, in which the freight had to be paid on the quantity of cargo delivered at the end of the voyage, and the ship was lost before the voyage was completed, the broker was held to be entitled to such a sum as the jury could estimate the amount at.

The mere fact that a broker has first introduced a customer does not give him a right to any commission on any *future* transaction which is not the direct result of further intervention on his part. But in a case where a charter was renewed for a second voyage on the same terms between the same parties, and for the same ship, it was held that the broker was entitled to a commission on that also.

The party to whom the commission is payable is the broker who actually procures the charter for the ship-owner. But if the charter party says how or to whom the commission is to be paid, then, after signing the charter, the ship-owner is bound by that.

If one broker introduces a customer to another broker, the introducing broker is entitled to receive from the other a share of the commission, according to the universal practice among brokers; but the connection of the introducing broker with the business must not be too remote.

If a broker, through some misunderstanding with the merchant, or by an error in the transmission of a cable dispatch or telegram from the ship-owner, closes the ship with the owner, and is subsequently unable to obtain the rates named to the owner, and the ship is afterwards fixed at a less figure, he is obliged to make up the difference of freight, and settle same when the bills of lading are signed.

The customary commission on all charters is five per cent. on the gross amount of freight and demurrage. This is divided up according to circumstances; the maximum proportion being received from steamers and sailing ships placed on the berth for general cargo, and the minimum from British freight steamers loading grain. Attendance fee, inward and outward, 10 cts. per register ton; inward or outward only, 5 cents per ton, when vessel is chartered through other parties. A regular charge of $25.00 is, however, made to owners or brokers of sister cities, who send all of their vessels to one broker only.

A ship broker is entitled to the commission on a charter effected, but not carried out, when the cancellation was due to the non-arrival of the vessel at loading port, on or before the date specified in the charter party.

STEVEDORES' RATES.

Revised to date by Murphy, Cook & Co., Master Stevedores.

DISCHARGING.

Ballast, per ton, . . .	25 to 30	Machinery, per ton, . .	$1. 25
Crockery, per ton meas-		Logwood, " . .	35 to 40
urement, ...	35	Coffee, per bag, . . .	02
Fruit, dry, per ton meas-		Fruit, green, per box, .	1½ to 02
urement, ...	35	Guano, per ton weight, .	35
Cotton, per bale, . . .	10 to 12	Cork, per bale, ...	04
General cargo, per bbl.,	2½	General Cargo, weight or	
Horns, per ton, . . .	60	measurement, . . .	30
Iron, " . . .	25 to 30	Lumber, per M, . . .	40
Labor, per hour, . . .	30	Labor, per day, . . 3 00 to 3 50	
Molasses, per hhd., . .	15 to 20	Lead, per ton, ...	30

Naval stores—pitch, tar,		Marble, per ton, . . .	$1 00
rosin,—per bbl., . .	2½	Rags, per ton measure-	
Naval Stores, turpentine,	03	ment, ...	30
Sugar, per hhd., . . .	15 to 20	Soda, per ton weight, .	30
" . " box, . . .	07	Saltpetre, per ton weight,	30 to 35
" bag, per ton, . .	30	Salt, per 1,000 bushels,	
Tin plates, per ton, . .	35	(W. I.), ...	10 00
Tea, per ton measure-		Salt, Liverpool and Italian	
ment, ...	35 to 40	per ton, ...	30 to 35
Sumac, ...	40	(Limit of time for dis-	
Scrap iron, per ton, . .	75	charging Salt, 1,000	
Sulphur, ...	35	bushels per day).	
Kryolite, ...	35	Wool, per ton measure-	
Mahogany, per ton, . .	75	ment, ...	35

LOADING.

Ballast, f. o. b., accord-		Syrup, per tierce, . . .	15
ing to quality. Stone,		" " hogshead, .	35
per ton, . , 50 cents to $1 00		Tallow, per " . .	35
Dirt, per ton, ...	20 to 30	Oil Cake, per ton, . . .	30
Bacon, "	40	Shooks, per bundle, and	
Coal, trimming, accord-		heads, ...	03
ing to size and number		Staves, per 1,000, . . $2 50 to 3 00	
of hatches, ...	06 to 07	Iron, pig, per ton, . . .	20
General cargo, per bbl.,	03	" railroad, per ton, .	30
" " " ton,		Lumber, per 1,000 feet, .	50
weight or measurement	40 to 50	Marble, per ton, . . .	1 25
Grain, per 1,000 bushels,		Naval stores,—pitch, tar,	
in bulk, ...	$2 50	rosin,—per bbl., . .	04
Grain, per 1,000 bushels,		Naval stores, turpentine,	06
in bags, ...	6 00	Tobacco, per hhd., . .	50 to 60
Petroleum, per round bbl.	05	Dunnagewood, per cord,	$4 50
" " case, . .	01	" boards, per	
Barrels, wet, ...	03	1,000, ... 10 00 to 15 00	
" dry, ...	02	Machinery, including	
Cotton, per bale, . . .	30	stowing, per ton, . .	1 25
Hoops, per M, ...	60	Car material, per ton,	
Syrup, per puncheon, .	30	measurement, . . .	60

PROPORTIONS TO DETERMINE A VESSEL'S APPROXIMATE CAPACITY BY HER NET REGISTER TONNAGE.

Weight from 50 to 70 per cent. for sailing vessels, according to nationality and where built. Freight Steamers built in Great Britain will carry from 80 to 100 per cent. in excess of their nett register tonnage, owing to the manner in which said tonnage is computed.

		FREIGHT STEAMSHIPS.
GRAIN,	7 Quarters to ton register	
Wheat,	56 Bushels to ton register	
Corn,	60 Bushels to ton register	
COTTON (compressed),	3¼ to 4 Bales to ton register	{ 3½ to 4¼ Bales to ton register, or 1,900 to 2,000 lbs. (compressed) cotton to ton register
DEALS (summer),	45 to 53 Standard to 100 tons register	55 to 60 Standard to 100 tons register
(winter),	40 to 45 Standard to 100 tons register	45 to 50 Standard to 100 tons register
LUMBER (including deckload),	75,000 running feet to 100 tons register	
LUMBER (without deckload),	10% less	
OIL–Petroleum,	{ 6 to 6½ round barrels to ton register. { 25% additional for barrels of 40 gallons	
Cases (high tops),	33 to 35 cases to ton register	
(low tops),	38 to 40 cases to ton register	
PROVISIONS,	65 to 67 cubic feet to the ton	

LIST OF PIERS.

NORTH FROM MARKET STREET.

Market Street.   Penna. R. R. and West Jersey Railroad Station.
  1.   Clyde's Line, Richmond and Norfolk.
  2.   "   "   Philadelphia and Charleston.
  3.   "   "   "   " New York.

Arch Street.   6.   River Steamers.
  7.   A. Groves, Jr., Baltimore Line.
  7½. Fruit Pier.
  8 and 8½. Alex. Kerr, Bro. & Co., salt.
  9.   Smyrna and Odessa Steamers.

Race Street.   10.   William Bumm & Son, salt.
  11. Taggart's Line, Bridgeton, Salem, Greenwich, Trenton and Port Penn.
  11½. Taggart's Line, Chester and Thompson's Point.
  12. Albany and Troy Canal Line.
  13. T. M. Uhler, Canal Line.
  14. C. A. Clement, oysters.
  15. Frank D. Watson, wood; Freeman Bros., fish.

Vine Street.   16.   Camden and Atlantic Ferry.
  17. Delaware Avenue Market Co.
  18. "   "   "   "
  19. Wharfage.
  20. J. B. Bloodgood, coal.

Callowhill Street. 21.   Northern Liberties Market Co.
  22. Reading Railroad.
  24. "   "

Willow Street.   25.   "   "
  26. Knickerbocker Ice Co.
  27. Reading Railroad.
  28. "   "

Noble Street.   29.   "   "
  30. C. S. Riley & Co., lumber.
  31. "   "   "
  31½. J. W. Gaskill & Sons, Lumber.

Green Street.
  32. J. W. Gaskill & Sons, lumber.
  33. John Wear, manure.
  34. J. Lukens & Bros., and J. S. Kent, lumber.

Fairmount Ave.	35.	J. A. J. Sheets, lumber.
Brown Street.	35½.	Haney & Rogers, J. B. Lewellen.
	36.	W. A. Levering, lumber.
Poplar Street.	37.	H. C. Patterson & Co., lumber.
	37½.	Lloyd & King, lumber.
	38.	Bruner & Davis, lumber.
	39.	Carpenter Ice Co. ; R. S. Shimer, lumber.
	40.	Philadelphia Iron and Steel Co., mill.
	41.	James Rowland & Co., mill.
	42.	Taylor & Betts, lumber.
Laurel Street.	43.	" " "
	44.	Watson, Malone & Sons, lumber.
	45.	J. W. Paxson & Co., foundry supplies.
	45½ and 46.	Pennsylvania Sugar Refining Co.
	47.	B. F.Taylor & Co., lumber ; Andress & Bryant,wood.
	48.	A. W. Von Utassy, lumber.
Shackamaxon St.		Camden and Atlantic Ferry.
	49.	Frank Merrihew, wharfage and coal.
	50.	Clement & Dunbar, logs.
	51.	S. B. Vrooman, lumber.
	52.	Woolverton & Tinsman, lumber.
Marlborough St.	53.	W. S. Ward, wood.
	54.	Marshall Bros. & Co., mill.
	55.	Knickerbocker Ice Co.
	56.	Chas. Lennig & Co., storage.
Hanover Street.	57.	Wainwright & Bryant, lumber.
	58.	Geo. H. Davie, lumber.
	59.	Wharfage.
	60.	Penn Iron Works, Neafie & Levy.
Palmer Street.	61.	Wharfage.
	62.	Cramp's Dry Dock and Railway.
	63.	" " " " "
	64.	Birely, Hillman & Streaker, Railway.
Warren Street.	65.	" " " "
	66.	Robbins' rolling mills.
Vienna Street.	67.	Kensington Engine Works.
	68.	Jos. Allen.
	69.	Butcher's Ice Co.
Otis Street.	70.	Kensington Water Works.
	71.	Manure and Sand.
Gunner's Run.		

Aramingo Canal.

	72.	Brenner's Glass Works.
	73.	Lehigh Coal and Navigation Co.
	74.	" " " " "
	75.	" " " " "
	76.	Reading Railroad.
	77.	" "
	78.	Manure.
	79.	Gillingham & Garrison, lumber.
Plum Street.	80.	Chas. Delaney, wharfage and storage.
Norris Street.	81, 82, 83, 84 and 85.	Cramp's ship yard.
York Street.	86.	I. P. Morris Co., machine works.
Cumberland St.	87.	Dan'l Brittain & Sons, coal.

PORT RICHMOND PIERS, READING RAILROAD.

	21.	Reading Railroad.
	19.	" "
	18.	" "
	17.	" "
	16.	" "
	15.	" "
	14.	Grain Piers.
	13.	" "
	12 to 1.	Reading Railroad Co.
Williams Street.	108.	" " "
	109.	" " "
Sorrel Street.	110.	" " " lumber and iron.
Ann Street.	111.	" " " Port Richmond Elevator.
Elkhart Street.	117.	
Alleghany Ave.	126.	Canal Boats Pier.
	129.	" " "

SOUTH FROM MARKET STREET.

Market Street.

	1.	Clyde's Line, for Washington and New York.
	2.	Bush's Line, Wilmington, Delaware.
	3.	A. Groves, Jr., Baltimore Line.
Chestnut Street.	5.	Pleasure Steamers.
	6.	Warner's Line, Wilmington, Delaware.
	7.	Jacob E. Ridgway.
	8.	Railroad, Atlantic City.
Walnut Street.	9.	Cope Bros.
	10, 11, 12, 13 and 14.	Pennsylvania Railroad.

Dock Street.	15. Fish market.
Spruce Street.	16 and 17. Delaware Avenue Market Co.
	18. Winsor's Line, Providence.
	20. Winsor's Line, Boston.
Pine Street.	21. S. B. Fotterall, wood and lumber.
	22. Wharfage.
Lombard Street.	23. "
	24. "
	25. Windmill Island Ferry.
	26. Kaighn's Point Ferry.
South Street.	27. Gloucester Ferry. Health and Boarding Officers' Station.
	28. E. C. Knight & Co., sugar refinery.
Bainbridge St.	29. " " " " "
	30. Harrison, Frazier & Co., sugar refinery.
Almond Street.	31. Wood and wharfage.
	32. " " "
	33. Coal.
	34. S. & J. Welsh, West Indies.
	35. Fitzpatrick & Pemberton, warehouses and wharfage.
	36. Coal wharf.
	37. Knickerbocker Ice Co.
Catharine Street.	38. Fitzpatrick & Pemberton, warehouse and wharfage.
	39. " " " " "
Queen Street.	40. Stevenson, Fernald & Co., sugar refinery.
	41. Fitzpatrick & Pemberton, storage and wharfage, Ocean Steamship Co. of Savannah, Lessees.
	42. Simpson's Dry Docks.
	43. " " "
	44. " " "
Christian Street.	45. Pennsylvania Railroad.
	46. Allan Line, Glasgow.
	47. International Steamship Co.
	48. Grain Elevator.
Washington Ave.	49. Pennsylvania Railroad.
	50. Philadelphia, Wilmington and Baltimore Railroad.
	51. " " " " "
Prime Street.	52. " " " " "
	53. International Navigation Co,
Wharton Street.	54. " " "
	55. Pennsylvania R. R.
	56. " "
	57. " " Sutton & Co., California Line.

Reed Street.　　58. Pennsylvania R. R.
　　　　　　　　59. Merrick's Estate, wharfage and storage.
　　　　　　　　60.　　"　　　　"　　　　"　　　　"　　　　"
Dickinson Street. 61. J. H. Scott, wharfage and storage.
　　　　　　　　62. Eugene H. Cathrall, wood and wharfage.
Tasker Street.　63. Reading Railroad, coal.
　　　　　　　　64. W. J. McCahan & Co., sugar refiners.
　　　　　　　　65. A. A. Ardis & Sons, wood, &c.
Moore Street.　70. Baugh's Fertilizer Works.

GREENWICH PIERS.

　　　　　　　　92. Pennsylvania Salt Manufacturing Co.
　　　　　　　　93.　　"　　　　"　　　　"　　　　"
　　　　　　　　94. Greenwich Land and Improvement Co.
　　　　　　　　Logan, Emery & Weaver, oil works.
　　　　　　　　J. E. Tygert & Co., fertilizers.

PIERS ON THE EAST SIDE OF THE SCHUYLKILL RIVER, BETWEEN CHEST-
NUT STREET AND SOUTH STREET BRIDGES.

Producers' Marble Co.	Consumers' Ice Co.
Phila. Granite and Blue Stone Co.	Knickerbocker Ice Co.
Wm. Struthers & Sons.	Smith's Planing Mill.
A. Adams & Co.	Donaghty & Son.
J. K. Freedley & Son.	Anthony Taylor & Co.
John Baird & Sons.	J. W. Lowery & Sons.
Barker & Bros.	Commercial Ice Co.
V. A. Sartori & Son.	National Fire Brick Co.
Warren, Lober & Co.	Frank K. Ward.

BELOW SOUTH STREET.

Maule Bros. & Co.	Wm. Pancoast.
Richmond Granite Co.	John J. Brady, coal.
Hugh Lafferty.	U. S. Arsenal.
Henry J. Devinney.	Harrison Bros. & Co.
John S. Lowery.	Atlantic Refinery.
Delaware Ice Co.	Girard Point Elevators.

WEST SIDE OF THE SCHUYLKILL RIVER, BETWEEN SOUTH STREET AND
CHESTNUT STREET BRIDGES.

The Allison Manufacturing Co.	Wm. Gray & Sons, stone.
New York wharfage and storage.	I. P. Thomas, fertilizers.
Stokes Bros., lumber.	

WEST SIDE, BELOW SOUTH STREET.

Gibson's Point, Lucent Oil Works, Bosshardt & Wilson.
Phenix Oil Co.
Ballast Wharf, Point Breeze.

BOARD OF WARDENS FOR THE PORT OF PHILADELPHIA.

Rooms 11 and 13, Chamber of Commerce.

President,
GEO. A. COTTON.

1. William R. Tucker, 414 South Delaware avenue.
2. Edward K. Stevenson, 133 South Front street.
3. George A. Cotton, 22 and 24 South Delaware avenue.
4. Samuel T. Kerr, Pier 8, North Delaware avenue.
5. Joel Cook, Office Public Ledger.
6. William Charlton, 2720 Brown street.
7. Chas. Halyburton, Jr., 1365 Beach street.
8. Samuel Disston, Front and Laurel streets.
9. A. C. Ferguson.
10. Frank T. Downing, 233 South Fourth street.
11. Chas. H. Cramp, 1736 Spring Garden street.
12. John B. Lewellen, Pier 35, North Delaware avenue.
13. Chas. S. Lowry, Lombard street wharf, Schuylkill.
14. William M. Neall, S. E. cor. Broad and Race streets.
15. Theodore Frothingham, 217 Walnut street.
16. Nathan McK. Wilson, 105 Walnut street.
17. Amos Gartside, Chester.
18. Joseph S. Pierce, Bristol.
19. Christian K. Ross, Master Warden.

Master Warden,
CHRISTIAN K. ROSS, Rooms 11 and 13, Chamber of Commerce.

Secretary,
JONA. GILLINGHAM.

Harbor Master,
JAMES P. LINDSAY, 516 South Delaware Avenue.

Vessel Clerk,
GEORGE F. SPROULE.

TIDE TABLE FOR THE PORT OF PHILADELPHIA, 1886.

WALNUT STREET WHARF.

Furnished by United States Coast and Geodetic Survey Office.

TIDE TABLE FOR THE PORT OF PHILADELPHIA.

Showing the difference between the time of High Water at Philadelphia (Walnut Street Wharf, Delaware River) and the following places.

The hours and minutes standing against the place in this table are to be added or subtracted from the time of High Water at Philadelphia on any given day, which will give (nearly) the time of High Water at the following points :

(+ *signifies* ADD ; — *signifies* SUBTRACT.)

DISTANCES.		DISTANCE FROM WALNUT STREET WHARF, PHILADELPHIA, IN *Nautical Miles*, TO THE FOLLOWING PLACES; AND THE DIFFERENCE IN TIME OF HIGH WATER AT EACH POINT.	DIFFERENCE IN TIME.
			H. M.
2½	miles.	Port Richmond Elevator, Philadelphia	+ .08
¾	"	Cooper's Point, New Jersey	+ .11
0	"	Walnut Street Wharf, Philadelphia	. . .
1⅜	"	Kaighn's Point, New Jersey	— .10
3¾	"	Greenwich Point, Philadelphia	— .18
7	"	Girard Point (Schuylkill River)	— .30
9¼	"	Point Breeze "	— .35
9½	"	Gibson's Point "	— .37
12⅛	"	Chestnut St. Wharf "	— .40
11⅛	"	Lazaretto, Pennsylvania	— .45
14¼	"	Chester, Pennsylvania	— .57
15⅞	"	Schooner Ledge, Delaware River, below Chester, Penna	— 1.05
23⅝	"	Cherry Island Flats, Delaware River, off Edgemore, Penna	— 1.40
24¼	"	Wilmington, Delaware (mouth of Christiana Creek)	— 1.45
26	"	Deep Water Point, New Jersey	— 1.42
29¼	"	New Castle, Delaware	— 1.51
33⅜	"	Fort Delaware	— 2.02
39	"	Reedy Island Lighthouse	— 2.17
44⅝	"	Liston's Point	— 3.15
48	"	Bombay Hook	— 3.27
65⅜	"	Cross Ledge Lighthouse	— 4.40
77⅛	"	Brandywine Lighthouse	— 5.37
82½	"	Cape May	— 5.20
89	"	Cape Henlopen	— 5.42
110⅜	"	Old Five Fathom Bank Lightship	. . .
9⅞	"	N. N. E. from the Old Light-ship is the New Light-ship	. . .

PHILADELPHIA STEAMSHIP LINES.

AMERICAN STEAMSHIP COMPANY, (American Line.)
Peter Wright & Sons, Agents, 307 Walnut Street.

Steamers sail every Wednesday, from Pier 46, South Wharves, for Liverpool, calling at Queenstown.

INTERNATIONAL NAVIGATION COMPANY OF PHILADELPHIA, (Red Star Line.)
Peter Wright & Sons, Agents, 307 Walnut St.

Sailing weekly for Antwerp, from New York and Philadelphia alternately.

ALLAN LINE, PHILADELPHIA TO GLASGOW.
William Brockie, Agent, 101 Walnut Street.

LORD LINE, PHILADELPHIA TO BELFAST.
William Brockie, Agent, 101 Walnut Street.

OCEAN STEAMSHIP COMPANY OF SAVANNAH.
William L. James, Agent, 13 South Third Street.

Steamers sail every Saturday, at noon, for Savannah, Ga., from Pier 41 South Wharves.

This line issues through passage tickets and bills of lading in connection with the Central Railroad of Georgia, Savannah, Florida and Western Railway, and Florida Steamers to all points South and Southwest.

BALTIMORE AND PHILADELPHIA STEAMBOAT COMPANY, (Ericsson Line.)
A. Groves, Jr., Agent, 28 South Wharves.

Steamers leave Chestnut Street Wharf daily, (Sundays excepted,) at 4 P. M., arriving in Baltimore early on the following morning. First-class accommodation for passengers. Freight received for South and West of Baltimore.

8

BOSTON AND PHILADELPHIA STEAMSHIP COMPANY.

Henry Winsor & Co., Agents, 338 South Delaware Avenue.

Providence Line, from Pier 18, below Spruce Street, sailing every Wednesday and Saturday from Philadelphia, at 11 A. M., from Providence at 5 P. M.

Boston Line, from Pier 20, foot of Pine Street, sailing every Wednesday and Saturday from Philadelphia, at 10 A. M., from Boston at 3 P. M. ; only direct Steamship Line.

THE CLYDE STEAM LINES.

William P. Clyde & Co., General Agents, 12 South Wharves.

Boston, Fall River, Providence and the New England States. Steamers leave Pier 2, North Wharves, every Wednesday at noon, and every Saturday at 3 P. M.

New York—Steamers leave daily from Pier 1, South Wharves. In winter, tri-weekly.

Charleston, S. C.—Steamers sail from Pier 22, South Wharves, below Pine Street, for the South, Southwest, and Florida Ports, every Saturday at noon.

Richmond, Norfolk, Portsmouth, City Point and Petersburg, Va.—Steamers leave Pier 1, above Market Street, every Tuesday, Thursday and Saturday at noon.

Washington and Georgetown, D. C., and Alexandria, Va.— Steamers leave Pier 1, South Wharves, every Saturday at 10 A. M.

LEHIGH TRANSPORTATION LINE.

Pier 13 North Wharves.

Freight forwarded on Lehigh and Delaware Canal, Union and Juniata Tidewater, and Pennsylvania Canal. T. M. Uhler, General Agent, 234 North Delaware Avenue.

FOREIGN CONSULATES.

[Corrected to April 1, 1886.]

Argentine Republic.—Edward Shippen, 532 Walnut street.
Austria and Hungary.—Lars Westergaard, 138 S. Second street.
Belgium.—Dr. Charles E. Sajous, 1630 Chestnut street.
Brazil.—John Mason, Jr., 138 S. Second street.
Chili.—Edward Shippen, 532 Walnut street.
Colombia.—Annibal Gonzales Torras, Girard House.
Denmark.—F. F. Myhlertz, Twenty-Second and Barker streets.
Ecuador.—Edward Shippen, 532 Walnut street.
France.—Pierre de Bouteillier, 524 Walnut street.
German Empire.—Charles H. Meyer, 227 Chestnut street.
Great Britain.—Robert Charles Clipperton, Consul; George Crump, Vice-Consul, 413 Locust street.
Greece.—A. H. Lennox, N. W. Cor. Second and Walnut streets.
Hayti.—A. H. Lennox, N. W. Cor. Second and Walnut streets.
Italy.—Cavalier Nicolo Squitti, 259 S. Fourth street.
Liberia.—Edward S. Morris, 4 S. Merrick street.
Mexico.—Rafael Varrios, 321 Spruce street.
Netherlands.—Lars Westergaard, 138 S. Second street.
Nicaragua.—Henry C. Potter, 813 Market street.
Orange Free State, South Africa.—Charles W. Riley, 1115 Race street.
Paraguay.—Francis Wells, 607 Chestnut street.
Peru.—George Blaese, 130 Walnut street.
Portugal.—John Mason, Jr., 138 S. Second street.
Russia.—Henry Preaut, 138 S. Second street.
San Domingo.—Thomas B. Wanamaker, S. W. Cor. Thirteenth and Market streets.
Spain.—Antonio Diaz Mirandi, Consul; Francisco Monjes Merino, Vice-Consul, 411 Pine street.
Sweden and Norway.—Lars Westergaard, 138 S. Second street.
Switzerland.—Rudolph Koradi, Consul, 314 York Av.; Werner Itschner, Vice-Consul, 712 Market street.
Turkey.—J. B. Hamel, Jr., 105 Walnut street.
Uruguay.—Charles W. Matthews, 212 S. Third street.
Venezuela.—Andres Entrena, 228 S. Broad street; Vice-Consul, J. B. Hamel, Jr., 105 Walnut street.

PROPORTIONATE RATES OF FREIGHT, CALCULATED IN STERLING, BASED ON THE DISPLACEMENT OF ROOM.

Column headings (left to right):

- Oil, per 40 gallons.
- Provisions, (Tallow and Lard) per Ton of 2240 lbs.
- Beef, per Tierce.
- Beef, per Barrel.
- Bacon, per 2240 lbs.
- Butter. — The rate for Butter per ton of 2240 lbs. is generally 20 per cent. higher than for Provisions.
- Cheese. — The rate for Cheese per ton of 2240 lbs. is generally 22 per cent. higher than for Provisions.
- Cotton ('Taylor's Compressing) per lb.
- Rio Coffee, per 2240 lbs.
- Flour, per Barrel.
- Flour, per Bag.
- Grain in Bags, per Bushel.
- Grain in Bulk, per Bushel.
- Measurement Goods, per 40 cubic feet.
- Asphaltum, per 2240 lbs.
- Rosin, per 280 lbs.
- Tobacco, (Virginia), per Hhd.
- Tobacco, (Kentucky), per Hhd.

For the Rate on—Tobacco in cases, Hardware and Woodenware, Knitting and Sewing Machines, Organs, Stoves, Shoe Blacking, Starch in Boxes, etc., see rate for Measurement Goods.—Add 33 per cent. to Sales Measurement of Cedar Wood, and 25 per cent. to Sales Measurement of Black Walnut, and take the rate of freight for Measurement Goods, with 2s. 6d. addit onal for extra stevedore expenses.

REDUCTION OF TONS INTO QUARTERS AND BUSHELS.

Tons of 2240 lbs.	Quarters.	Corn or Rye, Bushels.	Wheat, Bushels.
428 4/7	2,000	17,143	16,000
450	2,100	18,000	16,800
471 3/7	2,200	18,857	17,600
492 6/7	2,300	19,714	18,400
514 2/7	2,400	20,571	19,200
535 5/7	2,500	21,429	20,000
557 1/7	2,600	22,286	20,800
578 4/7	2,700	23,143	21,600
600	2,800	24,000	22,400
621 3/7	2,900	27,857	23,200
642 6/7	3,000	25,714	24,000
664 2/7	3,100	26,571	24,800
685 5/7	3,200	27,429	25,600
707 1/7	3,300	28,286	26,400
728 4/7	3,400	29,143	27,200
750	3,500	30,000	28,000
771 3/7	3,600	30,857	28,800
792 6/7	3,700	31,714	29,600
814 2/7	3,800	32,571	30,400
835 5/7	3,900	33,429	31,200
857 1/7	4,000	34,286	32,000
878 4/7	4,100	35,143	32,800
900	4,200	36,000	33,600
921 3/7	4,300	36,857	34,400
942 6/7	4,400	37,714	35,200
964 2/7	4,500	38,571	36,000
985 5/7	4 600	39,429	36,800
1,007 1/7	4,700	40,286	37,600
1,028 4/7	4,800	41,143	38,400
1,050	4,900	42,000	39,200
1,071 3/7	5,000	42,857	40,000
1,092 6/7	5,100	43,714	40,800
1,114 2/7	5,200	44,571	41,600
1,135 5/7	5,300	45,429	42,400
1,157 1/7	5,400	46,286	43,200
1,178 4/7	5,500	47,143	44,000
1,200	5,600	48,000	44,800
1,221 3/7	5,700	48,857	45,600
1 242 6/7	5,800	49,714	46,400
1,264 2/7	5,900	50,571	47,200
1,285 5/7	6,000	51,428	48,000

100 Quarters equal 21 3/7 tons.

PROPORTIONATE FREIGHT TABLES,

Including 5 per cent. Primage, on the Quarter, on the 100 lbs., and on the Ton of 2240 lbs.

CALCULATED IN STERLING.

Per 60 lbs.	Per 100 lbs.	Per 480 lbs.		Per 2240 lbs.		Per 56 lbs.	Per 480 lbs.		Per 2240 lbs.	
d.	*d.*	*s.*	*d.*	*s.*	*d.*	*d.*	*s.*	*d.*	*s.*	*d.*
4	7	2	9½	12	5⅓	4	3		13	4
4¼	7 7/16	2	11½	13	2⅔	4¼	3	2¼	14	2
4½	7⅞	3	1¼	14		4½	3	4½	15	
4¾	8 5/16	3	3¾	14	9⅓	4¾	3	6¾	15	10
5	8¾	3	6	15	6⅔	5	3	9	16	8
5¼	9 3/16	3	8	16	4	5¼	3	11¼	17	6
5½	9⅝	3	10	17	1⅓	5½	4	1½	18	4
5¾	10 1/16	4	¼	17	10⅔	5¾	4	3¾	19	2
6	10½	4	2¼	18	8	6	4	6	20	
6¼	10 15/16	4	4½	19	5⅓	6¼	4	8¼	20	10
6½	11⅜	4	6½	20	2⅔	6½	4	10½	21	8
6¾	11 13/16	4	8½	21		6¾	5	¾	22	6
7	12¼	4	10¾	21	9½	7	5	3	23	4
7¼	12 11/16	5	¾	22	6⅚	7¼	5	5¼	24	2
7½	13⅛	5	3	23	4	7½	5	7½	25	
7¾	13 9/16	5	5	24	1⅓	7¾	5	9¾	25	10
8	14	5	7	24	10⅔	8	6		26	8
8¼	14 7/16	5	9¼	25	8	8¼	6	2¼	27	6
8½	14⅞	5	11¼	26	5½	8½	6	4½	28	4
8¾	15 5/16	6	1½	27	2⅚	8¾	6	6¾	29	2
9	15¾	6	3½	28		9	6	9	30	
9¼	16 3/16	6	5½	28	9⅓	9¼	6	11¼	30	10
9½	16⅝	6	7¾	29	6⅔	9½	7	1½	31	8
9¾	17 1/16	6	9¾	30	4	9¾	7	3¾	32	6
10	17½	7		31	1⅓	10	7	6	33	4
10¼	17 15/16	7	2	31	10⅔	10¼	7	8¼	34	2
10½	18⅜	7	4	32	8	10½	7	10½	35	
10¾	18 13/16	7	6¼	33	5⅓	10¾	8	¾	38	10
11	19¼	7	8¼	34	2⅔	11	8	3	36	8
11¼	19 11/16	7	10½	35		11¼	8	5¼	37	6
11½	20⅛	8	½	35	9½	11½	8	7½	38	4
11¾	20 9/16	8	2½	36	6⅚	11¾	8	9¾	39	2
12	21	8	4¾	37	4	12	9		40	
12¼	21 7/16	8	6¾	38	1⅓	12¼	9	2¼	40	10
12½	21⅞	8	9	38	10⅔	12½	9	4½	41	8
12¾	22 5/16	8	11	39	8	12¾	9	6¾	42	6
13	22¾	9	1	40	5⅓	13	9	9	43	4

VESSEL OWNERS' AND CAPTAINS' NATIONAL ASSOCIATION.

This Association resolved itself into a permanent organization at a meeting held in the Board of Trade Rooms, at Boston, Mass., May 13, 1885. As the membership is so largely represented by the vessel owners and captains of Philadelphia and vicinity, it has been deemed proper to insert herein a copy of the preamble and resolutions which were unanimously adopted at that meeting, together with the schedule of the minimum rates of freight on coal which went into effect December 1, 1885, but subject to any change which may be determined upon thereafter. The coal bill of lading which has been approved by the Association as the regular agreement under which all vessels represented in the Association are to load and discharge coastwise, is also given below; and as the membership has now assumed so great a magnitude, embracing nearly all of the principal vessel-owners, a unity of action is assured, it being particularly apparent that the interests of each and all are thereby protected and harmonized.

The officers of the Association are as follows:—

President,
CHARLES LAWRENCE, of Philadelphia.

Vice-Presidents,
GUY C. GOSS, of Bath.   CLARENCE P. LOVELL, of Boston.

Secretary,
W. F. HUMPHREY, of Boston.

Treasurer,
J. A. VAN BRUNT, of New York.

Commissioners of Coasting Trade:

CHARLES A. PETTIT, *President*, Philadelphia.
HENRY SUTTON, New Haven.
✓ HENRY LORD, Bangor.   .
THOMAS M. BARTLETT, *Treasurer*, New York.
S. M. THOMAS, Taunton.
FRANK D. PETTIT, *Secretary.*

Preamble and Resolutions adopted, unanimously, at a Meeting of the Vessel Owners' and Captains' National Association, held in the Board of Trade Rooms, Boston, Mass., May, 13, 1885:—

WHEREAS the diversity of interests represented in this Convention demands unity of action, necessitating a permanent organization, therefore be it *Resolved:—*

First.—That an association be formed, to be known as the " Vessel Owners' and Captains' National Association." All owners and masters of vessels, upon signing the agreement, as hereinafter stated, and paying the annual assessment, hereinafter provided for, upon their respective vessels, shall be regarded as members.

All meetings of the Association shall consist of delegates, not exceeding five from each seaport town or city on the Atlantic Coast of the United States.

Meetings shall be called at least once a year, at such time and place as shall be fixed by the Executive Committee, which committee shall consist of one member from each seaport town or city, and shall be appointed at the annual meeting.

The officers of this Association shall consist of a President, two Vice-Presidents, Secretary, and Treasurer, who shall be elected at the annual meeting, shall serve for one year and be members of the Executive Committee, *ex officio*, and also five commissioners, whose term of office and duties are as hereinafter provided for.

Second.—That a Coasting Trade Commission be elected by the Convention, to consist of five representative members, two from the Middle States and three from the New England States. Said commissioners to get from the owners and captains of all coasting vessels engaged in the coal and ice trade authority investing them with full power to establish the minimum rate of coal and ice freights as hereinafter provided, to represent the coasting trade, and to consult with the interests auxiliary to this trade in making this rate.

Said commissioners to serve for two years and until their successors are elected. Vacancies in this commission, if any occur, shall be filled by the remaining members thereof for the unexpired portion of the term.

Third.—That said commissioners shall elect one of their members as president, one as treasurer, and appoint a secretary who shall not be member of the commission; and they shall have their office, for the transaction of business, at such convenient place as they may select. That the said commissioners shall have full power to make such prudential rules and regulations as they shall deem needful and proper to carry out the objects and purpose of this Association.

Fourth.—That the said commissioners shall be reimbursed for all travelling expenses incurred in the transaction of the business of said commission, also rent of office, printing, postage, and other necessary expenses.

Fifth.—That, in order to defray the expenses of this commission, an initiation fee of two dollars per vessel shall be paid, and an annual tax of two cents per ton on the registered tonnage of each vessel engaged in the coasting trade shall be assessed and paid, when called for by the commission.

Sixth.—That the commission shall have power to hear complaints, to adjust any differences that may arise between members of the Association, shippers, and consignees, and in its discretion to punish by fine or publication any violation of its rules and regulations.

Seventh.—That the managing owners and masters of all coast-wise vessels be requested to transmit their pledges to abide by the above regulations, to the commission, sending the name and registered tonnage of their vessels, and giving the commission full authority to bind their vessels for the general good of the coasting trade.

Eighth.—That the commission be empowered to provide :—

That, in contracts for carrying coal, the rate of freight shall be free of discharge, the shippers shall load vessels in turn, the consignees shall discharge in turn, and at a rate not less than one hundred and fifty (150) tons per day, and the rate of demurrage shall be reduced to six (6) cents per *ton of cargo* per day, and that this provision shall go into effect upon thirty days' notice being given by the commission.

Ninth.—That ten members of the Executive Committee constitute a quorum for the transaction of business.

Tenth.—That the Secretary be instructed to send to the Executive Committee notice of their election, accompanied by the following resolve :—

Resolved, That this Convention do most earnestly recommend the vessel owners and captains of vessels, engaged in the coasting trade in the various cities and towns (where no such association exists), to take immediate steps to form local organizations by enrolling members and electing officers, and thus strengthening this Association ; and, when the same is done, reporting the names of officers and such other information as may be valuable, to the Secretary of this National Association.

Eleventh.—That the vessel owners of the several places shall send to the Secretary of this Association the name of one person to serve upon the Executive Committee, in case such place is not now represented upon such committee, either by reason of the person now chosen to serve from such place declining so to do or because no person has yet been appointed from such place.

Twelfth.—That the Secretary be instructed to give notice to the Executive Committee that, in fixing the time of holding the annual meeting, they consider the advisability of calling the meeting in the fall of the year.

Thirteenth.—That the President and Secretary shall be authorized to audit any bills already incurred; and the Treasurer shall pay the same.

Fourteenth.—That the first meeting of the Executive Committee shall be called by the President and Secretary of this Association.

Fifteenth.—That, when this Association adjourns, it adjourns subject to the call of the President and Secretary.

CHARLES LAWRENCE,
President.

Attest; WILLIAM F. HUMPHREY, *Secretary.*

SCHEDULE OF MINIMUM RATES OF FREIGHT ON COAL.

The rate to be in all cases free of discharging the cargo.

FROM	New York.	Hoboken.	New Haven and Bridgeport.	Rhode Island Ports.	New Bedford.	Boston, Below bridges.	Portsmouth.	Newburyport.
Georgetown, D. C., ... to	$1 00	$0 95	$1 05	$1 05	$1 05	$1 15	$1 25	$1 30
Baltimore, ... "	1 00	95	1 05	1 05	1 05	1 15	1 25	1 30
Hampton Roads, ... "	90	85	95	95	95	1 05	1 15	1 20
Philadelphia, ... "	..	..	..	..	..	1 05	1 15	1 20
Rondout, ... "	..	..	..	..	..	1 05	1 15	1 20
New York, ... "	..	..	..	..	..	85	95	1 00
Weehawken, Hoboken and Port Johnson, ... "	..	..	..	..	..	85	95	1 00
Elizabethport, ... "	..	..	..	..	..	90	1 00	1 05
Perth and South Amboy, . . "	..	..	..	..	..	90	1 00	1 05

The minimum rate of freight for ports not mentioned in the above schedule shall not be less than the rates for ports nearest thereto. The Boston and Portland bridge rate shall be 3 cents per ton of cargo per bridge. The rate to Penobscot Bay, Calais, Me., and Eastport, Me., will be the same as Boston. Rhode Island ports will include all Rhode Island ports, and Fall River and Somerset, Mass.

BILL OF LADING OR AGREEMENT.

As approved by the Vessel Owners' and Captains' National Association.

SHIPPED, IN GOOD ORDER AND CONDITION, BY . . . on board the
good . . . called the . . . whereof . . . is Master for the present voyage, now
lying in the Port of . . . and bound for . . . to, say: . . . being marked and
numbered as in the margin, and are to be delivered in like good order and condition
at the aforesaid Port of . . . , the dangers of Seas and Fire only excepted, unto . . .
or Assigns, he or they paying freight for said Goods . . . together with all expenses
of discharging said cargo, and Average Accustomed. And 24 hours after the arrival
at the above named Port, and notice thereof to the consignee named, there shall be
allowed for receiving said cargo at the rate of one day, Sundays and legal holidays
excepted, for every one hundred and fifty tons thereof; after which the cargo, consignee, or assignee, shall pay demurrage at the rate of six cents per ton a day,
Sundays and legal holidays not excepted, upon the full amount of cargo, as per this
Bill of Lading, for each and every day's detention, and *pro rata* for parts and portions
of a day, beyond the days above specified, until the cargo is fully discharged; which
freight and demurrage shall constitute a lien upon said cargo. After arrival and
notice to the consignee, as aforesaid, and the expiration of said 24 hours, said vessel
shall have precedence in discharging over all Steam vessels arriving or giving notice
after her arrival; and for any violation of this provision she shall be compensated in
demurrage as if while delayed by such violation her discharge had proceeded at the
rate of three hundred tons per day.

In Witness Whereof, the Master of said vessel hath affirmed to . . . Bills of
Lading, all of this tenor and date; one of which being accomplished, the others to
stand void.

Dated at . . . this . . . day of . . . 18 . . .

. . . .

INDORSEMENT ON THE BACK OF CAPTAIN'S BILL OF LADING,
WHICH SHOULD BE SIGNED BY THE CONSIGNEE ON DISCHARGE
OF VESSEL.

Arrived at . . . 18 . . , at . . . o'clock, . . M.
Discharged at . . . o'clock, . . M.
Cargo received in good order, as per within Bill of Lading   The detention of the
Vessel was owing to no fault of the Master or Crew.

WEIGHT AND MEASUREMENT OF GENERAL CARGO GOODS.

Asphaltum.—In casks, measuring 43¼ cubic feet, averages 2120 lbs. gross.

Alcohol.—Barrels containing 40 gallons, measure 10⅓ cubic feet.

Beef.—Weighs in tierces 475 lbs. gross, 304 lbs. net, measures 2 feet 7 inches x 2 feet x 2 feet = 10⅓ cubic feet. Some tierces weigh 336 lbs. net, 550 to 560 lbs. gross.

Beef, weighs in barrels 200 lbs. net, 330 to 350 lbs. gross, measures 2 feet 5 inches x 1 foot 8 inches x 1 foot 8 inches = 6¾ cubic feet.

Bacon.—In boxes, 475 lbs. net; average of 25 per cent. for salt and boxes is generally added.

Barley.—48 lbs. per bushel (pays 17 per cent. more than Wheat per ton).

Beans.—In barrels containing 3½ bushels, weigh 242 lbs. gross, and pay the same freight as Wheat per ton.

Butter.—In firkins, averaging 125 lbs. gross, 1 foot 8 inches x 1 foot 4 inches x 1 foot 4 inches = 3 cubic feet.

Butter, in firkins, averaging 124 lbs. gross, 1 foot 8 inches x 1 foot 6 inches x 1 foot 6 inches = $3\frac{9}{12}$ cubic feet.

Butter, in tubs, averaging 55 to 60 lbs. gross = $2\frac{1}{16}$ cubic feet.

Currants.—2 feet 6 inches x 1 foot 5 inches x 1 foot 5 inches = 5 cubic feet.

Cheese.—In boxes 40 to 45 lbs.= per cubic foot according to size.

Cedar Wood.—(Florida) 2240 lbs. = 80 cubic feet.

Cotton.—Bales, compressed, 465 lbs. = 20 to 21 cubic feet.

$\frac{3}{32}$ *d.* per lb.	= 17 *s.*	6 *d.* for 2240 lbs.	
⅛	"	= 23 *s.* 4 *d.*	"
$\frac{5}{32}$	"	= 29 *s.* 2 *d.*	"
$\frac{3}{16}$	"	= 35 *s.*	"
$\frac{7}{32}$	"	= 40 *s.* 10 *d.*	"
¼	"	= 46 *s.* 8 *d.*	"
$\frac{9}{32}$	"	= 52 *s.* 6 *d.*	"
$\frac{5}{16}$	"	= 58 *s.* 4 *d.*	"
⅜	"	= 70 *s.*	"

Castor Oil.—In boxes weighing 179 lbs., measuring 1 foot 10 inches x 1 foot 10 inches x 1 foot = $4\frac{6}{12}$ cubic feet.

Coal.—Lehigh, Egg size, measures $34\frac{1}{2}$ cubic feet to 2000 lbs.

Schuylkill,	"	"	35	"	"
Red Ash,	"	"	36	"	"

Coffee.—Coffee bags are cut to measure unfilled 3 feet x 2 feet to hold $2\frac{1}{2}$ bushels, weighing about 160 lbs., average weight 2048 lbs. per 40 cubic feet.

Deals.—St. Petersburg standard 1980 feet = 165 cubic feet. American ships carry on an average, 1 standard as being equal to 27 to 30 bbls., or say : 4 to $4\frac{1}{2}$ standards for every 10 tons Register.

Fish.—Cod in cases weighing 700 lbs. = 19 cubic feet, equal to 1480 lbs. per 40 cubic feet.

Flour.—

1 s. 6 d. per barrel	= $10\frac{1}{2}$ barrels to the ton,	15 s. 9 d.
1 s. $7\frac{1}{2}$ d.	"	"	"	17 s.
1 s. 9 d.	"	"	"	18 s. $4\frac{1}{2}$ d.
1 s. $10\frac{1}{2}$ d.	"	"	"	19 s. 8 d.
2 s.	"	"	"	21 s.
2 s. 3 d.	"	"	"	23 s. 7 d.
2 s. $4\frac{1}{2}$ d.	"	"	"	24 s. 11 d.
2 s. 6 d.	"	"	"	26 s. 3 d.
2 s. $7\frac{1}{2}$ d.	"	"	"	27 s. 7 d.
2 s. 9 d.	"	"	"	28 s. $10\frac{1}{2}$ d.
2 s. $10\frac{1}{2}$ d.	"	"	"	30 s. 2 d.
3 s.	"	"	"	31 s. 6 d.
3 s. 3 d.	"	"	"	34 s. 1 d.
3 s. $4\frac{1}{2}$ d.	"	"	"	35 s. 5 d.
3 s. 6 d.	"	"	"	36 s. 9 d.
3 s. $7\frac{1}{2}$ d.	"	"	"	38 s.
3 s. 9 d.	"	"	"	39 s. 4 d.

Genessee measures $6\frac{9}{12}$ cubic feet. Southern measures $6\frac{4}{12}$ cubic feet. Island River 2 feet 3 inches x 1 foot 7 inches x 1 foot 7 inches = $5\frac{8}{12}$ cubic feet. Standard weight is about 216 to 218 lbs. gross, but rarely holds out in shipment, and in London and Liverpool rarely exceeds 211 to 212 lbs. per barrel.

Gunny Bags.—900 to 915 lbs. per 40 cubic feet.

Ginger.—1120 lbs. per 40 cubic feet.

Gum Copal.—3 feet 2 inches x 2 feet 1 inch x 1 foot 6 inches = 10 cubic feet = 330 to 340 lbs.

Guano.—15 ½ bags per ton weight of 2240 lbs.

Grain.—Standard weight.

Wheat,	60 lbs. per bushel	37⅓	bushels	=	2240 lbs.
Corn,	56	"	40	"	"
Rye,	56	"	40	"	"
Barley,	48	"	46⅝	"	"
Oats,	32	"	70	"	"
Clover,	63	"	$35\frac{35}{63}$	"	"
Beans,	63½	"	$35\frac{17}{63}$	"	"
Linseed,	50	"	$44\frac{4}{5}$	"	"

Hops.—As usually shipped, average 185 lbs. to 210 lbs. per bale, varying materially in measurement, viz.:

4 feet 6 inches x 1 foot 7 inches x 2 feet 7 inches = 18 cubic feet, 210 lbs. per bale.

2 feet 6 inches x 4 feet 3 inches x 1 foot 4 inches = 14.2 cubic feet, 185 lbs. per bale.

2 feet 9 inches x 4 feet 9 inches x 1 foot 6 inches = 19.7 cubic feet, 188 lbs. per bale.

Hemp.—Manila bales, averaging 280 lbs. gross, measuring 3 feet 5 inches x 1 foot 9 inches x 1 foot 6 inches = 9 cubic feet.

Sisal bales, averaging 375 lbs. gross, measure 14 cubic feet.

Tampico bales, averaging 360 to 365 lbs. gross, measure 12 cubic feet.

Hides.—Calcutta, 1350 lbs. = 40 cubic feet. Green, 2240 lbs. = 47 cubic feet.—(dried) three-eighths more than the freight, of (clean) Hemp per ton gross.—(Wet or salted) two-thirds the freight of clean Hemp per ton gross.

Hams.—Average 390 lbs., measure 2 feet 7½ inches x 2 feet 2 inches = 10 cubic feet 6 inches.

In Hhds. 1280 lbs. = 3 feet 9 inches x 3 feet 7 inches x 3 feet 7 inches = $48\frac{2}{15}$ cubic feet.

Hay.—Bales 350 lbs. per 40 cubic feet.

Indigo.—Calcutta, 1200 lbs. = 40 cubic feet.

Jute.—Calcutta, 1265 lbs. per ton of 40 cubic feet.

Lard.—38 to 40 lbs. per foot. Tierces 2 feet 8 inches x 1 foot 11 inches x 1 foot 11 inches = $9\frac{9}{12}$ cubic feet, weighing 387 lbs. gross.

Tierces 2 feet $10\frac{1}{2}$ inches x 2 feet 2 inches x 2 feet 2 inches = $11\frac{7}{12}$ cubic feet, weighing 468 lbs. gross.

Barrels 2 feet 6 inches x 1 foot 8 inches x 1 foot 8 inches = 7 cubic feet, weighing 265 lbs. gross.

Firkins 1 foot 5 inches x 1 foot 5 inches x 2 feet = 4 cubic feet, weighing 110 lbs. gross.

Racks 2 feet 4 inches x 2 feet x 2 feet x 1 foot 2 inches = 5.5 cubic feet gross, weighing 152 lbs. (4 in a rack).

Tubs measuring $2\frac{1}{16}$ cubic feet, each weighing 53 lbs. net, 56 to 58 lbs. gross.

Logwoods.—Campeachy and Laguna = 2240 lbs. per 60 cubic feet.

Jamaica, 2240 lbs. per 80 cubic feet.

Linseed.—50 lbs. per bushel, Calcutta measurement is 40 cubic feet for 1600 lbs.

Mahogany.—Average weight from 47 lbs. to 60 lbs. per cubic foot. 1880 lbs. to 2720 lbs., equal to 40 cubic feet.

Measures.—Prussian Lasts each 4000 lbs. = 2 tons.
Norwegian Lasts each 6000 lbs. = 3 tons.
Gallon = 231 cubic inches.
Bushel = $2150\frac{42}{100}$ cubic inches.
Petersburg standard = 1980 feet = 165 cubic feet.
Ton wheat in bulk = $46\frac{2}{3}$ cubic feet.
" in bags = 53 cubic feet.
100 Quarters are equal to $21\frac{428}{1000}$ tons.
1 Load of Timber and Deals = 50 cubic feet.
1 Ton Measurement = 40 cubic feet.
1 Ton Register = 100 cubic feet.

Oars.—Measuring 12 feet, 14 feet, 15 feet, 16 feet, 17 feet, 18 feet, weigh as follows: 10 lbs., 14 lbs., 16 lbs., $17\frac{1}{2}$ lbs., $20\frac{1}{2}$

9

lbs., 23 lbs., average about 1493 ft. which equals 2240 lbs. Piled
up they average to 16 feet long, 7 feet high, 14 feet wide—say

150 oars	12 feet long	10	lbs. each	= 1800 feet.
200 "	14 "	14	"	= 2800 "
300 "	15 "	16	"	= 4500 "
600 "	16 "	17½	"	= 9600 "
400 "	17 "	20½	"	= 6800 "
350 "	18 "	23	"	= 6300 "

Organs.—Vary in size and description, but weigh on an average
1100 lbs. per 40 cubic feet.

Oils.—Petroleum in barrels measure 2 feet x 2 feet x 2 feet 9
inches = 11 cubic feet containing between 48 and 52 gallons
gross. Oil weighs 6½ lbs. per gallon ; barrel weighs about 60 lbs.

Palm, in barrels and casks, weigh 1671 lbs. gross = 40 cubic
feet measurement.

Whale, in casks (varying in dimension and shape), 1 gallon
gross = about 10 lbs., and 200 gallons displace about 40 cubic
feet measurement.

Lubricating, 48 to 50 gallons gross in a barrel, weighs 6¾ lbs.
per gallon, barrel weighs about 60 lbs., gross weight barrel of
oil, 400 lbs., net weight, 340 lbs.

Cases, equal 2 cubic feet 2 inches, contain 10 gallons, 78 to 82
lbs. gross per case.

Oil Cake.—In bales: 2 feet 5 inches x 1 foot 6 inches x 1 foot
2 inches = $4\frac{3}{12}$ cubic feet, weighing 241 lbs.

1 foot 11 inches x 1 foot 10 inches x 1 foot = $2\frac{11}{12}$ cubic feet,
weighing 170 lbs.

2 feet 3 inches x 1 foot 9 inches x 1 foot 2 inches = $4\frac{7}{12}$ cubic
feet, weighing 231 lbs.

Pitch and Tar.—100 barrels equal to 97 quarters wheat.

Pork.—Barrels, 320 to 330 lbs. gross, 2 feet 5½ inches x 1 foot
10 inches = 8 cubic feet, 3 inches.

Tierces, 80 pieces iron-hooped, 515 lbs. gross, average 318 lbs.
net, measure 12 cubic feet.

Pepper.—3½ bushel bags, 318 lbs. net, weigh 125 to 130 lbs.,
35 lbs. per bushel.

Port Wine.—Pipes, 135 to 140 gallons $= 42\frac{9}{12}$ feet.

Hhds, 74 " $= 19\frac{3}{12}$ "

Casks, 35 " $= 8\frac{11}{12}$ "

Palm.—Leaf bales weigh 175 lbs. $= 12$ cubic feet.

Rosin.—Barrels measure 2 feet 7 inches x 1 foot 9 inches x 1 foot 9 inches $= 8$ cubic feet.

2 feet 9 inches x 1 foot 8 inches x 1 foot 8 inches $= 7$ cubic feet 7 inches.

2 feet $7\frac{1}{2}$ inches x 2 feet x 2 feet $= 10$ cubic feet 6 inches.

3 barrels $= 26$ feet 1 inch. The gross weight of the rosin varies from 250 to 500 lbs. per barrel.

Rice.—40 casks weight $= 2854$ lbs. gross, measure 75 cubic feet, averaging $713\frac{1}{2}$ lbs. per cask $= 18\frac{9}{12}$ cubic feet.

Rum.—Barrel of 40 gallons, measure $10\frac{4}{12}$ cubic feet.

Sugar.—St. Jago. Hhds. 1248 lbs. gross measure $26\frac{6}{12}$ cubic feet.

New Orleans, Hhds. measure $30\frac{9}{12}$ cubic feet.

Cuba boxes, 450 lbs., measure 12 cubic feet.

Stone.—Free Stone 154 lbs. per cubic foot.

Marble, 168 lbs. per cubic foot.

Spirits.—Turpentine in barrels. $41\frac{1}{2}$ gallons gross, measure 2 feet 8 inches x 2 feet x 2 feet $= 10\frac{8}{12}$ cubic feet, weight $7\frac{1}{4}$ lbs. per gallon. Barrels 75 to 100 lbs., 41 gallons per barrel $= 375$ lbs. gross.

Spermaceti.—In boxes, 56 lbs. 1 foot 4 inches x 1 foot x 1 foot $= 1\frac{4}{12}$ cubic feet. 42 lbs. each foot, 1680 lbs. to 40 cubic feet.

School-slates.—Cases measure about 4 cubic feet each and weigh on the average 1300 lbs. per 40 cubic feet.

Slate.—Roofing slate; 1 ton of 2240 lbs., displaces the room of 20 cubic feet.

Starch.—Boxes measure 16 cubic inches, weigh 48 to 50 lbs. gross; taken as small stowage.

Staves.—Pipes. Extra heavy, weigh 7 to 8 tons per gross mille of 1200 each.

Heavy, weigh 6 to 7 tons per gross mille of 1200 each.

Light, weigh 5 to 6 tons per gross mille of 1200 each.

Measure 54 inches in length for each stave.

Hogshead.   Extra heavy, weigh 5 to 6 tons per gross mille of 1200 each.

Heavy, weigh 4 to 5 tons per gross mille of 1200 each.

Light, weigh 3½ to 4 tons per gross mille of 1200 each.

Each stave measures 42 inches in length.

Barrel.   Extra heavy, weigh 4 to 5 tons per gross mille of 1200 each.

Heavy, weigh 3 to 4 tons per gross mille of 1200 each.

Light, weigh 2 to 3 tons per gross mille of 1200 each.

Each stave measures 32 inches in length.

The above weights and measurements are those of staves known to the trade as Western staves.

This distinction is necessary, as staves shipped from South Atlantic Ports and New Orleans differ from those mentioned above, in many ways.

New Orleans Staves average 80 per cent. to 100 per cent. more in weight than Philadelphia Staves, the wood heavier, size larger, back broader; measure about:

Pipes, 60 inches; Hogsheads, 48 inches; Barrels, 36 inches.

South Atlantic Port Staves, average 50 per cent. more in weight than New York Staves, the dimensions varying and the oak being much heavier.

(*Culls.*   This means those staves which have defects, however slight, and which consequently form a class by themselves.)

Tobacco.—Hhds. Kentucky averaging 1500 lbs. = 80 cubic feet.

Maryland averaging 925 lbs. = 40 cubic feet.

Virginia averaging 1200 lbs. about 60 cubic feet.

Stems in various Hhds.   1020 lbs. measure 40 cubic feet.

Boxes, manufactured 145 lbs. net, 2 feet 3 inches x 1 foot 2 inches x 1 foot 6 inches = 2½ feet, 121 lbs. net, 143 gross = 2½ feet.

Kegs 250 to 265 lbs. measure 2 feet 1 inch x 1 foot 6 inches x 1 foot 6 inches = 4½ cubic feet, ½ Tierce 457 lbs. = 7$\frac{10}{12}$ cubic feet.

Leafs in boxes, 395 lbs. gross, 3 feet 8 inches x 2 feet 8 inches x 2 feet 8 inches = 26½ cubic feet.

Tallow.—Hhds. 1240 lbs. gross, measure 3 feet 7 inches x 3 feet x 3 feet = $32\frac{3}{12}$ cubic feet, or 40 lbs. per 1 cubic foot; in barrels 2 feet 7 inches x 1 foot 9 inches x 1 foot 9 inches = $7\frac{1}{2}$ cubic feet, weigh 293 lbs.

Wool.—Round, uncompressed, 336 lbs. per 40 cubic feet. Beyrout 700 lbs. average $26\frac{1}{2}$ cubic feet.

Wood.—Elm, weighs 37 lbs. per cubic foot.

White Pine,	"	34	"
Ash,	"	50	"
Cedar in logs,	"	28	"
Maple,	"	47	"
Live Oak,	"	83	"
Forest,	"	60	"
Boxwood,	"	$64\frac{1}{2}$	"

Black Walnut in logs, weighs 50–53 lbs. per cubic foot.

Tonala Mahogany,	"	50–53	"

Logwood.—Camp and Laguna, 50 cubic feet = 2240 lbs.

Honduras,	52	"	"
Jamaica,	80	"	"
Limawood,	85	"	"
Japan,	90	"	"
Tabasco,	36	"	"

(180 tons weight occupies less than 11,200 feet measurement in store; equivalent to 62 cubic feet per ton weight of 2240 lbs.)

Woodenware.—Clothes pins in common sized boxes, measure $1\frac{1}{4}$ cubic foot each, weigh 22 lbs. per cubic foot.

Pails, various styles, measuring 5 feet x 1 foot x 1 foot = 5 cubic feet.

5 feet x 1 foot 2 inches x 1 foot 2 inches = 6 cubic feet 10 inches.

4 feet 3 inches x 1 foot 1 inch x 1 foot 1 inch = 5 cubic feet per dozen.

Usual size weighs 32 lbs. per dozen.

Buckets in nests: 1 foot 4 inches x 1 foot 4 inches x 1 foot 2 inches = $2\frac{1}{12}$ cubic feet.

Ice coolers in nests: 1 foot 5 inches x 1 foot 5 inches x 10 inches = 1 cubic foot 8 inches.

Washboards, in bundles containing a dozen: 16 inches x 14 inches x 24 inches = 3 cubic feet 1 inch.

Rolling pins in boxes 20 inches x 9 inches x 23 inches = 2 cubic feet 5 inches.

Lemon squeezers: 2 feet x 1 foot x 1 foot = 2 cubic feet.

Tubs: measure singly 25 inches x 15 inches x 25 inches = 5 cubic feet 5 inches. In nests: 5 feet 6 inches x 1 foot 11 inches x 1 foot 11 inches = 18 cubic feet 6 inches.

AVERAGE WEIGHTS OF THE PRINCIPAL ARTICLES OF AMERICAN EXPORT.

		LBS.
Hogshead of	Bark,	2,275
"	" Tallow,	1,250
"	" Tobacco (Maryland and Ohio),	900
"	" " (Kentucky and Wisconsin),	1,800
"	" " (Virginia, Indiana and Missouri),	1,500
Tierce	" Lard,	390
"	" Beef,	520
Barrel	" Refined Petroleum,	400
"	" Crude Petroleum,	390
"	" Residuum,	440
"	" Naphtha,	360
"	" Pork,	320
"	" Flour,	216
"	" Rosin,	375
Case	" Petroleum,	81
Box	" Bacon,	540
Bag	" Oil Cake,	220
Bale	" Cotton,	450
Bushel	" Wheat,	60
"	" Indian Corn,	56
"	" Rye,	56
"	" Barley,	48
"	" Oats,	32
"	" Clover Seed,	60
"	" Pease,	60
Gallon	" Refined Petroleum (gallon of water, 8 lbs.),	6½
"	" Naphtha,	5¾
"	" Crude Petroleum,	6½
"	" Residuum,	7½

ABSTRACTS

FROM

UNITED STATES LAWS

GOVERNING THE

FOREIGN AND COASTWISE SHIPPING BUSINESS

AT

PORTS OF THE UNITED STATES.

The Government of the United States has passed many laws of a maritime character, affecting all classes of tonnage and foreign trade of every description, which were presumably necessary for a proper and harmonious consummation of business and for the better protection of the several industries of the nation, as well as for the enhancement of the Government Treasury. Many of those laws were repealed and others substituted, and they in turn followed the fate of their predecessors. Regulations have been adopted and subsequently rescinded; rules have been laid down for the benefit of trades and protection of shipping which were enforced in some districts and ignored in others; edicts have gone forth from the Treasury Department, which a succeeding official recalled; decisions have been rendered on numerous appeals from the exactions of some over-officious collector whose limited business experience or lack of proper assumption of discretionary power disqualified him for the discharge of his duties, which were subsequently modified or completely transformed; bad enforcement of good laws and persistent inflictions of unpopular ones, have been sources of great annoyance and expense to vessel owners and merchants alike. But whatever may be the opinion of those having business to transact with the representatives of Uncle Sam as to the feasibility or practical usefulness of the voluminous laws, rules and regulations governing American tonnage and foreign trade, it is a fact absolute, definite and beyond dispute that the substance of the following abstracts relating principally to matters which are likely at any time to come within the duties of the ship-master, owner or broker, must be literally and absolutely complied with.

Vessels of the United States of five tons burden and upwards must be registered, enrolled and licensed, or licensed according to the requirements of the trade in which they are engaged.

A vessel's home port is that at or nearest to which the owner resides, or, if there is more than one owner, where the managing power resides. The name of every vessel and her home port must be painted on her stern in white letters of not less than three inches in length, on black ground; steamers must also have their names on each outer side of the pilot-house, if there is one, in plain letters not less than six inches in length. If steamer has side wheels, the name must be placed on the outer side of each wheel-house. Penalty, $500.00 for registered vessel; $20.00 if licensed.

A vessel's name cannot be changed after she has received her papers except by special Act of Congress. Penalty, forfeiture of vessel.

Steamboats employed only in a river or bay of the United States, owned wholly or in part by an alien resident within the United States, may be enrolled and licensed in the same manner as vessels of the United States.

Every documented vessel must obtain an official number.

A vessel's tonnage must be carved or permanently marked on her main beam.

The officers of all vessels of the United States must be citizens of the United States.

Certificates of registry are required for vessels engaged in the foreign trade.

The papers of a vessel must be shown to any officer concerned in the collection of the revenue, if requested. Penalty, $100.00.

A vessel enrolled or licensed for the coasting trade cannot engage in the foreign trade without first taking out a register.

A vessel changing her form, burden or rig, must be documented anew by her former name.

A change of masters must be endorsed upon the vessel's papers.

Vessels from foreign ports can make entry and discharge only at ports designated for those purposes according to law.

Merchandise cannot be brought into the United States from a foreign port in any vessel, unless the master shall have on board a full manifest of the cargo, in writing, and signed by such master, detailing all the items of the vessel's lading; the port or ports where the same may have been shipped; the names of the consignees and the different ports, if more than one, where the same is consigned or intended to be entered; the names of the several passengers on board, and the baggage belonging to each; and the remaining ship's stores.

Any form of manifest will be accepted which affords a substantial compliance with the requirements of the law.

The master must also produce for inspection, in like manner, to any officer of the customs who shall first come on board of the vessel upon arrival within the limits of any district of the United States in which the cargo, or any part of it, is intended to be discharged or landed, the manifest of such cargo, and deliver to him a true copy, provided and subscribed by the master. And the production of the original and delivery of the copy shall be certified by the officers of the customs on the back of the original manifest, with the date of such production of the original and receipt of copy; and said officer shall transmit the copy of the manifest to the collector of the district.

The master of every vessel is required to deliver a copy of each manifest to the officer first coming on board within four leagues of the coast, and another copy to the officer first coming on board within the limits of the district. He is also required to exhibit to any other officer, on demand, the original manifest, or manifests, with the certificates thereon. The original manifest should always be ready for production on demand; but if the copies are unprepared, a reasonable time will be allowed by the boarding officer for their preparation. The master must afterwards produce and deliver to the collector the original manifest or manifests; and when a manifest shall be produced to the collector not certified by the boarding officer, the master of the vessel must make oath or affirmation that no officer has demanded or indorsed a manifest of the cargo of the vessel.

The master of a vessel of the United States from a foreign port is required to exhibit the certified copy of his crew list to the first boarding officer at the first port of arrival, and produce to him the persons therein named. The bond is not forfeited by the failure to produce any of the persons named in the crew list who may have been discharged in a foreign country with the consent of the United States consul or consular agent therein residing, in writing, under his hand and official seal, to be exhibited to the collector; or who may have deceased, absconded, or been forcibly impressed into other service, of which satisfactory proof must then be exhibited to the collector.

Upon every arrival of a vessel of the United States from a foreign port, the master is required, before the vessel can be admitted to entry, to exhibit to the collector of the port a true account of the number of seamen employed on board such vessel since her last entry at any port of the United States.

Within twenty-four hours after the arrival of any vessel from a foreign port or place, within any port of the United States at which an officer of the customs resides, or as soon thereafter as the hours of business at the custom-house will permit, the master is required to make report of the arrival to the chief officer of the customs; and within forty-eight hours after arrival he is required to make a further report, in writing, to the collector of the district, in the form and containing all the particulars required to be inserted in a manifest, and declare to its truth, by oath or affirmation before the collector. The master, neglecting to make the reports and the declaration, or to make the oath as required, or not fully complying with the true intent and meaning of the law, as the case may be, shall pay the sum of one thousand dollars.

The master of any vessel having on board distilled spirits, wines or teas, is also required, within forty-eight hours after his arrival, whether at the first port of arrival or not, to report in writing, to the surveyor, the foreign port or place from which he last sailed; the name, burden, denomination of the vessel; his own name; to what nation the vessel belongs; the quantity and kinds of spirits, wines and teas on board, and the number of packages containing the same, with their marks and numbers; and the quantity and kinds of spirits, wines and teas on board as sea stores. Penalty, five hundred dollars and the spirits so omitted.

Before an entry of a vessel of the United States is made, the register, together with the clearance and other papers granted by the officers of the customs to the vessel on her departure from the port from which she may have arrived—are required to be produced to the collector with whom the entry is to be made, to remain in his office until a clearance is granted.

The master of every foreign vessel is required, before entry, to produce to the collector, the register or other document in lieu of same, together with the clearance and other papers granted by the officers of the customs to his vessel at the port of departure for the United States, and within forty-eight hours after entry, to deposit the same with the consul or vice-consul of the nation to which the vessel belongs, and to deliver to the collector the certificate of that officer that the papers have been so deposited. Penalty not less than five hundred nor more than two thousand dollars. This regulation does not apply to vessels of foreign nations, in whose ports consuls of the United States are not permitted to have the custody of the papers of vessels of the United States entering the ports of such nations.

If a vessel, which shall have arrived from a foreign port within the limits of a collection district of the United States, shall depart

or attempt to depart from the same, unless to proceed to some
" more interior district " to which she may be bound, before report
or entry shall have been made by the master of the vessel, to the
collector of a district of the United States, such master will be
liable to pay the sum of four hundred dollars ; and the collector,
surveyor, or naval officer, or the commander of any revenue
cutter, is authorized to arrest and bring back such vessel to the
most convenient port. The foregoing penalty will not be incurred if it shall be made to appear, by oath of the master or
other person in charge or command of the vessel, and of the
person next in command, or other sufficient proof to the satisfaction of the collector of the district into which the vessel shall
afterwards be brought, or of the court before whom the prosecution may be had, that such departure, or attempt to depart, was
occasioned by stress of weather, pursuit or duress of enemies, or
other necessity. The foregoing provisions comprehend foreign
as well as American vessels bound to the United States, but do
not extend to a vessel arriving from a foreign port and passing
through the conterminous waters of a river which forms the
boundary between the United States and the territory of a foreign
state, for the purpose of proceeding to such territory.

If merchandise be brought in a vessel from a foreign port and
specified in the manifest verified on oath or affirmation before the
collector at the first port of arrival, as destined for other districts
in the United States, the importing vessel may proceed with the
same from district to district in order to the landing or delivery,
the duties on such goods only as are landed or delivered in any
district, to be paid or secured in such district. But before such
vessel shall depart from the district in which she shall first arrive
for another district, if the departure be not within forty-eight
hours after arrival, with merchandise brought in her from a
foreign port or place, duties not having been paid or secured, the
master of such vessel is required to obtain from the collector of
the district a copy of the report and manifest, certified by said
collector, to which must be annexed a certificate of the quantity
and particulars of the goods landed within his district, or of the
goods remaining on board upon which duties are to be paid or

secured in some other district. And the master or person having charge or command of such vessel is also required to give bond, with one or more sureties, to the satisfaction of the collector of the district within which the vessel shall first arrive, in a sum equal to the amount of the duties on the residue of the cargo, according to the estimate of the collector.

Coasting papers will not be granted to a vessel having on board merchandise brought from a foreign port, unless it be wholly unladen and the duties paid or secured.

In the case of a vessel from a foreign port or place compelled by stress of weather, or other necessity, to put into any other port or place than that of her destination, the master, together with the mate or person next in command, within twenty-four hours after arrival, shall make protest, in the usual form, upon oath, before the collector of the district of arrival, or other person duly authorized, setting forth the causes or circumstances of such necessity. The protest, if not made before the collector, must be produced to him and the naval officer, if any, at the port, and a copy lodged with them. If such master shall also make report to the collector within forty-eight hours after arrival, as in other cases, and if it shall be made to appear to the collector, by the certificates of the wardens of the port, or other officers accustomed to ascertain the condition of vessels arriving in distress, or if there be no such officers, by the certificate of two reputable merchants, to be named for that purpose by the collector, that it is necessary to unlade the vessel, the collector and naval officer, if any, will grant a permit therefor, and appoint an inspector to oversee the unlading and keep an account thereof, to be compared with the report of the master of the vessel; and the merchandise so unladen will be stored under custody of the collector. At the request of the master of the vessel, or of the owner, the collector, together with the naval officer where there is one, and alone where there is none, shall grant permission to enter and pay the duties on, and dispose of, such part of the cargo as may be of a perishable nature, or as may be necessary to defray the expenses attending the vessel and her lading. And if the delivery of the cargo do not agree with the master's report, and the difference be not satisfactorily explained, the master of the vessel will become subject to the penalties provided in like cases by law. The merchandise, or the residue not so disposed of, may be reladen on board the vessel, under the inspection of the officer who superintended the landing, or other proper officer, and the vessel proceed with the same to her place of destination, subject only to the charge for the storing and safe-keeping of the merchandise, and the fees to the officers, as in other cases.

If, after the arrival of any vessel, bound to the United States from a foreign port, within the limits of any collection district of the United States, or within four leagues of the coast, any part of the cargo of such vessel shall be unladen before the vessel's arrival at the place where the whole or part of her cargo is to be discharged, and without authority therefor from the proper officers of the customs, the master or person in charge or command of such vessel and the person next in command shall respectively pay the sum of one thousand dollars for each such offence ; and the merchandise so unladen and unshipped, except in the case of accident, necessity, or stress of weather, shall also be forfeited. Where such unlading occurs by reason of unavoidable accident, necessity, or stress of weather, the master or other person in charge or command of the vessel, with two or more of the officers and mariners of the vessel, including the second in command, whom he shall duly notify, must make proof upon oath, before the chief customs officer of the district within which the casualty occurred, or before the chief customs officer of the first district at which such vessel shall afterwards arrive, if the casualty occurred within four leagues of the coast and without the limits of any collection district. If the merchandise so unladen be put or received on any other vessel or boat, except in the case of accident, necessity, or stress of weather, to be notified and proved as above required, the master or person in charge or command of such vessel or boat, and every other person aiding or assisting, shall forfeit and pay treble the value of said merchandise, and such vessel or boat shall also be forfeited.

The time allowed in which to discharge the cargo of a vessel is as follows:—Vessels of less than 300 tons, 8 days; vessels of 300 tons and less than 800 tons, 12 days; vessels of 800 tons and upwards, 15 days. Days of arrival and entry, Sundays, legal holidays and rainy days are excluded.

Vessels with salt are allowed one working day for each 1,000 bushels. An extension of time in all cases can be obtained.

Vessels bound to a port in California or Oregon from an Eastern Atlantic or Gulf port, are entered and cleared coastwise.

A vessel of the United States, bound from a port in the United States to a foreign port, or *vice versa*, is required, before clearance, to receive on board all such mails as the Post Office Department of the United States, or any minister, consul, or commercial agent of the United States abroad, shall offer; and also all such coin, bullion, United States notes and bonds, and other securities as the government of the United States, or any department thereof, or any minister, consul, vice-consul, or commercial or other agent of the United States abroad, shall offer; and securely convey and promptly deliver the same to the proper authorities, or consignees, on arriving at the port of destination, for which a reasonable compensation shall be paid. But a vessel departing from the United States for a foreign port cannot receive or convey any letters or other packets originating in the United States which have not been regularly posted at, and received from, the post-office at the port of departure, except letters or letter packets relating to the cargo and addressed to the owner or consignee of the vessel, and letters or letter packets enclosed in United States stamped envelopes of sufficient denomination to cover the postage. And it is the duty of the collector or other officer to require from the master, as a condition of clearance, an oath or affirmation that he has not under his care, or within his control, and will not receive or convey any letters or letter packets in violation of this provision.

If a vessel bound to a foreign port shall depart without the delivery of the manifest by the master to the collector, and obtaining from him a clearance, such master shall pay five hundred dollars.

The sea-coast of the United States is divided into five great coasting districts.

The first embraces the collection districts on the sea-coast and navigable rivers between the eastern limits of the United States and the southern limits of Georgia.

The second includes the harbors, ports, sea-coast, and navigable rivers between the southern limits of Georgia and the river Perdido.

The third comprehends the sea-coast and navigable rivers between the river Perdido and the Rio Grande.

The fourth includes the Pacific coast of the United States south of Alaska.

The fifth comprises the Territory of Alaska.

A vessel of twenty tons burden or upwards, licensed for the coasting trade, bound from one collection district to another within the same great coasting district, or between a State in one and an adjoining State in another great district; or a vessel of less than twenty tons burden, licensed for the coasting trade, bound from a collection district·in one State to a collection district in the same or an adjoining State on the sea-coast or navigable waters of the United States; in ballast or having on board goods, wares, or merchandise of the growth or product of the United States only, except distilled spirits, or distilled spirits not exceeding 500 gallons, or wine in casks not exceeding 250 gallons, or wine in bottles not exceeding 100 dozens, or sugar in casks or boxes not exceeding 3,000 pounds, or tea in chests or boxes not exceeding 500 pounds, or coffee in casks or bags not exceeding 1,000 pounds, or foreign merchandise in packages, as imported, not exceeding in value four hundred ($400) dollars, or foreign merchandise of any kind, including any or all of the articles before mentioned, the aggregate value of which does not exceed eight hundred ($800) dollars, the duties upon which have been paid or secured, may proceed from one place to another, within the limits stated, without delivering a manifest or obtaining from any officer of the customs a permit to depart.

In all cases, however, where any cargo is on board, the master is to be provided with a manifest subscribed by himself.

The master of such vessel is also exempted from making report or entry on his arrival at a port or place within the limits stated; he may, however, be required by any officer of the customs to exhibit the manifest subscribed by himself, and to give true information from whence the vessel last sailed, and, if in port, when she arrived.

The master of a vessel of the burden of twenty tons or upwards, licensed for the coasting trade, bound from one collection district to another within the same great coasting district, or from a State in one to an adjoining State in another great coasting district; or of a vessel of less than twenty tons burden, licensed for the coasting trade, bound from a collection district in one State to a collection district in the same or an adjoining State, on the sea-coast or navigable waters of the United States, having on board any of the articles of foreign growth or manufacture, or distilled spirits, exceeding the quantities or value before mentioned, or any or all of said articles, exceeding in the aggregate eight hundred dollars in value, must, previous to the departure of the vessel, make out and subscribe duplicate manifests of the whole cargo on board. If there be a collector of the customs or surveyor within five miles of the port where the vessel may be, the master must present such manifest to him, and make oath to its truth, and that the duties on the foreign articles have been paid or secured, according to his best knowledge and belief. On arrival of such vessel at the port of destination within the limits described, if there be a collector or surveyor within five miles, the master must, before unlading any part of his cargo, exhibit to the collector or surveyor the certified manifest before mentioned, or, if no certified manifest was obtained by reason of there being no collector or surveyor residing within five miles of the place of departure, then he must produce the duplicate manifest before mentioned, to the truth of which he must make oath or affirmation. If there be no collector or surveyor residing within five miles of the port of arrival, the master may unlade his cargo;

but he must deliver to the collector or surveyor of the first port
at which he afterwards arrives, and within twenty-four hours of
his arrival, the certified manifest or duplicate manifests before
mentioned, and must note thereon the time when, and the place
where, the cargo was discharged.

The master of every vessel of the burden of twenty tons or
upwards, licensed for the coasting trade, bound from one to
another great coasting district, except from a State in one to an
adjoining State in another great coasting district, or of a registered vessel bound from one collection district to another collection
district, or of a vessel of less than twenty tons burden, licensed
for the coasting trade, bound to any collection district other than
a collection district in the same or an adjoining State, on the sea-
coast or navigable waters of the United States, must, previously
to his departure, deliver to the collector residing at the port, or
if there be no collector at such port, to the collector of, or a surveyor residing within the district nearest to the port where the
vessel may be, duplicate manifests of the cargo on board such
vessel, to which he must make oath or affirmation. If there be
no cargo or lading, other than sea stores, on board such vessel,
the master or commander must make oath or affirmation that
such is the case. The collector or surveyor will then certify the
manifests, and grant a permit, as in the preceding case; or if
there be no cargo, and the master make oath or affirmation of the
fact, the collector or surveyor will grant a permit according to
form. On arrival of a vessel at the port of her destination, the
master must, within twenty-four hours thereafter, deliver to the
collector residing at the port of arrival, if there be one, or to a
collector or a surveyor within the district, if either reside within
five miles of the port, or within forty-eight hours after his arrival,
if there be no collector or surveyor residing within five miles,
before unlading any part of the cargo, a certified manifest of the
whole cargo on board, to the truth of which he must make oath,
according to form. The collector or surveyor at the port of
arrival will thereupon grant a permit for unlading a part or the
whole of such cargo, as may be requested; but in case a part
only of the cargo is discharged, the collector or surveyor will

endorse the articles so discharged on the manifest, and will grant a permit to the master to proceed with the vessel to the place of her further destination. If there be no cargo on board, the master must produce the coastwise clearance and permit granted by the collector or surveyor at the port of departure.

In case a vessel employed in transporting goods coastwise shall put into a port other than the one to which she is bound, the master must, within twenty-four hours after his arrival, if he continues so long, report to the collector his arrival, the place whence he came, and whither he is bound, with an account of the cargo on board his vessel.

Commercial intercourse with the Guano Islands that are bonded in pursuance of law forms a part of the coasting trade of the United States, and the laws relative thereto forbid foreign vessels from engaging therein.

Vessels engaged in the guano trade are not required to produce clearances or certified manifests from the islands, there being no customs officers stationed there. But masters of such vessels will be required to have manifests of the cargo, subscribed by themselves, and to exhibit the same, on demand, to officers of the customs for inspection. Entry at the custom-house must be made on arrival at the port of destination in the United States.

Steam-tugs, duly enrolled and licensed, when exclusively employed in towing vessels, are not required to report and clear at the custom-house; but when such steam-tugs are employed in towing rafts or other vessels without sail or steam motive power, not required to be enrolled or licensed under existing laws, they must report and clear in the same manner as other vessels.

The importation of cigars in less quantity than 3,000 in a single package, or in boxes containing more than 500; of spirituous liquors in casks of less than 14 gallons, or other packages of less capacity than 30 gallons; and of spirituous liquors and wines in bottles, unless in packages containing not less than a dozen bottles, is prohibited. Penalty, forfeiture.

In respect to liquors, the law is understood to regulate merely the size of the package immediately containing them, without regard to the actual quantity of the contents.

Merchandise picked up at sea derelict, or recovered from a wreck, will be taken possession of in the port where it shall first arrive, and retained in the custody of the collector as unclaimed. If not claimed and entered by the owner, on due proof of ownership, before the expiration of the usual period, it will be subject to sale for duties in the usual manner.

Salvors have an uncertain interest in the goods saved, dependent upon the decree of a competent tribunal. They have not such an interest as will justify the collector in permitting them to make entry, unless so decreed by the court. If the merchandise be libelled for salvage, the collector will notify the district attorney of the claim of the United States for duties, and to intervene for the same. All derelict or wrecked goods should be entered by appraisement.

Small parcels containing tokens of affection or presents, not intended for sale, and not exceeding two hundred dollars in value, will be admitted to entry upon appraisement, without invoice. When the value exceeds two hundred dollars, application must be made to the Secretary of the Treasury.

All goods unclaimed by the owner or consignee at the expiration of the period allowed by law for the discharge of the vessel in which the same may have been imported, and all goods of which the entry shall be at that time for any cause incomplete, so that the duties thereon are not paid or secured, will be forthwith taken possession of by the collector and deposited as hereinafter directed.

And, in any case, one day after receiving notice of the consent of the owner or master of the vessel, or of the owner or consignee of the goods, the collector may take like possession of the goods and deposit them in public store or bonded warehouse.

But merchandise imported in steam-vessels, appearing by bill of lading to be deliverable immediately after entry of the vessel, may be taken like possession of immediately.

Merchandise cannot be carried from one port in the United States to another port within the same, in a vessel belonging wholly or in part to a subject of any foreign power, except for the purpose of unloading the cargo from the importing vessel, or of proceeding in ballast, or with a part of her outward cargo, from one port of the United States to another, to complete such cargo.

PRINCIPAL ARTICLES OF EXPORTS OF VARIOUS COUNTRIES.

Arabia.—Coffee, aloes, myrrh, frankincense, gum arabic.

Asiatic Islands.—Pepper, cloves, nutmegs, camphor, opium.

Belgium.—Grain, flax, hops, woolens, linens, laces, etc.

Brazil.—Cotton, sugar, coffee, gold, diamonds, dye-woods.

Nova Scotia and New Brunswick.—Furs, lumber, fish.

Central America.—Logwood, mahogany, indigo, cocoa.

Chili.—Silver, gold, copper, hemp, hides, sugar, fruits.

China.—Tea, silks, nankeens, porcelain, ivory, pearl articles.

Denmark.—Horses, cattle, beef, pork, butter, cheese, grain.

Africa.—Gold, ivory, diamonds, ostrich feathers.

Egypt.—Rice, linseed, fruits, indigo, cotton, sugar, grain.

Ecuador.—Coffee, cotton, indigo, fruit, sugar, cocoa.

France.—Silks, woolens, linens, wine, brandy, porcelain, toys.

Germany.—Linen, grain, various manufactures of silver, etc.

Great Britain.—Woolens, cottons, linens, hardware, iron.

Greenland.—Whale oil, whale bone, seal skins.

Holland.—Fine linens, woolens, butter, cheese, etc.

Italy.—Silks, wines, marble, oil, fruits, rice.

Ireland.—Linens, hides, tallow, potatoes, barley, beef.

Japan.—Silk, tea, japanware, porcelain, indigo.

Mexico.—Gold, silver, logwood, cochineal, fruits.

Persia.—Carpets, shawls, wines, silk, rhubarb, guns, swords.

Peru.—Peruvian bark, mercury, silver, gold, sugar, fruits.

Russia.—Hemp, ivory, linen, grain, timber, furs, platina.

Spain and Portugal.—Silks, wool, wines, oil, fruits, salt.

Sweden and Norway.—Iron, steel, copper, timber, fish.

Switzerland.—Watches, jewelry, paper, laces, silk goods.

Turkey.—Grain, fruits, cotton, oil, wines, carpets, muslin.

Venezuela.—Sugar, coffee, cocoa, cotton, indigo, fruits.

West Indies.—Sugar, rum, molasses, coffee, spice, cotton, indigo, fruits.

UNITED STATES.

Eastern States.—Lumber, beef, pork, fish, cottons, woolens, watches, clocks, etc.

Middle States.—Flour, wheat, salt, coal, cottons, woolens, watches, sewing machines, oil.

Southern States.—Cotton, rice, tobacco, lumber, pitch, beef, whiskies, and fruits.

Western States.—Corn, wheat, lard, coal, iron, salt, lime, beef, pork, gold, silver.

ABSTRACTS

FROM

ADMIRALTY DECISIONS AND GENERAL MARITIME LAW.

AUTHORITY AND DUTY OF MASTERS, ETC.

In this country the Constitution of the United States has conferred upon the Courts of the National Government cognizance of all cases of Admiralty and Maritime jurisdiction. The words "Admiralty" and "Maritime," as they are used in the Constitution and Acts of Congress are by no means synonymous, although many distinguished lawyers seem sometimes to have so considered them. They were evidently both inserted in order to preclude a narrower construction which might be given to either word, had it been used alone. The English Admiralty had jurisdiction of all cases arising beyond the sea, although not maritime in their character. These are excluded by the use of both terms. The District Court of the United States has been given cognizance of all civil causes of Admiralty and Maritime jurisdiction, including all seizures under laws of imports, navigation, or trade of the United States, where the seizures are made on waters navigable from the sea by vessels of ten or more tons burden, within their respective districts, as well as upon the high seas; and by an act passed in 1845 Congress extended the jurisdiction to similar cases arising upon the lakes, and navigable waters connecting the same.

The Admiralty jurisdiction generally has been, of late, so much expanded by the decisions of the Federal Courts, as to make the practice of those tribunals of great consequence.

The various phases of Admiralty practice render it almost impossible to give any definite outline of forms, and for this reason those who have Admiralty cases are advised to consult attorneys who make this branch of legal science a specialty. The number of maritime lawyers in Philadelphia is comparatively few, but they make up in wisdom and nautical lore what they lack in numbers, and what they don't know about maritime jurisprudence is of little value.

The following abstracts are presented as concisely and simply as possible, avoiding all unnecessary technicalities, details and case references, in order that those not familiar with legal verbiage may readily understand what the sum and substance of it is, without being compelled to wade through the confusing profundity with which such information is generally clothed, and finally emerging therefrom in a perspiring state of wonderment and ignorance of what it all means. These notes are therefore made as clear to the understanding of the average mortal as possible, and may be considered correct and trustworthy.

But as the old maxim that "circumstances alter cases" is as applicable in matters of a nautical nature, if not more so, than the ordinary events of domestic life, it is often discovered that much depends upon the eloquence of the lawyer and the caprices and brain capacity of the jury, and that the sauce prepared for one case is not the dressing necessary in another of an apparently coincident character.

The following, however, will be found of benefit to the "sad sea dogs" who brave the elements at home as owners, and those who face the dangers of the deep as masters, as well as to ship brokers, and all whose business occupation is in any way connected with the maritime commerce of the country; and in the transaction of all business of that character a knowledge of these facts is very desirable and necessary. There are many captains who are skillful sailing masters, but poor business men, and others who combine the merits of both, but from inexperience are unqualified to act promptly and correctly in important matters affecting the interests of the owners, and the consequent pecuniary loss which owners thereby suffer in the course of a year is, in the aggregate, very large. A thorough familiarity with the following abstracts would, therefore, be of great assistance to ship-masters, especially at times when communication with the owners is not convenient or wholly impracticable; and as they are based upon cases upon which decisions have been rendered by eminent American and British judges and jurists, and applicable in either country, as well as upon prevailing customs where there is no special law to take the precedence, they can be confidently relied upon as correct. Evident tautology must be accepted, as under some circumstances and connections repetition is not only admissible, but necessary.

A mere verbal agreement between a ship-owner and merchant for the employment of a ship, and acted on by the parties, has been held to be equivalent to a charter party. But to prevent uncertainty, and in order that the terms of the agreement may, in case of dispute, be more easily proved by either party, it is better that the charter should be in writing. The captain has an implied authority to enter into all necessary contracts for the navigation of the ship; but he has no authority to substitute a different contract from any which may have been previously made by the managing owner, except under very special circumstances. The captain should in all cases sign charter parties as agent for the owners, otherwise he may be sued by the charterer in case of any dispute. If a charterer signs as agent, he should state the name of the principal in the body of the charter. Care should be taken that a charter party should contain no provisions which are unusual, or which may be prejudicial to the rights of either party. As the writing alone will bind the parties, no independent verbal promises can be enforced by either party, it being presumed by the law that the whole of the terms have been inserted in the writing. But a charter may be explained by verbal evidence of the custom of the trade to which it relates, provided that the express words of the charter are not inconsistent with, or opposed to the custom, in which case the custom would be excluded. When various kinds or qualities of goods are mentioned in the charter party, the proportion of each should be specified, otherwise the charterer will be entitled to load the goods in any proportion he pleases.

As the ship-owner will only have a lien on the cargo for the amount of freight named in the bills of lading, care should be taken that the charter party provides for the payment of the difference between the charter freight and the bill of lading, if any, at port of loading, and before the bills of lading are signed, if in favor of the ship, otherwise the claim for the balance will be against the charterer only.

In order to secure a lien on the cargo for payment of freight, the freight should be made payable in cash on delivery, as the lien is lost if freight is made payable after delivery.

After a ship is on demurrage, all days thereafter are counted up to and including the day of the termination of detention.

Where a certain number of days is specified for *loading and discharging*, it should be clearly expressed that the number stated is for *both included*.

The charterer has power to sub-let either the whole or any part of the ship to another, and if the contrary is desired by the ship-owner it must be so stated in the charter.

Any merchandise carried on deck must be so specified in the bills of lading. If the charter party does not provide for deck-load, and any merchandise is placed on deck, it is at the risk of ship-owner, and if jettisoned, the value cannot be recovered from the underwriters.

If a ship is chartered for a lump sum, the draft of water or dead weight of cargo guaranteed by ship-owner should be named in the charter to prevent the charterer from overloading the ship.

The penalty usually inserted at the end of the charter does not increase the liability of either party in case of a breach of the charter. The amount of damage actually sustained can only be recovered unless the charter stipulates that the amount named for the penalty is to be considered as the amount of "liquidated" (or ascertained) damages in case the charter should be broken. The naming of a penalty prevents the recovery of more than that amount.

A case has recently been decided in a British Court in favor of the ship making claim against the *shippers* for demurrage at this port for detention in discharging a cargo of pig iron, the cargo having been removed from the ship's side as fast as discharged, and no lien for demurrage was placed upon it here.

If the ship is chartered to load at a certain place, " or so near thereto as she may safely get, and there take a full cargo," this has been held to mean a place to which the ship can safely get, and from which, *when loaded*, she can safely get away at a suitable tide, and if necessary the merchant is bound to load a part of the cargo in the roads at his own expense.

All warranties in a charter must be strictly complied with. In a case where the vessel was described to be "now at sea, having sailed three weeks ago," the vessel having only sailed a fortnight, the charterer was released from his contract. In another case the vessel was stated in the charter to be "now in the port of Amsterdam," whereas, in fact, she was not there on the day the charter was signed, but was at sea sixty-two miles distant, and reached Amsterdam the next day. In that case also it was held that the merchant had a right to abandon the charter. In another case, when a ship was wrongly described to be at sea, when, in fact, she had not left port, the statement was held to amount to a warranty, and the merchant was discharged from all liability.

If the carrying capacity of a ship be warranted, and the charterer is unable to discover whether the ship will actually carry the quantity named until after he has loaded the cargo, still he cannot, after loading the ship, refuse to carry out the charter.

If the register tonnage of a ship is described as a certain number of tons " or thereabouts," that is considered a representation only, and not a warranty; and the charterer will be bound to carry out the charter, notwithstanding that the ship is larger or smaller, unless the difference is particularly unreasonable, and that is a question for the jury to decide.

As the question of whether any stipulation in a charter party is a warranty or not, depends upon the intention of the parties, as shown therein; each case must depend upon the words which the parties make use of. If the words do not amount to a warranty, or if the whole object of the voyage is not lost, the stipulation is considered merely a collateral agreement, the breach of which by one party will not justify the other in refusing altogether to carry out his own part of the contract, but it will only give him a right to sue the other party for damages for his breach of the contract.

In construing the meaning of the terms adopted by the parties in the charter, the Courts endeavor to adopt an interpretation which is liberal, and according to the true intention of the parties. The contract will not be construed so as to lead to absurd or unreasonable results, for the law will not presume that the parties intended to make an absurd or unreasonable contract; but if the words are clear and positive, they will be adhered to, however hard they may prove, for the parties should be more cautious before they enter into the contract.

A charter is construed so as to make it conformable to the custom of the trade to which it relates, unless such custom is at variance with the express terms of the contract. The parties are supposed to intend their contract to be carried out in the usual and customary manner.

Both the validity of the contract and the interpretation of it depend on the law of the country where the contract is made; but the mode of enforcing it is governed by the law of the country where it is to be enforced.

If the voyage becomes illegal before it is commenced, the charter is considered to be rescinded; for instance, if war is declared with the country to which the ship is about to sail, or if the exportation of the cargo is prohibited by our Government.

When a charter party has been signed, the parties cannot *verbally* make any alteration in its terms so as to be binding. If it is wished to alter the terms, such alteration should also be reduced into writing, and be signed the same as the original charter; or else the old charter should be cancelled, and a new one, containing the amended terms, substituted. A charter may, however, be *wholly rescinded* by a verbal agreement.

Generally, a consignee taking goods under a bill of lading incurs no other liability than that of paying the freight. If it is desired that the assignee of the bill of lading should observe the terms of the charter other than that which relate to freight, it should be provided for in the bill of lading by inserting therein the clause, "all other conditions as per charter party dated," etc.

If the merchant endorses bills of lading, and parts with all property in the goods, he cannot afterwards stop the goods from coming into the hands of the consignee, unless the consignee is merely his agent, or has become bankrupt in the meantime.

The bills of lading should be signed as soon as possible after the shipment of the goods; but on receiving the goods, the captain is to give a receipt for them, if required to do so, until the bills of lading are made out, and he should not sign them until the receipts are returned to him.

If, after the lay days are expired, the merchant delays the captain in sailing by preventing him signing proper bills of lading, the merchant will be liable to pay demurrage for the detention; but if the captain refuses to sign them without a sufficient cause, then the consequences will fall on the ship-owner only.

After signing one set of bills of lading, the master cannot be compelled to sign another set for the same goods, unless the former set is returned to him; otherwise he might become liable to deliver the goods to the holders of both sets.

The charter party generally provides that the ship shall be tight, staunch and strong, and furnished with all proper necessaries, and a sufficient crew; but this is also required by the law, even if there is no charter party. If the ship is in a leaky state, and the cargo be damaged, or the merchant be otherwise injured thereby, the ship-owner will be liable to pay damages.

If it is necessary to put ballast in the ship, as well as cargo, the captain has the right to put in heavy merchandise instead of ballast ordinarily used, provided that it occupies no more space than such ballast would have done, is not injurious to the cargo, and leaves to the charterer the entire cargo space.

The ship-owner is liable for all damage which the cargo may sustain by the want of proper and firm dunnage. The captain has the right, however, to use merchandise as dunnage, provided that it does not occupy more space than ordinary dunnage, and is equally effective.

The merchant must supply the vessel with the same cargo stipulated in the charter party, and in the manner which is customary at the port. In one case where the charterer had agreed to supply a cargo of "tallow, deals, and battens," and no tallow was loaded, but only deals and battens, which paid a less freight than tallow, the ship-owner was held to be entitled to damages.

When the charter party calls for a cargo of certain specified goods "and other merchandise," the charterer is restricted to goods of the same nature as those specified, and paying an average freight with them.

Accidents over which the charterer has no control is not sufficient claim to allow him to refuse to load the vessel.

The agent of the charterer has not any implied authority as agent to arrange with the ship-master for substituting another voyage or cargo in the place of the voyage or cargo named in the charter made by his principals. To empower him to do so, he should have an express authority to that effect from his principals.

The charterer has no right to put any goods into the cabin, or to load the deck, unless that is specially agreed for, or unless a deck cargo is both lawful and customary. The expression "full cargo" in a charter does not include the cabin or the deck, but only the full range of the ship's hold, from bulkshead to bulkshead.

While the cargo is being loaded, if the ship is in a bar harbor, the captain should see that she is not loaded so deep that she cannot go over the bar. He is not bound to receive any more cargo in port than he can safely leave the port with, at a good tide; and, if necessary, the merchant is bound to load the remainder of the cargo in the roads; but if the captain consents to receive the cargo in port, and then tries to leave, but fails to do so for want of water, the cost of discharging a portion of the cargo, and reloading it from lighters outside the harbor, will fall on the ship, as the merchant is not bound to load the vessel twice.

If the merchant refuses to load a part of the cargo in the roads, when bound to do so, the captain should note a protest when the lay days are expired, and, if necessary, sail with such cargo as he can safely leave the port with; and the merchant will be liable to pay dead freight for the remainder of the ship's capacity. The captain, however, would not be justified in insisting on sailing to prevent his being neaped, but he would have to receive in the harbor as much cargo as he could leave the port with at a spring tide, unless an arrangement is made with the merchant to load a part of the cargo outside the harbor to save the tides.

If the merchant has agreed by the charter to supply a full cargo, he is bound to furnish whatever broken stowage is required to complete a full cargo, unless there is some customary mode of stowage at the port of loading which exempts the merchant from this liability. The ship-owner is bound to accept broken stowage to fill up.

If the charter provides for a full cargo, and describes the vessel a little below her actual burthen, still the merchant is bound to supply her with a full cargo, provided the ship-owner has not made any wilful misrepresentation of the size of the ship, and the merchant has had the opportunity of seeing the ship to judge for himself. If the captain suspects that the contents of any packages are damaged, he can demand to see the contents; but he is not justified in opening a package, except in the presence of the shipper or his agents.

If the goods are of a dangerous or destructive character, the shipper is bound to inform the captain of their nature, and obtain his leave to send them on board, otherwise the shipper will be liable for any damage which they may do.

The captain has the power to have a suspected parcel opened, to ascertain whether it contains any dangerous articles, but if he does so, he should request the shipper or his agent, if possible, to be present at the time, and if the articles are found to be dangerous they may be thrown overboard without any liability for so doing.

After the merchant has shipped goods, he has no right to require them to be unshipped until they arrive at their destination, unless he first pays the full freight on the goods and the cost of relanding them, and also returns to the captain all bills of lading he may have signed for such goods; or, at his own expense, gives the captain a proper indemnity against all liabilities on such bills of lading. If this is not done, it is the captain's duty to retain the goods for the benefit of the ship-owner, and to secure the freight which will be due upon them.

If the merchant neglects to load the ship, he cannot be considered to have broken the contract until the end of the lay days, and demurrage days, if such are stipulated for in the charter, unless before that time arrives he positively refuses to carry out the contract; and if such refusal is acted on by the ship-owner or captain, then the breach of contract by the merchant is rendered complete, and the captain will be at liberty to re-charter the ship, and hold the first charterer liable for all consequences. But if the captain, instead of accepting the refusal, continues to demand the cargo after the merchant has refused to supply it, he cannot still consider the charter as broken, but he must then wait until the end of the time stipulated in the charter before he is entitled to re-charter the ship.

If the merchant refuses to load the ship, the captain should get the merchant to state his refusal in writing; or, if this cannot be done, he should note a protest.

If the charterer does not load the ship according to the charter, the amount of damages which the shipowner is entitled to recover is the amount of freight which the ship would have earned if she had been loaded according to the charter, deducting the expense the ship-owner would have had to incur in earning the freight, and also deducting the net profit he has made, if any, by the employment of the ship in the meantime; and the owner is not justified in keeping his ship idle after breach of contract, but he must accept employment if he can obtain such with safety and profit.

The amount of damages the merchant is entitled by law to recover from the ship-owner, in case the latter improperly refuses.

to carry a cargo which he is bound by the charter party to take, will be the amount of the loss actually sustained by him; and thus the amount will depend upon whether the merchant could obtain another ship to carry the cargo or not. If he could not obtain another ship, the damages will be the amount he has lost by having the cargo left on his hands. If he could obtain another ship, then the ship-owner will only be liable for the extra freight, if an increased amount of freight has been paid; but if the new freight is not more than that named in the original charter, then, as the merchant would sustain no loss, he can recover no damages, unless the merchant show special damage, as, for instance, that arising directly from the breach of a time contract owing to the default of the ship-owner, or any other clear and undoubted damage. If the charter contains a provision that a certain sum is to be paid as the ascertained damages, or "liquidated damages" in case the charter is broken, then the amount so named will be the amount payable. If, however, the amount stated to be payable on non-performance is expressed to be a *penalty*, or is in its amount of a nature evidently intended to operate as a penalty, then the merchant can only recover such amount of damage as he can prove he has sustained.

If the charter does not fix any time for the commencement of the voyage, it must be commenced with despatch, and within a reasonable time, wind and weather permitting, after the necessary clearance at the Custom House. In one case, the master had omitted, during the loading of the ship, to take in his stores and provisions for the voyage; and after the cargo was loaded, and while he was engaged in taking on board his provisions, ice set in, which prevented the sailing of the ship for several months, and the ship-owner was held liable for all damage caused to the charterer by the delay.

A ship's register cannot be made a security for money advanced for the ship's benefit.

If the vessel deviates improperly from the direct course of the voyage, the underwriters may be relieved from their liability in case of a loss if the ship is insured for the voyage only; and if

11

any goods on board the vessel are captured, lost, or damaged during such deviation, the ship-owner is liable to the merchant, even if the loss was not caused by the deviation, and the ship-owner cannot relieve himself from liability by proving that the same thing would have happened even if the master had made no deviation. In the same way, if there is any fall in the market price of the goods composing the cargo, the ship-owner will be liable to make good the loss of price sustained by the merchant in consequence of the delay or deviation of the ship.

If an accident occurs which renders it necessary to discharge the cargo before the end of the voyage, the master has a right to detain it a reasonable time, until the ship is repaired; but if it is found that it is impossible to repair the ship, so as to enable her to complete the voyage, or if she is not worth repairing, the master has the right to tranship the cargo, and send it on by another vessel; but it has been decided that he is not compelled to send the cargo on. If the captain tranships at a higher rate of freight than is named in his own charter, his ship-owner will have to pay the difference of freight himself, as he cannot charge the higher rate against the merchant. Therefore, the captain should not tranship unless he can send the cargo on for the same or a smaller freight than that named in his own charter. If the merchant *accepts* the cargo at a port short of its destination, he will be liable to pay the freight for it *pro rata*, according to the distance the cargo has been carried; but if he does not accept the cargo, he cannot be compelled to pay the freight until it is carried to its destination. The captain should communicate with the merchant at once, if possible, and obtain his instructions. If this cannot be done, and the cargo cannot be transhipped, he should either send it back to the port of loading, or leave it safely deposited at the place where it happens to be; or in case of *urgent* necessity he can sell it, but this should never be done unless there is an absolute necessity to adopt that course, and until the captain has taken the best independent advice he can get on the subject. The cost of unshipping and reshipping the cargo will generally fall on the insurers of the freight, if the freight is fully insured, but the cost of wages and provisions during the detention are not chargeable to them. If the cargo is transhipped, and the goods are sent on solely for the purpose of earning freight, the extra cost of transhipment beyond the amount of the original freight will fall on the underwriters of the freight.

A celebrated English jurist says :—" The disposal of the cargo by the master is a matter that requires the utmost caution. He should always bear in mind that it is his duty to convey it to the place of destination, and this purpose he is bound to accomplish by every reasonable and practical method. It is obvious that this purpose cannot possibly be affected by a sale of the whole of the cargo. What, then, is the master to do, if by any disaster he is unable to carry the goods to their destination? To this, as a general question, no answer can be given. Every case must depend on its own peculiar circumstances ; the conduct proper to be adopted with respect to perishable goods will be improper with respect to a cargo not perishable; one thing may be fit to be done with fish or fruit, and another with timber or iron. One method may be proper in distant regions, another in the vicinity of the merchant; one in a frequented navigation, another in unfrequented shores." What, then, is the master to do? In general it may be said that he is to do that which a wise and prudent man will think most conducive to the benefit of all concerned. In doing so he may expect to be safe, because the merchant will not have any just reason to be dissatisfied. Some regard may be allowed to the interest of the ship, but the interest of the cargo must not be sacrificed to it. Transhipment for the place of destination, if it be practicable, is the first object; if that be impracticable, return, or a safe deposit, may be expedient. The merchant should be consulted if possible. A sale is the last thing a master should think of, because it can only be justified by that absolute necessity which supersedes all human laws.

If it is absolutely necessary for the captain to have money to do repairs necessary for the prosecution of the voyage, and for the benefit of all interested, and if the captain cannot obtain it on the credit of the owner, he may either obtain it on bottomry

of the ship and cargo, or he may pledge the whole or sell a part
of the cargo, in order that the remainder may arrive; but he has
no right, under these circumstances, to sell the whole or an
unreasonable proportion of the cargo, because then no benefit
would result to the owner of the cargo, the object of the venture
being that at least a considerable portion of the cargo should
arrive at its destination. If any part of the cargo is sold by the
captain to raise money for the ship's necessities, then on the
arrival of the vessel at her destination, the ship-owner will have
to pay the merchant the price which the goods sold would have
brought at their destination, and then the owner receives freight
on the whole cargo; but if the merchant prefers it, he has the
right to claim the price the goods were actually sold for, and in
that case the ship-owner is only paid freight on the quantity of
cargo actually brought to the port of delivery. In either case
the merchant has the right to deduct from the freight the amount
due to him for the portion of the cargo which has been sold.
If the ship never arrives at her destination, then the merchant
has no choice but to accept the amount the goods actually sold
for.

In the absence of the owner, or in the absence of means of
communicating with the owner, the captain has the power to
pledge the owner's personal credit for all things that are *necessary* to conduct the navigation to a successful termination. He
may, therefore, borrow money to pay for services which will
have to be obtained and paid for in cash, but he has no right to
pledge the owner's credit by borrowing money to pay for services which have already been rendered, unless a very strong
case of necessity exists. If the captain borrows money to pay
for anything which is not necessary, then the owner will not be
liable to pay the amount.

If any damage occurs during the voyage, or if it becomes
necessary to put into a harbor for repairs in consequence of any
accident, the captain should note a protest, if possible, within
forty-eight hours after he is first able to leave the vessel, but he
must not neglect his duty to the ship in times when his services

are required at the ship. The protest need not be at once extended, as that can be done at any time subsequently. He
should also get the damage to both ship and cargo surveyed by
competent persons, and should send full particulars of the damage to the ship-owners, that they may inform the underwriters
and the merchants if necessary. If the ship's bottom is injured
by being struck by a sea which strains her, and causes her to
make water, the underwriters will be liable ; but if she is injured
by being struck by a succession of seas, that will be considered
mere wear and tear, and will fall on the ship-owner, and not on
the underwriters.

If there is likely to be any delay, and the surveyors are of
opinion that the cargo will spoil by keeping, and they accordingly
advise a sale of it, then the captain should advertise a sale by
public auction ; and when he proceeds on the voyage after his
repairs are completed, he should obtain other goods, if possible, in
the place of those he has sold, so as to earn freight.

If any repairs are necessary during the voyage, the captain
need not go to any *extraordinary* expense (especially if the ship
is at a place where repairs are very expensive) in having the
repairs done in an absolutely perfect manner, for that can
generally be done better and more cheaply at the end of the
voyage. But he must make the ship seaworthy, or the ship-
owner will be liable to the owners of the cargo for any damage
they may sustain in consequence of the ship's unseaworthiness.
If the ship becomes unseaworthy after the commencement of the
voyage, it is the duty of the ship-owner, as towards the charterer,
to repair her if he has the opportunity, or at least not to proceed
with the voyage in an unseaworthy state. The captain should
have the vessel surveyed by two or more practical men, and
obtain a written report from them, stating in detail the repairs
which have to be done, and (if such is the fact) that after such
repairs she is in a fit state to complete the voyage. The captain
should not allow his own judgment to be superseded by any
person whose interest it is to advise expensive repairs, and he
should not do anything which is not absolutely necessary. It is

the duty of the captain to act on his own judgment in ordering repairs, assisted by the advice of such independent practical men of experience and respectability as he may himself consider best able to advise him.   Lloyd's surveyors have not any official authority, and he is not bound to follow their directions.   If they should recommend repairs which he and the surveyors whom he consults consider unnecessary, it is his duty to act on his own judgment, and do what he considers best for all concerned.

The shipwright who does the repairs will have a *lien* on the ship for the amount of the bill, unless, before he is employed, an agreement is made with him as to how he is to be paid.

The ship-owner's liability for repairs rests entirely upon contract, and it must be shown that the captain had express or implied authority to order the repairs.

In ordering the repairs, the captain should not order anything which is not really necessary, merely because he expects the cargo will have to bear its proportion in a general average contribution, for it may turn out that the cargo is not liable to contribute.

If the repairs are only temporary, a statement should be made in the surveys and protests to the effect that the damage is to be finally surveyed and repaired when the vessel arrives home.

If the cargo has to be landed for the purpose of doing repairs to the ship, it is the duty of the captain to land it in his own name, on behalf of the ship-owner, and keep it until the repairs are finished, and not to return it to the merchant or his agent. The merchant cannot require the cargo to be delivered back after shipment, and if the captain delivers it back after the ship has met with an accident, he may be unable to borrow money on bottomry to pay for the repairs (as he could then only offer a security on the ship, instead of on the ship, freight and cargo); or if money cannot be borrowed on bottomry, he has power to sell *part* of the cargo to pay for the repairs—an additional reason for not returning it to the merchant.   Besides, if the cargo is returned, he may not be able to obtain another cargo in its stead.

If repairs are done, the captain is bound to have them executed without any unnecessary delay.

If the cargo will not spoil by keeping, the captain should not tranship, if his own vessel can be repaired within a reasonable time, and he should not sell it, unless compelled to do so by the absolute necessity of raising money which he cannot obtain in any other way, but even then pledging the goods will generally answer the same purpose, instead of selling them. If, however, the cargo is a perishable one, and would be completely spoiled by keeping, the captain should either tranship it, and send it on to its destination, or sell it where it is for the benefit of the merchant. If it would merely deteriorate, and not spoil completely, the captain should not sell it, but deposit the goods in safe custody in his own name until the merchant orders what is to be done with them. No freight will be payable on any part of the cargo which may be sold by the master.

If in consequence of some accident during the voyage it should become impossible to repair the ship, so as to take the cargo to its destination, and the completion of the voyage has thus become absolutely hopeless, or if the cost of the necessary repairs would exceed the value of the ship after she is repaired, the master should hold a survey, and then, *if the surveyors recommend that course*, he has power to sell the wreck for what it will bring for the benefit of all concerned. But in selling, the captain must act perfectly *bona fide*, and before selling he must try by every means in his power to complete the voyage, either—first, by borrowing the money on his owner's credit; second, by bottomry; or third, by selling a *part* of the cargo. If the master, in a case of extreme necessity, sells the ship, the person who purchases her is bound to see that the master is justified in selling, as he may afterwards have to prove that he *was* justified in doing it.

If the ship is so much damaged that she is not worth repairing, it is a "constructive total loss." If the owner wishes to claim for a constructive total loss, he must give notice of abandonment to the underwriters as soon as he has received certain intelligence of the casualty which renders it improbable that the ship will ultimately be recovered. If the information received by the owner is *doubtful*, he may wait a reasonable time to enable him, if possible, to obtain more certain information.

If the ship-owner abandons to the underwriters, still it is the duty of the master to continue his exertions to save as much as possible, and do the best for all concerned the same as if no abandonment is made. Anything which he does after the ship is abandoned to the underwriters is considered to be done as agent for them for their benefit.

In writing home to the ship-owners, after any accident, the captain should give full particulars of the damage done, and the chances of getting it repaired, so that they may be able to decide what course should be taken.

As the money loaned on bottomry is payable only in case the ship ultimately arrives at her destination, the lender should therefore insure. But if the ship deviates from her course during the voyage, then the ship-owner is liable to pay the money secured by the bond, even if the ship is lost.

If the bond expressly states that the money is to be repaid in any event, whether the ship completes her voyage or not, the security will not be considered a bottomry, and the lender will not be entitled to that prior claim on the ship which a regular bottomry bond would have given him.

A bottomry bond takes precedence over any other claim of any nature, excepting for crew's wages earned after the bottomry and subsequent salvage services.

A later bottomry has priority over an earlier one, as the money lent on the second bond assists the vessel to complete her voyage, and thus prevents the holder of the first bond from losing his claim.

At the end of the voyage, the holder of a bottomry bond is bound to endeavor first to obtain his money from the ship; and if that is insufficient, he can then look for payment to the cargo, if that has been secured to him by the bond.

The holder of the bond should enforce it within a reasonable time after it becomes due, or he may lose his right to priority over other creditors.

SALVAGE.

The ingredients of salvage service have been defined by good authorities to be—

First.—Enterprise in the salvors in going out in tempestuous weather to assist a vessel in distress, risking their own lives in order to save their fellow-creatures, and to rescue the property of their fellow-subjects.

Second.—The danger and distress from which the property is rescued is to be considered; whether it was in imminent peril, and almost certain to be lost, if not at the time rescued and preserved.

Third.—The degree of labor and skill which the salvors incur and display, and the time occupied, is to be taken into account.

Lastly.—The value of the property saved. Where all these circumstances concur, a large and liberal reward is given; but where there are none, or scarcely any, of those circumstances, the service can hardly be deemed a salvage service, and remuneration for ordinary work and labor only will be due to the parties.

No salvage remuneration is payable unless the services have been successful in saving the property.

Salvors forfeit their claim if they expose the property to unnecessary risk.

A salvor must be a volunteer, who is not under any obligation to perform the service; and for this reason, the crew of the ship saved cannot claim to be paid as salvors, for it is their duty to do all in their power to save her, so long as their contract in the service of the ship lasts. For the same reason, a passenger cannot be a salvor unless the services are very extraordinary and meritorious.

The salvage service must be performed personally, and not by an agent; but the owner of a salving ship is entitled to a share of the salvage reward if his vessel has been in any risk.

If one set of salvors are engaged with a vessel, and they are competent to save her, they have the right to reject the services of a second set of salvors. But if the first set are unable to save the ship, they must not refuse further assistance, or they may thereby forfeit their claim to salvage. In case of a derelict ship, however, if one set are in possession, then, as no further services are needed, a second set has no right to interfere.

The salvors may be dismissed by the master or owner of the ship when their services are no longer considered necessary (unless the ship was derelict), but they are entitled to be paid for the services rendered by them before dismissal, and also for such services as it is found they could have further rendered if they had not been so dismissed.

In assessing the amount of salvage payable, the total value of the ship, freight and cargo, is to be reckoned as the amount of the property saved ; and the compensation payable is divided between the owners of those three items, according to the value of their several interests.

It may be stated, generally, that where a boat or vessel is found at sea, deserted and abandoned by the master and crew, without the hope or intention of returning and recovering possession, she is in the sense of the law derelict ; and goods abandoned in the same way, whether found floating or cast ashore, are derelict. But where the master or crew abandon vessel, boat, or goods temporarily, with an intent or hope to return, they are not considered legal derelicts.

In case of derelict, the amount awarded generally varies from about one-third to one-half the value of the property saved ; in other cases it varies according to circumstances, but never more than half the value is allowed.

If a special and distinct agreement is made as to the amount which is to be payable for the services, then that amount only can be claimed, and not salvage, provided the agreement was a fair one. The parties must also have had a clear understanding of the nature of the agreement, and it must be for a certain stated sum, otherwise it will not be binding on the salvors. The sum agreed upon must not be grossly exorbitant, showing that the salvors have used the misfortune of the ship in distress to exact a species of blackmail, or the agreement can be set aside by the proper tribunal.

Salvors have a lien on the ship or property saved, and can, therefore, retain possession of it until they are paid for their services.

The captain is not bound to take his vessel to a place which is not safe and convenient, and where her safety would be imperilled, and if a wharfinger or dock company place a ship in a berth where the ground is uneven, and not in a proper condition to receive vessels, they are liable to make good all damage which may be caused by the bad berth.

The ship-owner or captain is not bound to give notice to the consignee of the arrival of the ship ; but the consignee is bound to watch for the arrival of the ship.   It is better, however, for the captain to notify the consignee, if his address is known.

If the ship is to discharge at a certain place, " or so near thereto as she may safely get," that means so near as she can safely get, unless she is prevented by some permanent obstruction.   If the ship can get to the place named at a suitable tide, she will have to wait until the tide suits without receiving any demurrage, and the lay days will not begin to count until she arrives at the place named.

If the charter requires the ship to discharge *at* a wharf, that has been held to mean *alongside* the wharf, and the ship may have to wait until the tide suits before the lay days begin.

The consignee, however, has not a right to order the ship to discharge at any place excepting the usual and customary places of discharge in the port, unless otherwise stipulated in the charter, or at a place which can only be reached during a few days in each year.

If any general average contribution is due from the cargo, the captain has also a lien on the cargo for that amount, and if the consignees are insolvent, or doubtful, he should get it paid in cash, if possible, or obtain a proper security from the receiver of the cargo, guaranteed, if necessary, by some responsible parties.

As a general rule, the ship-owner is bound to deliver the cargo in as good a condition as it was in when it was delivered to him, and it is the duty of the master to take all possible care of it. If he neglects to do so, the ship-owner will be liable for all damage which is caused by the negligence or misconduct of himself, or his captain, or crew, even if the bill of lading says he is not to be liable for any damage. If the cargo has received damage *prima facie*, the ship-owner is liable, and it will rest with him to prove that the damage was not caused by the fault of himself, or the ship, or any of his crew; therefore, if anything has occurred which may have damaged the cargo, the captain should be careful to have both the damage, and also the hatches, stowage and dunnage, properly surveyed.

The ship-owner is liable for damage caused by the unseaworthiness of the ship, or by overloading, or by bad stowage, or want of proper dunnage, or by rats (unless such damage is excepted in the charter and bill of lading), or by the ship not being properly pumped, or by not having the cargo ventilated.

The phrase, "dangers and accidents of the seas," excepted by the charter and bill of lading, has been held to mean those dangers naturally incident to navigation, and which cannot be avoided by human agency or care.

A loss caused by an unavoidable collision is a loss by the perils of the sea, and therefore the ship-owner is not liable to the merchant for any damage to the cargo occasioned thereby. An unavoidable accident has been defined to be an occurrence which could not have been prevented by that *ordinary* skill and diligence which is generally found in persons who properly discharge their duty. Extraordinary skill or diligence is not legally required.

The ship-owner is liable for errors of judgment, or for the negligence or unskilfulness on the part of the master while he is in the execution of his duty, but he is not liable for an illegal, or for a wilful or malicious act, done by the master or the crew beyond the scope of his or their duty.

If a part of the freight is paid in advance, under an agreement to that effect in the charter, and the ship is lost, the money so advanced cannot be recovered back from the ship-owner. But if it was advanced merely as a loan, and not as part of the freight, or if the amount is described in the charter not as freight, but merely as an advance of money to meet disbursements, or if the charter contains no agreement to advance it, or if the loss of the ship has been caused by the negligence of the captain, then the merchant can recover it back if the ship is lost.

If the charter says the amount is to be advanced " subject to insurance," it is then considered part of the freight and cannot be recovered back.

If the charter stipulates that the freight, or a portion of it, is to be paid at the expiration of a certain time after the sailing of the ship, before the right delivery of the cargo, and if before that time arrives she is totally lost, still the ship-owner can enforce payment of the freight as agreed when the stipulated time arrives.

The charterer is always liable to pay the freight (unless there is some special agreement to the contrary in the charter party), and so also is a consignee, who receives the goods as owner of them, by endorsement of the bill of lading. Therefore, after the cargo is delivered, if the freight is not paid, the ship-owner has the option of suing either the charterer or the consignee. If the master signs bills of lading expressing that the freight is to be paid by the consignee, that will not release the charterer from his liability.

In order to make the consignee liable for the freight, it is necessary that he should *receive* the goods as *owner* of them. If the consignee has no interest in the goods he does not, by accepting the goods as agent, make himself personally liable to pay the freight. If the consignee endorses over the bill of lading to another person, he does not continue liable to pay the freight, but the actual receiver is liable.

The parties entitled to receive the freight are the persons who are owners of the ship at the time when the freight becomes due by the completion of the voyage.

If the cargo is so much damaged that when it arrives at its destination it is not worth the freight, the merchant cannot avoid payment of the freight by abandoning the cargo to the ship-owner, whatever may have been the cause of the damage.

"Right and true delivery," means delivery of the right quantity, although the quality may be damaged.

If the charterer agrees to supply a full cargo and does not do so, he is bound to pay to the ship-owner the sum which would be payable for a full cargo, whether he actually loads a full cargo or not, and the amount is to be reckoned on the tonnage which the ship is actually able to carry. If the charter stipulates for the payment of the freight in cash, the consignee has, in general, no right to claim any deduction for discount or interest in pursuance of any alleged "custom" of the port. A custom of that kind will not override the express terms of the charter.

The ship-owner, or the captain on his behalf, has a right to retain possession of the cargo until the freight is paid, if the freight is payable on delivery of the cargo. If the amount is to be paid by bills of exchange, then there is a lien on the cargo until the bills are given.

If a good and approved bill has been agreed for in payment of freight, the merchant is bound to offer a bill to which no reasonable objection can be made, and which ought to be approved by the ship-owner. If the ship-owner negotiates the bill, he cannot afterwards make any objection to it.

Technically speaking, the freight is not due until the *whole* cargo is delivered; but if there is a partial delivery of cargo at one time and place, the ship-owner may become entitled to freight on such portion. The law considers then that the ship-owner has given up his lien on the goods delivered, because the merchant has undertaken to pay the freight thereon.

The master can detain any part of the cargo for the freight due upon all the cargo that is consigned to the same person.

If the cargo is damaged, or if there is a short delivery, still the captain can hold it until the whole freight due on the quantity delivered is paid, even if the damage has been caused by the negligence of the captain, and the amount of damage exceeds the amount of freight; and no alleged custom to the contrary will make any difference in this. If any damage has been caused by the negligence of the master, the merchant will have a separate claim for that against the ship-owner, but one amount cannot be set off against the other so as to override the lien except by consent of both parties.

If the amount of freight named in the bill of lading is different from that named in the charter party, the master can only claim from the consignee the amount named in the bill of lading, and he has only a lien on the cargo for that amount, and the balance must be claimed from the charterer. But if the cargo still continues the property of the charterer, or if the consignee, before receiving the bill of lading, had full notice of all the terms of the charter, then he is liable to pay the amount of freight named in the charter, and the ship-owner will have a lien for the whole sum. If the freight is for a lump sum, and cannot be divided, then the lien would be for the amount named in the bill of lading.

The ship-owner also has a lien on the cargo for any general average contribution which may be due from it; but there is no lien for demurrage, port charges, wharfage, or dead freight, unless specially agreed for by the charter party and bill of lading.

A demand of more than is due is not a waiver of the lien, neither is the delivery of a portion of the goods. A delivery of a portion is only an abandonment of the lien so far as the portion of cargo delivered is concerned.

When goods are detained by the ship-owner, subject to the claim of a lien which is disputed, the owner of the goods must either pay the amount claimed under protest in order to obtain possession of the goods, and then sue the person who claimed the lien, to recover the amount which he has thus wrongfully obtained; or he can make a formal tender of the amount he considers really and legally due, and if that is refused, he can then sue the person detaining the goods to recover the goods, and also damages for their detention. If the amount in dispute is not large, it is the duty of the owner of the goods to pay under protest the sum claimed; if he does not do so, he cannot recover full damages for the delay in case the detention was illegal.

In the absence of any special agreement to the contrary the merchant is liable to pay demurrage if the delay arises from any cause which is not attributable to the ship-owner or his agents. By law, the party who charters a vessel is considered to detain her, if at the end of the stipulated time, he does not restore her to her owners; he is bound by the terms of his contract, and if he wishes to make any exception from the liability, it is his duty to provide for it specially in the contract, otherwise he will be liable for all delays whatever which are not attributable to the ship-owner. The original charterer is liable to pay demurrage even though he has parted with the cargo and has nothing to do with the delay. It is sometimes provided by the charter party that the liability of the charterer shall cease on the completion of loading. But in the absence of any special agreement, or exceptions in the charter party, the merchant is liable to pay demurrage if he has agreed to load or discharge the ship in a certain specified number of lay days and he is prevented from doing so in consequence of:—

The crowded state of the docks.

Frost, or the state of the weather after the ship is ready, and until she is completely loaded. But the merchant is not liable for demurrage caused by ice, etc., *after* the vessel is loaded or discharged.

Strikes among workmen, or riots, which may prevent the merchant from obtaining the cargo.

Disputes with railway companies, along whose line the cargo is to be brought to the place of loading.

The non-arrival of the bill of lading.

The non-production of the landing permits.

The consignee being ignorant of the ship's arrival.

Quarantine regulations which may delay the loading by prohibiting intercourse with the shore.

Custom-house regulations.

Illegal acts of custom-house officers.

Prohibition by a foreign government to export the stipulated cargo.

Impossibility of obtaining a cargo at the port.

Dispute improperly caused by the merchant, which delays the ship, such as preventing the captain from signing proper bills of lading, etc.

Alterations and repairs which have to be made to the ship by the *merchant* to enable him to load the cargo.

Refusal of the merchant to pay freight when bound to do so.

Having to discharge a portion of the cargo outside the port to lighten the ship, and enable her to enter the harbor, or reach her discharging berth.

If, however, the merchant has only agreed in the charter party to load or discharge the ship in regular turn, or in a reasonable time, then he is only bound to load or discharge her within such a time as would be considered reasonable under *ordinary* circumstances, and he will then not be liable for delay caused by custom-house regulations, or other unforeseen circumstances.

If no definite number of lay days are named in the charter for unloading the cargo, then there is an implied contract on the part of the consignees to discharge the ship in the usual and customary time for unloading the cargo, and he is bound to unload with reasonable despatch.

It has been held that the clause in the charter party exonerating the charterer from liability after the loading of the cargo does not exonerate him from demurrage for detention at the port of loading.

It has been held that the charterer is not liable to pay demurrage if the delay is caused by—

The detention of the ship by a hostile force.

The hostile occupation of the intended port.

The wrongful interference of the ship-owner, or any fault or negligence attributable to him.

Repairs which the *ship-owner* is bound to make before the cargo is loaded.

The damaged condition of the ship, which may prevent her sailing.

Impossibility of the ship obtaining clearance, or accidents of any kind, or frost or bad weather *after* the loading of the cargo is completed.

12

Where the charterer undertook to load the ship before the
1st of September, but did not complete loading until the 28th of
October, and just after sailing she met with an adverse wind, and
had to put back, and was frozen up all the winter, it was decided
that the ship-owner was only entitled to demurrage up to the
28th of October, the day when the ship was cleared and ready to
sail. The ship, however, might have returned home in ballast
after the 1st of September, and then claimed dead freight.

If neither party has contracted, either expressly or impliedly,
that there shall be no delay, then the owner of the cargo is not
liable for any delay caused by unforeseen circumstances over
which neither party had any control.

Where a given number of days are allowed for loading or discharging, there is an implied contract on the part of the charterer that from the time the ship arrives at the usual place of
loading or discharging, he will take the risk of any ordinary
vicissitudes which may occur to prevent his releasing the ship at
the expiration of the lay days.

Captains should always note a protest under the following circumstances: If the ship has been wrecked, or if any damage
occurs, or there may be fears that damage may have occurred to
the ship or cargo for which there will be a claim against the
merchant or underwriters, or if the merchant refuses to load or
discharge the cargo, or if he does not load the right kind of
cargo, or if he does not load a full cargo when bound to do so,
or if he causes any detention in loading or discharging, or if he
refuses to sign a charter party according to agreement, etc.

It is *generally* advisable merely to *note* the protest, and not to
extend it, as it can be extended afterwards, and it is not necessary
that the extended protest should be made before the same notary
who noted the protest.

If the merchant who is to supply the homeward cargo has no
interest in the outward cargo, the captain is bound to give notice
to him or his agents that the ship is ready to receive her homeward cargo, and if this notice is not given, the charterer will not
be liable to pay damages if no cargo is supplied to the ship.

If the merchant refuses to furnish a homeward cargo when that has been agreed for by the charter, or if he does not load the vessel within the stipulated time, the master can then either charter the vessel for another cargo, or if that cannot conveniently be done, he can sail home in ballast, and the ship-owner will be entitled to recover from the charterer a sum equal to the full freight the ship would have earned if she had been loaded according to the charter. The captain, however, should not return in ballast if he can obtain another cargo; he is bound to do what is reasonable in endeavoring to earn a freight, to reduce the amount of the loss, and he should, therefore, as soon as the charterer has finally and definitely refused to supply a cargo, or as soon as the time he has agreed by the charter to wait for a cargo is expired, re-charter the vessel at the best homeward freight he can find, and then the deficiency of freight only, with the expenses of obtaining the new charter, will have to be paid by the original charterer.

To constitute a breach of the charter, the refusal must be clear and positive, and if, after the merchant does refuse, the captain declines to accept this refusal, or continues still to demand a supply of the cargo, then the ship-owner or captain cannot treat such refusal by the merchant as a breach of the charter, but the captain will be bound to carry out his portion of the charter, and wait until the whole of the lay days are expired before re-chartering or sailing home.

The captain is bound to wait the whole of the lay days before he is justified either in sailing home, or re-chartering, unless the charterer or his agent specially requests him to re-charter, or states positively that no cargo will be furnished; and in either event it is advisable to note a protest before either re-chartering or taking in ballast.

If there is any fear of ice setting in, and the ship being frozen in port during the loading of the cargo, the merchant will not be liable to pay demurrage during the whole time the vessel is frozen up; his liability will cease as soon as he completes the loading of the ship. If the time during which the merchant should have loaded the ship is expired, he cannot require her to remain any longer ; and the captain should, therefore, sail with such cargo as he has already received on board, rather than run the risk of being frozen up over the winter.

If, when the ship arrives at her destination, the captain is unable either to deliver the cargo or to dispose of it by leaving it in safe custody, and he is forced to bring it back again, a return freight will be recoverable from the charterer.

It is the custom at Philadelphia for the shippers, especially of petroleum, to request the captains to sign an agreement that, in case the vessel is loaded inside of the specified number of lay days, she will not be cleared from the custom-house before all the lay days have expired ; and such an agreement is generally signed when it is of advantage to the vessel, such as enabling the captain to procure a berth elsewhere in the meantime at a lower rate of wharfage, or to move and anchor the vessel at the usual anchorage grounds in the river until the expiration of the lay days, or some concession is made by the shippers in the regular charges for wharfage at the loading pier.

Captains of vessels sailing from a foreign port with cargo for Philadelphia should send a copy of their charter party and bill of lading, or a copy of the *terms* of the agreement or charter party, to their ship-broker at Philadelphia before sailing, to enable him to make all necessary arrangements regarding the several matters which may come under the terms therein stated, before the arrival of the vessel. This would save expense, time and annoyance, and greatly facilitate dispatch.

Loss by leakage having arisen through the exposure of casks of oil to the sun, at New Orleans, for two days before shipment, through the negligence of the ship-owners, it was held that the consignees could claim for the loss, although it happened prior to the date of the bills of lading, as the liability of the carrier commences with the receipt of the goods.

The date of the shipment of goods is the date of the bill of lading, provided all of the goods were on board when the bill of lading was signed. The sailing of the vessel has no connection with the date of shipment where the latter is part of a transportation contract.

A vessel is liable for the number of pieces specified in bill of lading, which also names the number of superficial feet of lumber *more or less.* The last clause refers to the superficial feet, and not to the number of pieces. The same holds good where the cargo is iron and the number of pieces and weight are specified, and the words " more or less " are added.

Shippers losing a ship's receipt can obtain bills of lading by indemnifying the master against the subsequent presentation of the receipt, giving him a bond for an amount approximating the value of the goods, or depositing in the hands of a third party, mutually agreed upon, a sufficient sum of money, to be cancelled on completion of the voyage and delivery of goods to consignee. The dangers of the sea to be considered.

It is the duty of a ship-master to issue a bill of lading in the form commonly used for the special class of goods received on board, although no statute exists obliging him to do so, and he may be held liable for any damages arising from a refusal, and a suit may be brought against the vessel.

" Primage and average accustomed." This term usually found in bills of lading refers to a specified percentage of the freight which is to be added to the freight on collection of same. This was formerly a portion of the captain's emoluments, but it is now generally considered as a part of the ship's freight, and is accounted for to the owners. *Average* in this connection refers to the right reserved to divide *pro rata* between the owners of the ship and cargo, respectively, any items of expense incurred in which both may be mutually interested.

Whenever bills of lading do not state the character of bankers' drafts for payment of freight, whether *sight* or *sixty days*, the freight is payable at the sixty-day rate.

An indorser of a bill of lading may be held responsible for the genuineness of the document only, and has nothing to do with the delivery of the goods.

The master of a ship may demand from the consignee a copy
of the original bill of lading, to which he has previously affirmed,
before delivering the cargo.

A bill of lading signed by the master for goods which were
never delivered to the ship or in the master's custody, does not
bind the ship or owners, unless authority is first given by the
owners to the master to sign same. Goods are considered in
the master's custody when they are delivered alongside within
reach of his vessel's tackles.

No carrier, either by sea or land, is responsible for any loss
occurring by the act of God. A fire at sea, or the destruction
of a vessel through an agency beyond human control, excludes
liability. But the destruction by fire or otherwise, through negligence of the company, of goods in transit by car or other con-
veyance, does not release the carrier from liability, unless the bill
of lading provides for same.

Barges or lighters used for harbor or river transportation are
liable for damage to cargo, if arising from neglect or carelessness
on their part. If damage should arise through a collision by
another vessel's fault, the claim must be held against the colliding
vessel. Damage by the act of God must be borne by the owners
of cargo.

Short cargo must be paid for by the vessel. The value to be
fixed by the market price of the goods at port of discharge named
on bill of lading.

Prospective profits are not considered in claims for damages to
cargo.

Although bills of lading may specify that the vessel is not
accountable for cooperage or leakage, if carelessness or mis-
management can be proved, the vessel is liable.

The delivery of cargo to a vessel depends upon the usage of
the port where loading. "Alongside within reach of vessel's
tackles" signifies that the cargo or goods must be sufficiently
near so that the actual gearing of the ship may reach and handle
it. If taken from a lighter or barge with covered deck, it must
be placed on deck.

"Running days" commence as customary and continue without omission or intermission under all circumstances. "Working days" exclude Sundays, holidays and rainy weather. "Days" count all the days in the calendar, unless the usage or custom of the port, or some law forbidding work on Sundays or holidays is shown.

A steamer chartered for a direct voyage from port to port cannot deviate therefrom for the purpose of obtaining coal for its own use, without the knowledge and consent of the charterers. A sufficient amount of coal for the intended voyage must be placed on board at port of loading. Any deviation, unless arising from some unforeseen emergency due to the peril of the seas, or without the consent of the underwriters, would vitiate the insurance policy.

No American statute or State regulation controls the depth to which a vessel may be loaded. It is entirely within the practical control of the underwriters.

A master must sign bills of lading, notwithstanding any claim which he may have against the shippers for demurrage. Action may be taken against the shippers the same as for any other claim, and collected accordingly.

Cargo on board at port of loading may be held for demurrage actually due at loading port, providing the usual clause to that effect is in the charter party; and any refusal of shipper to clear the cargo pending a possible compromise subjects him to continued demurrage for the time the vessel is thus delayed.

When a vessel is chartered to be ready for cargo at a stipulated date, and is not ready until a later date, it is the duty of the master to advise the charterer when ready, and the charterer then has the option to accept or decline the vessel. It is not necessary for the charterer to give notice of his non-intention to load before receiving notice of vessel's readiness. Should the date expire while the vessel was at another port, it is still binding on the vessel to proceed to the loading port named in the charter party and receive the decision of the charterer, if the charterer should not previously signify his purposes and cancel the charter.

Whenever it is stipulated that a vessel is to be loaded and cleared on or before a certain date, a clearance of the cargo only upon that date does not constitute a clearance of the vessel where good and sufficient time is not given for the clearance of the vessel at the Custom House and *Consulate* when bound to a foreign port. Demurrage may be collected up to the time the master can obtain the necessary clearance. But where the charter party calls for days for *loading*, and clearance is not mentioned, the charterers may use the whole of the remaining day for loading, even if the vessel has no opportunity to clear upon the same day.

Whenever a certain number of running lay days are allowed for loading, and the cargo is delivered alongside, and rainy weather prevents loading, no claim can be made for demurrage for the detention caused thereby. Should the vessel stop by orders of the charterer when she might have been loading, the charterer is liable to that extent.

Although bill of lading may contain the clause " contents unknown," the vessel is liable for any shortage discovered, if it can be proved that the goods were put on board as per invoice. To avoid liability, vessel must be able to prove that the goods were delivered as received.

If a vessel is discharged under "general order," and before the consignee is legally bound to receive cargo (unless provided for by charter party), the vessel is responsible for the safety of the cargo so discharged. After that time the vessel's liability is ended.

After due notice has been given to consignees, and goods are allowed by them to remain on the wharf all day, the master has the legal right to send such goods to the public store, providing they have been legally discharged.

Where a special provision is made in the bill of lading for demurrage at the port of delivery, the person claiming and receiving the goods under the bill of lading is answerable for the paying, and not the party who shipped the goods.

A vessel making fast to more than one wharf or bulkhead is liable for wharfage to each.

An American citizen can obtain an American register for a wrecked foreign vessel, only by purchasing same, and having her repaired by a citizen of the United States to an extent equal to three-fourths of her cost when so repaired.

A change of ownership does not interfere with a just claim against a vessel, but prompt efforts are necessary always in collecting claims.

To constitute a specified shipment, goods must be placed in possession of the ship, either on board or within reach of her tackles, within the time stated.

The responsibility of tow-boats having vessels in tow depends upon circumstances. The principal decisions say that the tug is responsible for both vessels in case of collision. Another decision is to the effect that the tug is not responsible unless it can be proved that the injury was occasioned by want of care or skill of the master or person in charge. Where the tow is lashed to the side of the tug, and depends upon it entirely for motion, the responsibility is entirely with the tug. The tug is liable for damages occasioned by taking a tow around a dangerous point with a long hawser. Where the accident to the tow was occasioned by a sudden gust of wind, the tug was held not liable. Also, where the damage was caused by a sudden and unexpected shearing of the tow. Where a tug undertook to tow a barge, and ran the barge on a sunken pier, the master of the tug being aware of its existence, the tug was held liable for the loss. These decisions have been rendered by the various United States and States courts.

The liability of ship-owners for any loss, damage or injury by collision incurred without the privity or knowledge of the owners, is limited to their interest in the ship and her freight then pending.

If a foreign ship contracts bills for stores and outfits, and the seller takes the managing owner's or agent's note for same, and the owner or agent subsequently fails and the note is unpaid, the ship is liable for the amount of the note, unless it can be shown that the seller agreed to accept the personal credit of the managing owner or agent at the time the purchase was effected, or settlement by note was made.

In settling vessel's accounts with the owners, the master is obliged to deliver up all *vouchers* which may be named in his accounts.

"Not accountable for breakage" in bills of lading refers only to breakage caused by means beyond the control of the vessel. If negligence or carelessness can be shown, the vessel is liable.

The owners of vessels are liable for seamen's wages, seamen having a threefold protection in any case, regardless of any contract between the owners and captains, viz., the master, the owner and the ship.

The owners of vessels are liable for damage done by vermin to cargo.

As the ship-owner is responsible only for the proper transportation of the cargo, any loss occasioned by the decay of perishable goods does not affect the claim for freight on same. The master can collect from shipper in such cases, if consignee refuses settlement on account of the decay or rottenness of cargo delivered, even if it is of no value.

Goods stowed on deck without the consent of the shipper are not protected by an ordinary policy of insurance, and the risk is with the ship or master. If the shipper should be aware of the fact, and is willing to accept a clean bill of lading, he should at the same time protest against the fact, as in case of loss or damage his knowledge of the fact might be used as evidence of his approval of the same. A bond of indemnity from the master would answer the same purpose.

A foreign adjustment, made at any port at which it ought for sufficient reason to be made, is binding upon all the parties to it. Exceptions to this are seldom allowed.

All goods shipped for transportation by sea are subject to the laws of general average. If any part of the cargo is jettisoned for the purpose of saving the vessel and balance of cargo, the ship and remaining cargo are assessed to pay for the amount jettisoned. If by stress of weather the ship is driven into a port other than her destination for repairs, all the expenses of such repairs as may be necessary to complete the voyage, the necessary port charges, expenses of discharging and reloading, if required, can be assessed on the ship and cargo. If the cargo is not insured, the assessment must be paid before the cargo is delivered. If a copy of the invoice cannot be obtained, the adjusters may examine the cargo and assess its value.

Freight cannot be collected on goods or cargo not delivered at the port named in bill of lading. Neither can any proportion of same be collected where the goods or cargo have been delivered elsewhere and abandoned to the consignees or their agents, *unless previously provided for in charter party*, as in case of ice preventing vessel from reaching her destination.

Freight can be collected on casks which have been filled at port of loading with molasses, whether the casks are delivered full, part full, empty, or in staves, provided the charter party or bill of lading calls for " freight payable on gross gauge of the casks delivered."

Freight cannot be collected on part of cargo lost, except in general average. Cargo saved in a damaged condition is entitled to full freight.

A natural increase of goods on a voyage does not add to the freight bill.

A lien on cargo for freight may be filed at the Custom House where the cargo is landed, the lien being only for freight on the actual amount landed, irrespective of bill of lading. Liens cannot be filed with the collector for demurrage.

The master or agent of a ship arriving with cargo has a right to retain the goods until the freight is paid, but they must be discharged and ready for delivery on payment or tender of the freight. Any part of the goods consigned to one party may be detained for the freight of the whole due from that party.

HINTS ON STOWAGE OF CARGO.

As the ship-owner is a common carrier, it is necessary that all possible care and diligence should be used in the stowage of cargo, as he is responsible for the proper carrying and safe delivery of all goods taken on board. Nothing exempts him from liability but the act of God. All bills of lading contain more or less exceptions for the vessel's benefit, but if bad stowage can be proved, the owner of the goods is entitled to damages from the ship-owner. If the captain receives his cargo in good order he is bound to deliver it in like good order, the dangers of the seas excepted. This is generally understood, and the captain provides against all contingencies if the vessel has experienced heavy weather during the voyage, and he apprehends damages therefrom, by noting a protest immediately upon his arrival at the port of destination. If the surveyors of the hatches and cargo report that the damage was caused by improper stowage, even if the vessel experienced heavy weather, the ship-owner is liable. This fact is sufficient to induce all captains to make a special study of the stowage of cargo, and to employ stevedores whose experience and good judgment are well known.

The following rules and information for the proper loading of vessels, &c., are taken from the most trustworthy and experienced sources, and are compiled in an abridged manner, and in such a way as to be easily understood. They are not only adapted to the requirements of masters and mates of the world's merchant marine, but to stevedores and shippers whose interests are vitally connected with the proper stowage of cargo.

Much depends upon the build of vessels, regarding the manner in which they should be loaded, and it is very important that masters in charge should be fully informed as to the carrying capacity, stowage, &c., of their vessels, and all necessary and important points explained in full to the stevedore before loading.

The duty of supplying ballast belongs to the ship. All ballast should be kept dry especially when cargo of an absorbent nature is to be taken. Some deadweight cargoes do not require any ballast, and with mixed cargoes heavy goods are often made to answer the purpose of ballast. The quantity of ballast depends largely upon the build of the vessel, and captains taking charge of vessels, the build of which they are not familiar with, should make special inquiry regarding the quantity required and the trimming of same with different cargoes, provided the vessel is not new, in which case the builders or owners should be consulted. As a rule, very little, if any, ballast is required for vessels loading case oil. When any is taken it is usually found that just that quantity of cargo has been thrown out.

The dunnaging of cargoes is a matter which should be very carefully considered, as claims for damage to cargo through want of proper dunnage are not infrequently made. The quantity and quality required varies with different merchandise. Dry deals or plank are best for dunnaging grain and other cargo liable to injury from contact with water. Staves placed so the water can pass freely between them make good dunnage, and they are often taken on freight with the understanding that they are to be used for that purpose, more especially when the cargo consists of bagged grain only. The rules for loading grain and petroleum at Philadelphia, are given in full elsewhere under this head.

Flat bottomed vessels with little dead rise need more dunnage in the bilge than sharp bottomed ships, and should be fitted with bilge pumps.

Coals and other articles not liable to injury from contact with the ceiling, do not need dunnage, but a maximum of twelve inches in the bottom and fifteen inches in the bilges, with three to four inches up the sides, should be allowed for all dry goods and valuable merchandise.

Coals, grain, etc., require shifting boards, and iron of various kinds should be shored and care taken to have the weight properly distributed in the ship. Shifting boards in a green state, and all other stowage wood in that condition will injure grain that comes in contact with it.

In vessels constructed with caulked ceilings, dunnage will probably do more harm than good, as there is always a doubt about its being perfectly dry. These vessels, however, are liable to damage their cargoes by " heat from natural causes," in consequence of the retention of the steam through deficient ventilation ; and where there is probability of leakage, good dry dunnage will be necessary to protect from any wetness which may lodge on the ceiling and be unable to escape in consequence of its tightness.

All acids should be carried on deck, and the bill of lading should contain a clause giving the captain authority to throw the same overboard if necessary for the safety of the ship.

Alkali, or Soda Ash, is injured by water, and if stowed near any kind of manufactured goods, is very likely to damage them if any of the alkali is washed out. At Newcastle it is generally stowed on the ceiling or in the ends. It should be placed well off from the bilges. It is usually packed in casks of ten hundred-weight each, 16 tons being equal to 850 cubic feet.

Barrels of Apples should be first perforated with holes to admit air, and also to let out water in case they should get wet; they should be stowed between decks, as near the hatches as possible. For long voyages, it is better to stow them on deck, especially if there is any petroleum in the cargo, as they absorb the fumes.

Bone Ashes from the River Platte and the Brazils are dunnaged with bones covered with hides ; they should be shipped perfectly dry, to prevent spontaneous combustion. Pearl and Pot Ashes are also injured by water, and when wet will damage manufactured goods ; dunnage 9 inches in the bottom and bilge, 2½ against the sides.

Asphalt, shipped at the Island of Trinidad, is taken from inland lakes. Care should be taken to prevent amalgamation and shifting of cargo. Spars laid athwartships, planks laid against them, and branch-wood, five or six feet long, fixed to the planks and well whitewashed, is recommended; also fore and aft shifting-boards, rising four feet from the surface, to keep the cargo from shifting.

Bacon should be kept dry and cool, and not near dry goods. Freight of hams at Philadelphia and Baltimore is computed at 200 lbs. net, equal to a barrel of five cubic feet. American bacon is usually packed in boxes of three hundred-weight each.

Bale goods should never be suspended by sharp hooks, but slung when hoisted in or out. They should be stowed on their flats in midships, and on their edges in the wings, excepting the ground tier, and should never be placed near sand ballast, or near any damp goods. Unprotected bales are often injured by chafing, and should be well blocked off and firmly chocked; for long voyages it is better to use chafing pieces.

Bark should be dunnaged about six inches at the keel, and ten in the bilge, sharp vessels less in the bilge; it must be well rolled down, for no vessel can take her tonnage of bark. Peruvian bark is in small bales of about 112 lbs. each, well packed in dry hides, and sewn together carefully. It requires great care, and should always be stowed between decks and away from the masts, chain lockers and pump-well.

Beam Fillings.—To stow these properly should be the special study of a stevedore. When the cargo reaches from the ceiling up to the hold-beams, it becomes necessary, with most descriptions of goods, to alter the stowage; a sufficient amount of suitable articles should be retained for this purpose. Loss of bulk should be avoided as much as possible. The fillings should be carried high enough to prevent the upper cargo from resting on them, or they may break, especially in heavy weather; two inches is considered sufficient for timber, while other goods, not so compact, will require a greater height; the forecastle deck and the half-deck should not be overloaded with heavy goods.

Bones.—Ground bones are so very dry that, if insufficient dunnage is used, the heat will crack the ceiling and open the seams. Unboiled "yellows" are likely to injure certain goods, on account of their strong effluvia. A bushel of crushed South

American heavy cattle bones weighs about 56 lbs. Russian and Mediterranean light cattle and mixed, 42 lbs.; and Belgian fine and coarse mixed, steamed, 60 lbs.

Boots and Shoes, in trunks and cases, 40 feet to a ton.

Borate of Lime.—Large quantities in bags of a quintal each, 102 lbs., are shipped all the year round at Iqueque. It is much lighter than coal, and about one-half the weight of nitrate of soda. It is not so susceptible of injury by dampness as nitrate, on which it is usually stowed, but requires to be sufficiently dunnaged.

Bricks should be stowed in the hold in tiers; a large quantity should be placed in the middle if possible. They will readily absorb one-fifteenth of their weight in water, and are liable to be damaged by sea-water.

Brimstone requires six inches dunnage in the flat, and nine in the bilge. When stowed in bulk it should be kept as high as possible; it should lie in the hold just as it falls, excepting the necessary trimming off to prevent shifting, and thus avoid laboring and straining at sea. A full cargo cannot be taken, generally a little over three-quarters. Empty casks are occasionally used to keep the cargo up; if they are broken by the rolling of the ship, very great danger may be apprehended. Brimstone and sulphur are greatly damaged by contact with oil, which they will attract from casks. A small quantity of oil will spoil a full cargo of brimstone intended for bleaching purposes. In general cargoes it should be kept as far as possible from saltpetre, nitrate of soda, charcoal, and all goods liable to spontaneous combustion, for should fire break out and communicate with the brimstone, its suffocating vapors may prevent all efforts to extinguish it.

Butter should be stowed as low down as possible for the sake of coolness; it will not, however, bear much pressure. It is exported from Ireland and Holland all the year round; large quantities are also shipped from the United States, Canada, France and Hamburg; also from Gijon in Spain. Spanish butter is always computed by measurement for freight. 530 firkins, 70 lbs. each, 16½ tons, will occupy 850 cubic feet. In Ireland it is generally packed in firkins, but in Belfast a fresher quality is

13

packed in crocks; for freight, 32 firkins are reckoned to a ton; 55 on an average weigh 2 tons. Butter shipped at Philadelphia and Baltimore, is computed as 200 lbs net weight to a barrel of 5 cubic feet.

Candles should be stowed in a cold, dry part of the hold, and the boxes carefully placed on their bottoms, or the candles will be broken.

Canes are usually shipped in India for broken stowage; the bundles are of various sizes, and are frequently unfastened when stowing, much to the objection of the consignees on delivery. 3,000 (16 cwt.) go to a ton at Bombay.

Canvas must be kept free from oils, liquids, moist goods, or dampness of any kind, as it is liable to mildew.

Cement in sacks, occupies about the same space, and is of the same weight as coal in bulk; in casks 60 tons to 100 tons of coal. It should be stowed in a dry place, as it is liable to cake, and consignees will claim damage as being improperly stowed.

Chalk.—Considerable lump chalk is shipped at London for the United States, vessels usually taking all they require, reserving privilege of filling up with empty oil barrels or other light cargo. A whiter and somewhat better quality is shipped at Dieppe. Vessels generally receive a fair rate of freight for Philadelphia, and are discharged with good dispatch.

Coal.—Ships sail best when coal is heaped up towards the hatchways, in a line corresponding with the direction of the keelson; this mode is considered far more necessary with heavier goods, such as mineral ores, iron, etc. Small vessels cannot, however, afford to lose any space. Coasting colliers are always fully laden, unless their construction will not admit of it. With between-deck ships, the lower main hatches are left open to replenish the hold, as the cargo settles; the loss of several large ships has been attributed to neglect in not removing a sufficient number of planks from the 'tween decks to permit the cargo to be fairly distributed in the main hold. When loading, the large coal naturally falls away to the wings, and a quantity of small coal is thus produced, and is often found immediately under the hatchways; this obstructs the approach to the large, however much there may be, and the consignee declines, possibly, to receive the cargo until the dust is thrown on deck; the consequent delay might be avoided by trimming off the small at the loading port.

Gas coals are the most friable, steam coals the least. Coal is liable to danger of two kinds, totally different, although often confounded together; one is from spontaneous combustion, and the other the liability of ignition and explosion of the gas evolved from the coal, and remaining in the ship. Any coal containing a large quantity of iron pyrites, is apt to heat when saturated with water, and after sometime, to burst into flame; the only prevention is said to be to keep the coal dry. Some kinds of coal are free from iron pyrites, and therefore not subject to spontaneous combustion.

Cochineal is exported from Mexico, Honduras and the Canary Islands. Peru also produces a very small quantity. An inferior quality is obtained at Java. The chief places of export are Belize, in Honduras, Vera Cruz in Mexico, and Santa Cruz, Teneriffe. The average weight of packages from Central America is about 1½ cwt., and is called a seron; from Mexico, 200 lbs., and Teneriffe, 150 lbs. In bulk it weighs less than wheat. It must not be stowed in a hot place, or contiguous to oils or liquids, the melting or leakage of which will injure it; so will the moisture from nitrate of soda, sugar, tobacco, &c.

Cocoa is the seeds or kernels of the cocoa or chocolate plant which grows in South America and other tropical climates; the usual seasons for gathering the fruit are June and December, in bags, dunnaged 9 inches. bilge 14, sides 2½. Large quantities are shipped at Guyaquil. It should be kept perfectly dry. A bag of cocoa weighs about 1 cwt., a cask 1¼ cwt. *Tare:*—At Hamburg the tare is,Carraccas in serons, 12 lbs.; Guyaquil, bags 2 to 3 lbs.; Trinidad bags 3 lbs.; Maranham and Para, casks real. Cocoa husks and shells, the refuse of the chocolate factories, is brought from Gibraltar and other places, as well as from the West Indies.

Coffee.—The plant is now extensively cultivated in the West Indies, Brazil, the southern extremity of India, and in Java. In the East Indies it is shipped all the year, chiefly from October to May; the new crop comes in in October. Very little is grown in Bengal, Manilla or Madras, whence it is shipped in cases containing 200 lbs. each, of which ten are reckoned to the ton for freight. In Ceylon, the gathering commences usually in October, and finishes in December. It is packed chiefly in casks containing 8 cwt. each, of which two are reckoned to the ton. The crop grown by the natives, which is small is exported in bags. Coffee in bags requires to be dunnaged in the bottom 9 inches, bilge 14, and sides 2½; it should always be shipped in double bags, as single bags will not stand handling; the dunnage ought to be well covered, so as to save the coffee, in case the lower tiers are burst by the pressure from above. Masters must be sure that the casks or bags are in good condition before signing bills of lading or even the receipts. Coffee readily imbibes exhalations from other bodies, guano especially, and thereby acquires a disagreeable flavor ; sugar and rum will also injure the flavor. A few bags of pepper once spoiled a whole cargo of coffee. It should never be stowed near salt. If shipped perfectly dry it will gain in weight on the passage, and unless well ventilated, it will steam, and if in a green state it is liable to ferment. At La Guayra, mats for lining the bottom and sides of vessels loading coffee, can be obtained at about 20 cts. each. There are two kinds of coffee shipped at Colombo ; native and plantation. Native weighs 14 to 15 cwt. to the measurement ton, and plantation 18 to 19 cwt. Masters should be careful that the kind to be shipped is specified in the charter. Coffee shipped at Rio Janeiro should not be dunnaged with hides. In the West Indies it is shipped all the year, but less during the hurricane months. Coffee alone is dunnaged there with 8 or 10 inches of logwood carefully covered with mats or old sails; in bags it should have staves or matting all up the sides.

Copperas.—(Green Vitriol). Twenty hogsheads weighing 17 tons will occupy 850 cubic feet, or one keel. With wheat at 1s.

per quarter freight, copperas is rated at 4s. 10¼d. per hogshead, which weighs from 16 to 20 cwt.

Cork.—Specific gravity, 0.240. In Spain and Portugal the bark is removed in July and August. It is usual to calculate 120 tons register to every 30 tons of cork; sharp vessels one-sixth or one-eighth less. Ships require full two-thirds of their ordinary ballast when loading cork; the heavier the ballast the larger the freight. At St. Uber salt can be obtained for ballast; occasionally sulphur ore is taken, but a plentiful supply of matting should intervene, and the roughest cork placed next the ore. Sand is not desirable, as the motion of the ship drives it into the cork. Cork on deck should have a water-course under and tarpaulins or sails over. Cork is not packed so closely at Lisbon as at Faro; the packages there vary in weight from 130 to 170 lbs. each. Four and one-half tons Faro cork will occupy a space of 850 cubic feet.

Cotton.—It is impossible to lay down any arbitrary rule for determining the quantity of ballast required with cotton. Serious mistakes have been made by masters, through acting upon some imaginary belief as to the stability of their ships, not only by taking an insufficiency of ballast for their ordinary capacity, but by filling an immense poop with freight. The construction of the ship, her stability when light, the amount of the compression, and the nature of the specific gravity of the other parts of the cargo, if any, have to be considered. When the ballast is laid the height should be carefully measured from its level to the beams, to determine the number of edge and flat bales of cotton that can be stowed without losing space. The dunnage should be at least 9 inches on the floor and to the upper part of the bilge; the wing bales of the second tier kept 6 inches off the side at the lower corner, and 2½ inches at the sides; sharp-bottomed ships one-third less dunnage in floor and bilges; for large ships 12 inches in the bilges and 9 inches on the floor is customary. Of course it is desirable to get as much as possible in the hold, but time is sometimes lost in screwing hard to gain a little space; it frequently results in breaking posts, and starting beams or stanchions. Cotton shipped in India for Europe, and occupying four or five months in transit, should be carefully inspected before it is struck into the hold, to see that there are no marks of mildew or other signs of dampness on the bales, as if stowed in bad condition, much danger may be apprehended from spontaneous combustion. Side ballast-ports should be carefully fastened and caulked.

Messrs. A. K. Miller & Co., Ship and Steamship Agents, of New Orleans, state that the average number of bales loaded to register ton is $4\frac{1}{4}$ to $4\frac{1}{2}$ for steamers, and $3\frac{1}{2}$ to $3\frac{3}{4}$ for sail, and that the present average weight of a bale is 470 lbs. 18 weather working days, Sundays and holidays excepted, are allowed for loading steamer of about 5,000 bales capacity, and about 30 days for sail. The stevedores' rates at New Orleans, are 50 cents per bale for steamers, and 65 cents for sail. The exports from September 1, 1884, to September 1, 1885, to foreign ports, amounted to 1,335,360 bales.

Messrs. Street Brothers, Ship Agents, of Charleston, S. C., report that steamers loaded at that port, average 4 bales to the net register ton, and sailers $3\frac{1}{4}$ to $3\frac{1}{2}$ bales. The average weight per bale is 475 lbs. Lay-days for steamers, 16 to 18 working days, and sailing vessels, 15 to 30 working days. Stowage, 45 cents per bale for steamers, and 50 cents for sailers. The receipts at Charleston, during 1885, approximated 600,000 bales.

Messrs. Myers & Co., Ship Brokers and Steamship Agents, of Norfolk, Va., state that steamers average about $4\frac{1}{4}$ bales to net register ton, and sail $3\frac{1}{8}$ bales. Average weight, 470 lbs. per bale. The customary time allowed for loading is about as follows :—

A steamer of 1400 net tons, about 16 days, except Sundays.
      "   1000   "   "   12   "   "
Sailer of   1500   "   "   35   "   "
      "   1000   "   "   25   "   "
Stevedores' rates, 50 cents per bale.

In order to show the importance of Norfolk as a cotton shipping port, the full report of the Superintendent and Secretary of the Norfolk and Portsmouth Cotton Exchange, made August 31, 1885, is herein given, as follows :—

NORFOLK AND PORTSMOUTH COTTON EXCHANGE.

SUPERINTENDENT'S OFFICE,
NORFOLK, VA., August 31st, 1885.

To the President and Board of Directors Norfolk and Portsmouth Cotton Exchange :

GENTLEMEN:—Herewith I have the honor to submit the eleventh annual statement of the cotton movement of the port of Norfolk for the twelve months ending August 31, 1885—season of 1884–85.

The movement, owing to the shortness of the crop, has not equalled that of the previous year, but notwithstanding this, the direct exports show a material increase during the same period, thus demonstrating that the reputation of the port, both as a market and a shipping point, has been well maintained in the leading cotton marts of Great Britain and the Continent.

The splendid facilities for the handling and shipment of cotton which have signalized this port, through its powerful compresses and its magnificent coastwise lines of steamships, have been further augmented by the opening of the New York, Philadelphia and Norfolk Railroad which commenced operations in November last.

The movement of cotton at the ports of Virginia has attained such volume that I beg to direct your attention to a summary of the same, both at West Point and Newport News, and which will be found further on in this report. In the Newport News report will be found 6,137 bales which have been ferried to Norfolk and exported through our Custom House.

Norfolk has handled	548,823	bales.
West Point has handled	211,753	"
Newport News has handled	58,712	"
Making total handled at three Virginia ports,	819,288	"

Receipts this season from September 1st, 1885, to January 21st, 1886, 394,623 bales.

The receipts and shipments of cotton at the port of Norfolk for the twelve months ending August 31, 1885, are as follows :—

RECEIPTS.

Route.	Through.	Local.	Total.
Norfolk and Western Railroad, .	85,676	140,397	226,073
Seaboard and Roanoke Railroad, .	60,647	158,024	218,671
Norfolk Southern Railroad, . . .	11,505	41,067	52,572
Chesapeake and Ohio Railroad, .	6,137	614	6,751
Albemarle and Chesapeake Canal,	3,810	43,693	47,503
Dismal Swamp Canal, ...	......	757	757
Nansemond and James Rivers, &c.	......	2,633	2,633

Total receipts for Norfolk, . .	167,775	387,185	554,960
Deduct received from			
Wilmington, . . 2,384 ⎫			
Deduct received from ⎬	8,521	......	......
Newport News,. . 6,137 ⎭			
Deduct received from			
Mobile, Ala., . . 800 ⎫			
Deduct received from ⎬	......	1,021	9,542
Charleston, S. C., . 221 ⎭			
Receipts at Norfolk, ...	159,254	386,164	545,418

RECEIPTS IN ELEVEN YEARS.

	Through.	Local.	Total.
Receipts season 1884–5, .	159,254	386,164	545,418
" ten years previous,	2,815,495	2,751,332	5,566,827
Receipts in eleven years, .	2,974,749	3,137,496	6,112,245

EXPORTS AND SHIPMENTS.

The direct exports, coastwise shipments, and other details of the distribution of the movement are as follows :—

	Bales.
Exported direct to Great Britain since September 1, 1884, ...	277,667
Exported direct to France, ...	6,375
" " " Continent, ...	11,775
Total direct foreign exports, . .	295,817

```
Coastwise movement—New York, . . .      90,846
                    Boston, . . . .     74,506
                    Providence, . .     31,172
                    Baltimore, . . .    46,571
                    Philadelphia, . .   13,301
                    Liverpool, via
                       Newport News,       593
                                        ———————
    Total coastwise shipments, . . . .              256,989
                                                    ———————
    Total shipments, . . . . . . . . .              552,806
Withdrawn for consumption since Feb. 1,
    1885, . . . . . . . . . . . . .        642
Burned February 25, 1885, . . . . . .    1,968
Shipped overland to Petersburg and
    Suffolk, . . . . . . . . . . . .       399
                                        ———————
                                                      3,009
                                                    ———————
    Total distribution, . . . . . . . . . . .       555,815
```

RECAPITULATION.

```
                                                     Bales.
By stock on hand, August 31, 1884, . .                  980
By total receipts, 12 months ending
    August 31, 1885, . . . . . . . . .              554,960
To direct exports, . . . . . . . .      295,817
To coastwise shipments, . . . . . .     256,989
To consumption burned and overland, .     3,009
To stock on hand August 31, 1885, . .       125
                                        ———————
                                                    555,940
```

Following is a summary of the exports and shipments from this port for the past eleven years :—

	Foreign.	Coastwise.	Total.
Shipments 12 months, Aug. 31, 1885, ...	295,817	256 989	552,806
Shipments 10 years ending Aug. 31, 1884, ...	2,187,083	3,367,894	5,554,977
	2,482,900	3,624,883	6,107,783

The value of our direct exports for season 1884-85 amounts to $14.279,835, an increase of $2,697,010 over the season of 1883-84, and for the past seven seasons are as follows:—

Season.	Bales.	Value.
1878-79,	203,536	$9,143,015
1879-80,	257,085	13,785,209
1880-81,	328,818	17,286,947
1881-82,	331,817	17,573,410
1882-83,	372,529	17,869,682
1883-84,	243,381	11,682,825
1884-85,	295,817	14,279,835

There have been shipped on through bills of lading to Great Britain and the Continent, via Boston, New York, Philadelphia and Baltimore, 65,917 bales, exclusive of 593 bales shipped via Newport News to Liverpool. These shipments do not appear as our exports, being credited at port where finally cleared.

The shipments via coastwise lines on through bills of lading for the past seven seasons have been as follows:—

Season.	Bales.
1878-79,	30,270
1879-80,	25,614
1880-81,	40,873
1881-82,	42,749
1882-83,	91,288
1883-84,	82,818
1884-85,	65,917 } 66,510
Liverpool, via Newport News,	593 }

Through the courtesy of P. H. Adams, Esq., General C. and F. Agent at West Point, Va., I am enabled to give the receipts and shipments of cotton at that port:—

Receipts at West Point, Va., 12 months ending Aug. 31, 1885,		211,753
Exported to Great Britain, (Liverpool),	12,762	
Exported to Continent,	13,895	
Total direct exports,		26,657
Coastwise shipments:—		
New England towns,	26,636	
New York,	105,728	
Philadelphia,	12,411	
Baltimore,	40,294	
Returned home,	27	
Total domestic movement,		185,096
Total amount West Point,		211,753

Through the published figures I am enabled to give following statement of movement of cotton at Newport News for twelve months ending August 31, 1885, and to Hon. Baker P. Lee, Collector of Customs, I am indebted for the official exports of cotton for same period:—

Gross receipts at Newport News for 12
    months ending August 31, 1885, . .   59,316
Less cotton direct for Norfolk, and ferried
    to destination, ...   614

Net receipts Newport News, ...   58,702

DISTRIBUTION.

Exported direct to Liverpool, as per
    Custom House returns, ...   22,976
Ferried to Norfolk for export to Liverpool,   6,137
Shipped to coastwise ports, New England
    towns, &c., ...   29,589
                          58,702

' I desire to express my appreciation of the courtesies extended this office by the officials and their representatives of the various transportation lines, and also the Honorable Collector of the Port.

I remain, dear sirs, very respectfully, your obedient servant,

NORMAN BELL,
Superintendent and Secretary.

NEW METHOD OF LOADING COTTON.

The bark Queen of the Fleet, cleared from Norfolk, Va., on March 22d for Liverpool, loaded with 4,589 bales of cotton. The vessel was loaded by the National Compress Association under a new patent process of stevedoring by which she carried five bales to the ton, or twenty-eight per cent. more than she had carried heretofore. The old process of screwing cotton will be dispensed with by this method. It is claimed that the development of this system, which is known as the Grader Compound Bale System, will revolutionize the business and attract many thousands of bales of cotton annually to Norfolk which now go in other directions.

Drugs and Chemicals.—Alkalies, liquid potassæ, liquid ammonia and some other chemical preparations, such as chloride of lime in solution, are sometimes put in corked vessels; these substances will destroy the cork, and therefore glass stoppers should be used when possible, otherwise such goods require great care.

Earthenware in bulk should lie on a flat surface, the nearer the bulkhead the better; if on coal, first cover with a plentiful supply of straw. Crates should either be slung or hooked with can-hooks to the twist and not to the bars. All flat goods such as dinner plates, platters, etc., being heavy, are packed in the bottoms of the crates; the light ware and hollow ware on the top. Full-faced crates contain nearly half as much more as flat-faced crates. Salt will rot straw used in packing and stowing and cause breakage; crates should therefore be kept at a distance from it; water will have nearly the same effect.

Fruit.—Care should be taken to keep dry fruit from green. Raisins are very liable to become heated, especially when shipped in bad condition; they will then cause leakage from any casks of liquid near; in a heated state, maggots and other insects are speedily brought to maturity, to the great injury of the cargo. All unripe fruit is liable to ferment. The hatches of vessels in some fruit trades are built up temporarily three or four feet above the combings, and are fitted with lids to admit air at sea when the weather is favorable. Almonds being light are stowed in the upper part of the cargo, where most convenient for trimming. Sweet almonds are imported in serons, casks and boxes; the bitter in serons; 15 cwt. to a ton. Barcelona nuts are usually packed in bags weighing about 130 lbs. each, gross; 14 of which go to a ton. Currants are packed mostly in barrels and cases. Although cases stow closer than barrels they are very disadvantageous to carry, because freight is paid on the net weight, and a case which contains 1 cwt. of currants, has as much wood in it as a barrel which contains 2 cwt. Importers, however, find that cases are more convenient for sale. Steamers specially adapted for carrying every description of green or dried fruit are given the preference in freighting, as the position of the engines and

boilers in reference to the cargo has been duly considered and
arranged, and their certain and rapid passage is assured. As a
rule the shipping season for fruit, nuts, etc. in Europe is in
September, October and November; oranges much later. After
a wet harvest or gathering time, fruit may be delayed considerably
before it is ready to ship. Currants, in the Ionian Islands, are ripe
in August; fourteen days to three weeks are required for drying,
and they are all shipped by the end of November, principally
in steamers. Raisins and almonds, in the Ionian Islands, Coast
of Spain, etc. (Malaga and Denia) are all shipped before January,
commencing in August or September. In Malaga, the harvest
for raisins is in June. The first shipments of Smyrna figs occur
usually the first of September, and shipments are completed by
the first of November. Patras currants are shipped in casks of
various sizes. Certified stevedores are employed to stow them;
if the casks are not stowed sufficiently compact, the stevedore is
fined. Morea fruit shipped at Patras is often very dirty. Raisins
from Valentia are generally freighted at 20 cwt. per ton. At
Leghorn, vessels remain in the roads until half their cargoes is
discharged. The expense of lighterage and packing at this port
is high. For oranges and lemons, a ship will ordinarily require
one-fourth of her tonnage for ballast; boxes of oranges are
stowed on their sides, bilge to back, as many tiers as the hold
will take; top tier bilge up. Lemons, being heavier, are generally stowed below oranges. They must be discharged in dry
weather. Vessels should be ballasted with iron, metal dross,
stone or shingle, and nothing that would be prejudicial to fruit.
Hatches should be kept open at all times when the weather will
admit. Importers complain that green fruit cargoes are often
damaged through the inattention or want of information of
masters, some of whom will deliver fruit in better condition after
a passage of thirty days or more than others after a shorter
passage.

Fruit Packages.—Currants: 17 tons occupy a space of 850
cubic feet; a butt weighs 17 to 20 cwt.; box, 1½ to 3 cwt.;
barrel, 2½ to 2¾ cwt.; sack of Grecian, 140 lbs. ordinary, or

about 123 lbs. avoirdupois. Raisins: A drum, 24 lbs.; barrel, 1 cwt.; cask Malaga, 1 cwt.; Turkey, 2½ cwt.; box Malaga, 22 lbs.; Valentia, 56 lbs.; half-box, 28 lbs.; a seron is a kind of skin package, containing usually, 87½ lbs.; Admiralty barrel, 336 lbs. net; half-hogshead, 224; kilderkin, 168; and small cask, 112 lbs. Figs: A frail of Faro, 32 lbs.; Malaga, 28 lbs.; Malaga drums, 14 lbs. Prunes: A barrel, 1 to 3 cwt. Plums: Quarter-box, about 20 lbs.; carton, 9 lbs.; half carton, 4 to 6; quarter carton, 2 to 4 lbs. Almonds: A box of Jordan, 28 lbs.; a basket contains 1¼ to 1½ cwt.; and a seron, 1¼ to 1½ cwt. A seron of Barbary contains about 2 cwt. Nuts: At Barcelona, 14 bags of 130 lbs. gross, go to a ton. Grapes: At Malaga, 20 barrels go to a ton for freight; some say 25.

General Cargo.—Select the strongest casks for the ground tier, and not dry goods if it can be avoided, reserving wines, oils, vinegar and molasses for the second or third tier, to reduce the pressure, according to size of ship. Dry goods in bags or bales, should not be placed near leakage goods or moist goods, such as salted hides, bales of bacon, butter, lard, grease, etc.; dry goods should, if possible, be stowed in the after hold. Manufactured goods, dry hides and other valuable articles should have dunnage 2½ inches thick, against the sides, to preserve a water course. Miscellaneous goods, such as boxes of cheese, kegs and tubs of lard, or other small or slightly made packages, not intended for broken stowage, should be placed by themselves and dunnaged as other goods, and, if practicable, stowed at each end of the vessel. Tea, flour (in barrels), flax, clover and linseed, or rice in tierces, coffee and cocoa in bags, should always have 9 inches of good dunnage in the bottom, and 14 to the upper part of the bilges, with 2½ inches at the sides; allowed to stow six heights of tierces and eight heights of barrels. Some stevedores consider that four heights of seeds, etc., in tierces, and five of flour in barrels, is sufficient, but that where small battens are laid across, a great relief of pressure will ensue. All ships above 600 tons, should have 'twixt decks or platforms laid for these cargoes, to ease the pressure. Caulked 'twixt decks should have scuppers in the ceiling at the sides, and 2½ inches of dunnage, laid athwartship, and not fore and aft-ways, when in bags or sacks, and when in boxes or casks not less than one inch. When mats can be procured, they should be used at the sides for tea, etc. Such articles as guano, super-phosphate, bone dust, etc., ought not to be shipped with a general cargo of dry goods. Liverpool cargoes are usually stowed for Philadelphia and New York, as follows: About 150 or 200 tons of coal are levelled fore and aft in the bottom. Then a proportionate quantity of pig or bar iron, with strips of board, at intervals, to prevent the iron from burying itself in the coal. Crockery in the wings fore and aft. In the after hold, articles of particular value, such as cloths, laces and other dry goods, with plenty of dunnage and chocks, not only against leakage, but to prevent chafe, an injury worse than any other. In the fore hold and forward part, rough freight, such as crates and hogsheads of stone and earthenware, chocking and dunnaging all safely. Sacks of salt in the main hold, near the centre.

Glass.—Crates of glass should be packed perpendicularly by each other and firmly wedged together, so that the glass will not sound when the ship rolls. Keep at a distance from salt or wet, or the straw will rot and breakage ensue. In loading or discharging, hook the crates at each end and not across. When stowing with coal it should be carefully trimmed into the cants or ends of the crates; other goods are preferable, as coal soils the crates. More damage is usually done in receiving and delivering than during the voyage; the outside table is the one most frequently broken. Masters should refuse crates of glass or bottles, if the straw is wet. A cubic foot of crown glass weighs 156 lbs., green 169, flint, 187, and plate 170 lbs. Boxes of German sheet glass should be stowed on their bottoms; about 40 of these boxes occupy 850 cubic feet or 4½ tons weight. Plate glass is packed in cases; the chief cause of breakage arises from their not being stowed with their proper edge up, as marked. When not marked they are safer on their edges than on their flat. Great care must be observed when slinging, especially before the cases are fastened

in the slings and when they are passing the combings of the
hatchway, in loading or discharging. Silvered glass must be
kept off from everything of a damp nature.

Grain.—The rules adopted by the Board of Underwriters for
loading grain at Philadelphia, will be found under the special
head of The Grain Trade (see index.) The commercial name
of wheat and Indian corn in the United States, is grain. If
rye, barley, oats, etc., are to be shipped, their names must be
specially stated in the negotiations. In England, the bread corn
is chiefly wheat; in the United States, the name corn applies to
maize only; in Scotland it is given to oats before they are ground,
and in Sweden and Iceland it denotes barley. Generally speaking,
grain may be shipped all the year round from open ports. Baltic
shipments commence when the navigation opens in May, and
continue to its close in October. Petersburg and the other higher
ports however, close earlier and open later than the lower ports.
The navigation at Cronstadt is not open until June and closes in
November. Archangel shipments are made only during June,
July and August. From the Danube, Galatz and Ibrail, exports
take place usually from April to December, inclusive. The port
of Odessa is usually frozen for two months between December
and March; in mild winters there is no ice in the port. In the
Delta of Egypt, wheat and barley are ripe in May, a month later
than in upper Egypt. Wheat grown on the banks of the Nile is
usually so dirty as to require to be washed or cleaned; the earth
and stone amounting to about 4 per cent. Exports from Alexandria take place chiefly in November, December and January.
In New Brunswick, the crop is generally secured before October.
The ports of Quebec and Montreal are open from May to October and November. Montreal is the chief port of shipment, but
when ice closes its navigation, grain, flour, etc., is conveyed by
rail, either to Portland or Boston for shipment. The shipment
of grain from New York is very extensive, especially during the
opening of canal navigation, which closes about the first week in
October, but sometimes not until the middle of November, and
is opened in May. Very little grain is shipped from the East

Indies, it being susceptible to weevil from its dry nature and the heat of the climate. On the plains of South Australia, the wheat harvest commences in November, but in the hilly districts not until December or the beginning of January. At Adelaide the harvest is in January; the chief exports thence are made two months later, say in March, chiefly to Melbourne, Sydney and the Mauritius, both wheat and flour. Wheat from Australia to England is generally shipped in bags and stowed near a hatchway which is opened in the tropics to let off the damp air generated on the passage to Cape Horn. At San Francisco, the wet season extends from the middle of November to the middle of May; the dry season extends through the balance of the twelve months. The dry season commences earlier in the South and continues longer. The principal shipping ports of grain on the west coast of South America, are south of Valparaiso, viz.: Constitucion, in the river Maule, Tome, Penco, Lirquen, and Concepcion in the bay of Telcahuano. A fine description of red wheat is shipped at Tscapilla, between Valparaiso and the river Maule. Chili wheat is very dry and weighs heavy, but it is liable to weevil, especially on long voyages. All American and Canadian wheats and corn are freighted at 480 lbs. per quarter. The stowage of 100 quarters of wheat (eight bushels to the quarter) is considered as about equal to 21 tons of coal; this is at the rate of $4\frac{3}{4}$ quarters to a ton; $4\frac{1}{2}$ quarters is a safe calculation for an ordinary ship. A good carrying ship will stow 50 to 60 quarters barley to every 10 tons dead weight. Iron ships are generally preferred to wooden for carrying grain, as timbers and planking are liable to produce an injurious steam when saturated, or liable themselves to steam when heated by grain. A vessel, the hull of which is pickled, or which has recently discharged salt, or one the ceiling of which has just had a coating of varnish or tar, is not in good condition to receive grain. The effects of bilge water are most insiduous and pernicious with such cargoes, and the mischief is increased by the introduction of loose grain into the limbers, where decomposition creates an exhalation of a very offensive and detrimental character; this liability is increased by rats which sometimes eat holes through the ceiling; the pumps

14

are likely to be choked by this or other means and should be well protected. The heels of the pumps should have nailed round them with a few tacks lightly, some coats of tarpaulin to prevent the grain from falling into the limbers. The decks and waterways should be perfectly tight before loading, and kept so by throwing water over them; more injury is done by a small leak here than by a large one elsewhere; for although considerable leakage occurs in the hull, yet if the pumps be regularly attended to, the cargo remains uninjured, while a pint of water, weeping through a deck seam, may commence the heating, and lead to the damage of the entire cargo. The custom in some of the Mediterranean ports is to cover the dunnage of a cargo of grain with a large quantity of mats at a very heavy expense, and frequently to the injury of the cargo. Mats are often laid three deep, and when wet, either through neglect of the pumps or from other causes, commence rotting immediately, and extend their damage to the surrounding cargo, which is injured much more than if the grain had received wet which had not been in contact with the mats. Injury is also done to cargoes of grain by shifting boards in a green state.

In mixed cargoes it is better to stow grain in one distinct compartment, whether in bulk or bags, to prevent injury to other cargo, such as flour, etc., by sweating. A partial cargo should be covered with a layer of stout dry shifting boards, on which strong temporary stanchions should be fixed with their upper ends secured against the deck beams.

With grain in lots for different consignees, it is absolutely necessary to keep each separate by bulk-heads, compartments or mats, or disputes and loss of freight will occur on discharging. It may be taken for granted that fermentation and heating of grain cargoes, however long the voyage, will never take place without the presence of moisture; for in the case of hard Taganrog wheat in a perfectly dry state, if free from weevil, it may remain for an indefinite time without injury, provided moisture be entirely excluded. But there is always a dampness about the hold that in time will have some effect in producing damage which increases after once commencing. When fermentation does commence, and a portion of a cargo begins to heat, a vapor will arise, and be condensed against the under part of the deck, whence it falls back in drops on the grain, and so increases the damage. If a master supposes that his cargo has been wetted, either in the bilges or by leakage from the deck, he cannot err by ventilating as much as possible, even though there may be weevil in the cargo; for although ventilation may cause the weevil to increase, the damage thereby will probably be less than by the additional fermentation and injury from condensed moisture, if ventilation be neglected. It may be inferred also that there is considerable moisture in all new grain, unless it be the produce of an exceedingly dry climate; this moisture is not apparent or sufficient to cause damage during short voyages; the exterior may appear perfectly dry, but on biting, a degree of toughness and mealiness is apparent. When grain is brittle, approaching to rice in its character, it will sustain the longest voyage uninjured.

Indian corn from American ports is more liable to heat than that from the Black Sea, which is drier. Black Sea and Danubian Indian corn is kept nine months before shipment, as it only comes down in May and June; whereas American is shipped more immediately after harvest, and often has not been properly matured by time or frost, and become sufficiently dry. French maize, shipped before February, is sure to become hot on a voyage, and is often scarcely safe until March or April. Indian corn does not shrink by heating; it expands and gains in measure, and loses in weight the same as other grain.

The matter of stowage of grain cargoes, lining, etc., in the ports of the United States, is exclusively in the hands of the Underwriters' Surveyors, and no certificate of proper loading can be obtained unless the master has strictly conformed to the rules laid down, and complied with the instructions given by the Surveyors. It may be well to state in this connection that there is good authority for considering grain in bulk very liable to affect a new ship with dry rot, on account of its tendency to engender heat. It seems that even yellow pine, which is generally considered not liable to decay on account of its resinous quality, is not proof against the effects of grain. The same may be said of guano, which has extensive heating qualities.

Guano.—Guano weighs from 50 to 70 lbs. per bushel and will absorb 20 per cent. additional of water, which it will attract in a most extraordinary manner, for when well dunnaged off in a dry ship, all that part near the side becomes dark, by moisture drawn through. When moist, it has a tendency to undergo decomposition, with the production of inflammable gases, which form with the air, a mixture liable to explosion on exposure to naked flame. Every precaution is necessary to keep the pump well perfectly clear; iron knees and hoops around masts should be painted or tarred, as they are liable to corrosion by the action of guano. The decks and topsides require to be well caulked and seams paid. A ship will ordinarily carry as much guano as coal, and if she sails well on an even keel, may be loaded " chock up," if otherwise, space must be allowed for trimming.

At the Chinchas guano measures about 40 feet per ton ; usually 15 bags go to a ton, but they are various, the lesser about 12 inches by 18, made of fine cloth, the larger two feet square, of a material so coarse that it is very possible for the finer parts of the guano to pass through while stowing.

Dunnage of from 15 to 20 inches is required ; some recommend two feet. Guano should be stowed on a platform similar to that used for copper ore, or it should be well dunnaged, say as high as the keelson ; then bags, two tiers fore and aft, so stowed as to prevent any air from being drawn through by the suction of the pumps, or the loose guano from finding its way between. The ship's sides should be well dunnaged, say not less than three inches, and a tier of bags carried up to the lower beams; the hold stowed so that a man can go on and around the cargo daily, to watch if any drainings are visible from the deck, and if so, the wet spots should be taken up immediately, as a small portion of water will dissolve a large quantity of guano. On no account should the crystallized part of the guano be stowed among the cargo, but separately, in casks. The cargo should not be interfered with after it is stowed, for the article will lose a portion of its quality every time air is admitted, as well as evaporate and decrease in bulk. It is very rare that a vessel will carry her hold full, and it is seldom that a ship will turn out what she takes in.

A thin coating of gypsum or plaster of Paris, moistened with sulphuric acid, laid over the top of the cargo, will, it is said, abate if not entirely prevent the annoyance and danger of injury to health; it can be removed again before discharging, and will readily sell for more than it cost. Some merchants contend that there is no danger of injury to health. After discharging a cargo of guano, first remove the ballast, scrape and brush every part of the hold, &c., then put a few pounds of chloride of lime with water into a bucket, adding sulphuric or muriatic acid. Place the bucket at the bottom of the hold, and at intervals add acid until a strong smell of chlorine issues from the hatchways. After a few hours the chlorine will be absorbed or pass off, and the cleansing may be completed by washing with water, and white-washing with fresh lime. Guano is injured by contact with salt, nitrate of soda, &c., and it injures almost every article of human consumption, on account of the large proportion of ammonia which it contains; it will turn nuts, leather, &c., almost black. There is a guano obtained from the Kooria Maria Islands, which is sometimes called guano crust, and is described as a small, soft rock. The island of Navassi, belonging to the United States, which lies a little to the eastward of Hayti, towards Jamaica, is two miles east and west by 1¼ north and south, and is about 300 feet high; it produces a species of guano weighing about 125 lbs. per bushel. Navassi guano partakes almost entirely of the character of a mineral phosphate, contains about 70 per cent. of phosphate of lime, and scarcely a trace of organic matter, and consequently contains no ammonia, and is free from smell. In its natural state it is of scarcely any agricultural value, and is imported solely for the purpose of being manufactured into such artificial manures as derive their value from the soluble phosphates they contain. The prevailing winds at Navassi are southeast, and the current sets heavily against the wind.

Gunpowder.—Gunpowder should be very carefully handled, especially in the vicinity of iron, and stowed immediately on reception, and near the hatchway, for facility of access in case of accidental fire, and for convenience of stowing and discharging, powder being generally the last article shipped and the first discharged.

Hay requires a full amount of ballast; dunnage with board in the wings. In a damp hold hay is liable to become heated, and should be stowed so as to allow a current of air to pass from one hatchway to another. There should also be a well of about four bales space, kept clear from the upper deck to the bottom of the ship. 500 lbs. pressed hay is usually allowed to a ton. Ordinarily compressed hay in trusses measure about 2 feet 4 inches x 2 feet 6 inches x 3 feet, and will average about 270 lbs. per truss, occupying 140 feet per ton for stowage, which hydraulic pressure will reduce to 105 feet per ton. A bundle will weigh about 4½ lbs. per cubic foot.

Hemp.—Riga produces the best in Europe; the next is Petersburg, then Konigsberg, Archangel, Sweden and Memel. Russian hemp shipped in the Baltic, is usually of the growth of two seasons previous. It generally arrives at Riga about the middle of May; this hemp, especially if gathered in wet seasons, and if great care is not taken in its preparation, is very liable to get heated in the hold, and will become seriously damaged from natural moisture when the voyage is a long one. The hatches during fine weather should be kept open to counteract the injurious effects of heating. Particular care must be taken to ship hemp and flax in fine dry weather, and every vessel should be furnished with mats when loading. The ballast used in Cronstadt, St. Petersburg and Riga is generally stone, which is planked and double matted. In some Russian ports the ship is ballasted on dunnage of light wood, with bar iron stowed cross-ways, so as to admit the air; the iron is covered with mats to receive bales, and in large ships they are covered with mats to receive a second ballasting of iron. Hemp should be dunnaged about 9 inches on the floors and to the upper part of the bilge; the wing bales

of the second tier kept 6 inches off the side at the lower corner,
and 2½ inches at the sides; sharp bottomed ships one-third less
dunnage in floor and bilges.   Double mats are also carried up
the sides and are placed round the masts, pump-well, etc., and
under the hatchways.   Iron knees, bolts, etc., must be well
dunnaged, as by contact they greatly injure hemp, more especially
when leakage occurs near.   At Riga the ship finds dunnage, the
merchant mats; lathwood is generally used.   Oil, linseed oil
especially, and tar, if allowed to leak on hemp, may produce
spontaneous combustion.   The steam from artificial manures will
ruin hemp and flax.   Ships will not stow their register tonnage
of hemp.   Italian hemp is packed closer than Baltic; iron bands
are sometimes used.   A ship will stow 10 or 15 per cent. more
flax than hemp.   A stone of hemp is 32 lbs.; a bale nearly 20
cwt.; a bale of St. Petersburg clean hemp weighs from 55 to 65
poods; 63 poods an English ton.   A ton will occupy 88 cubic
feet.   A bale, well screwed, averages 2½ feet thick, 5 feet high and
7 feet long.   Bales of St. Petersburg are now mostly 6 cwt. to 10
cwt. each pressed.   A bale is made of a number of bundles
weighing 16 to 18 lbs. each.

Hides are shipped in immense quantities at Buenos Ayres,
Monte Video, and other ports in the River Platte, and at Rio
Grande do Sul, 300 miles north.   The harbors are shallow; good
anchors and cables are necessary.   The season of shipment is
from November to July; the largest shipments occur from
December to May.   A heavy ox-hide will measure 7 feet long by
5 feet 9 inches wide; light hide, 4 feet 10 inches by 4 feet 4
inches; average, 6 feet 6 inches by 4 feet 6 inches.   A salted
ox-hide weighs from 42 to 89 lbs.

It is usual to calculate that the carcasses of 7,000 animals will
produce 280 pipes of tallow, and when freighting a ship with
hides and tallow, about 35 pipes to every 1,000 hides is generally
agreed upon.   One thousand ox-hides, with the necessary salt,
weigh about 30 tons.   Masters should see that the number charged
is received.   In the River Platte, pipes of tallow are ordinarily
stowed on the ground floor, with a layer of bones or horns to

receive hides, otherwise there should be at least eight or nine inches of level dunnage in the bottom, with two or three inches in the wings, and a single spread of hides nailed up and down against the skin of the ship, to keep the dunnage in its place, and prevent loss of salt and pickle. These hides are brought into the cargo as the stowage progresses upwards. As salted hides are very heavy, more dunnage is required below to keep the cargo higher up. A layer of pipes of tallow from end to end is recommended; sometimes a layer in each wing also, if there is more than will fill the ends of the ship. The main object is to get a level bed for the hides. When stowing at Buenos Ayres, Monte Video, and Rio Grande, great care is taken to maintain an exact level with every layer. It is the universal practice to stow hides with the hairy side upwards; where it becomes necessary to turn in a part of the hide, the hairy part should be turned in carefully supplied with salt and pickle to prevent decomposition. Hides will quickly decompose if allowed to touch any article not of such a kindred character as bones, horns, &c., and will be burned by turpentine, and stained by oak wood, both of which, like iron, require to be well dunnaged by bones, etc. The masts, beams, and pump-casing should be well dunnaged. A vessel of three hundred tons requires about twenty tons of steamed bones for dunnage. Merchants prefer to have the entire cargo stowed in one bulk; when there are more bulks, the risk of injury is increased by the waste of pickle from the ends of the bulks, and the consequent decomposition of the outer hides; when more than one bulk is absolutely necessary, the space between should be well filled with salt, covered so as to prevent leakage coming into contact with it. Through the inconvenience of creeping about under the beams, the crew will sometimes double up the top hides; in this case, the folds will be sure to rot, and loss will fall on the ship.

The pickle should be made with fresh water. Some masters consider that there is sufficient salt when a potato will float in it when stirred with a stick. It is preferable to put too much rather than too little salt. Pickle should not be made with salt water, or the hides will turn black immediately afterwards, send forth a

most disgusting effluvia, and then rot. It is admitted by some
merchants that although fresh water is always preferable, salt
water can be used if made into very strong pickle. It is a good
plan to throw salt on top of the hides on the passage; the dampness of the ship will soon convert it into pickle, and they turn
out much better when discharged. The fore and after hatches
should also be kept open in fine weather, to let off the steam from
the hides. When a ship loads dry hides or wool, masters ought
to provide themselves with dead-weight goods for ballast, generally salt hides, and rarely casks of tallow. Dry hides from the
River Platte and Rio Grande are sent chiefly to Antwerp, Hamburg,
and other Continental ports; a ship will usually carry about half
her burden of dry hides. As pressed dry hides can be better
stowed than unpressed, it is calculated at Buenos Ayres that dry
should pay double as much as salt hides. Horns, like shinbones,
are used for dunnage; 1,000 are rated against one ton of bones.
Horns are preferable; but with an entire cargo of salt hides,
bones are preferable to horns; but with dry hides (having salt
hides for ballast), a master must be guided by his experience.

In the East Indies hides should be engaged only from first-
class firms, with a specification that they are well dried. Native
shippers have sent them on board insufficiently cured, and fever
and sickness have resulted therefrom. At Calcutta the bales are
about five or six feet long. At Melbourne, hides are salted,
folded into a squarish parcel, and tied with yarn. Seventeen tons
of salted hides occupy 852 cubic feet. Bengal and Bombay ton
50 cubic feet, screwed hides; Madras, 14 cwt.; Bombay, 12 cwt.
loose and small bundles; Manillas go by weight. Australia,
20 cwt.; Bahia, 12⅔ dry hides, 16 salted, 20 green; New York
and Philadelphia, 10 cwt. dry; Baltimore, 1,120 lbs.

Ice is sawn into square blocks, generally not less than twelve
inches thick. The holds have a space between the planking of
the ship and the ice, boxed in and filled usually with sawdust, or
some other substance reckoned a non-conductor of heat. Bulkheads and hatches are closed as tightly as possible, to prevent the
admission of heated air, which will diminish the cargo and

endanger the safety of the ship. Many thousands of tons are annually shipped from Maine to the Atlantic and Gulf ports, and to the West Indies and points even further south.

Iron.—With iron cargoes some ships are liable to leak in the bilges when the bilge timbers are short and the joints frequent. The precise points of leakage are not always observable after the cargo is discharged, because the whole frame of the hull may have resumed its original position, and the outer planks will close again. With too much weight in the ship's bottom, the upper works are generally liable to great strain, and everything above becomes very tight. Masters should avoid overloading, and see that the quantity is stipulated in the charter-party, and under no circumstances exceed it. The correct principle of stowing any cargo whatever should be to distribute the weight fairly over the ship's hold, so that no part of her frame be overloaded ; and as regards the ship's trim and power of carrying sail, the centre of gravity of the cargo should not be too low or too high. Iron or other metals are generally stowed too low in the hold, making the ship so stiff as to cause her to labor and strain greatly in bad weather. Very long bars should, if possible, be avoided, especially if the vessel is short, and the hatchways small. Large hatchways save much time both in loading and discharging. It is impossible to give specific instructions for stowing bar, railway or pig iron ; the character of the ship, her size, the nature of the voyage, and the season of the year, have all to be considered ; also, whether it is a complete or partial cargo. In the latter case the condensity or the lightness of the other cargo should have a powerful influence as to whether the iron should be stowed solid or open. One master says, "protect the ceiling from chafe by putting three rows, with their ends shifted, between it and the bars, then lay fagots or wooden slabs with three or four tons of iron on them, and so on."

Another says, "Bar iron should be stowed diagonally, bringing it up pyramidically from the ends ; this is the mode at Cardiff and Newport. At Porthcawl they stow iron light some way, say one-third up the cargo, then solid, say one-fourth, and the remainder light; this mode has been found very advantageous."

A third says:—"Place, say one-fourth of the iron below in open order, well secured; one-half compact, fairly distributed; the remaining one-fourth in open order. The centre of gravity will then not be too low." "It is of the greatest importance that the ground tier should be carefully laid with a uniform level bearing throughout the length of the bars. The first tier should be stowed as closely as possible. The keelson should have a full share of the weight." Stevedores occasionally endeavor to persuade masters to allow them to stow railway bars, etc., solid each side the keelson, pretending that it will enable the ship to sail better. Their real object is to place a large proportion of the cargo on the ceiling, because it is easier for them, and it leaves more space in the hold to handle the remainder of the bars, particularly if long, than when the hold is half full. To save extra pressure in the bilges, one experienced owner recommends iron to be kept as much as possible fore and aft on the flat of the floor, and that when chequering, the chequers should be closer over the keelson and amidships than toward the sides. When stowed close in the bilges, and the ship heaves over, the pressure must be excessive. The keels and keelsons of iron-laden ships have been sometimes injured when they have taken the ground, in consequence of all the weight being placed on the frame, and none on the keelson. Care should, therefore, be observed to lay the bottom iron as high only as the top of the keelson, so that the first 'thwartship tier should have a bearing on it; the keelson would thus sustain a fair proportion of the weight of the cargo.

Jute is shipped in the East Indies all the year round, but chiefly during the north-east monsoons, and nearly all at Calcutta; very little at Bombay, and some at Manilla. Bales average 300 lbs. each. For freight, a ton consists of five bales; this rule prevails at Manilla, where the bales weigh almost invariably 280 lbs. Ballast the same as for cotton, say 300 tons to 1,000 tons register. Jute is very liable to ignite through friction, and for this reason special attention should be paid when it is stowed in the same hold with other goods liable to be loosened by the movements of the ship at sea. Some masters will never stow jute near spirits, turpentine, or other inflammable liquids, for by the proximity of two such dangerous articles, there would be no chance for the escape of the ship should fire commence in the locality. With grain in the same hold a height of other goods should intervene. Bales of jute are roped very tightly, but they have a tendency to swell, and there is some degree of danger in taking a full cargo, especially if damp, or if the ground tier becomes wet. The bales require to be closely examined when shipped, to ascertain that they are not damp inside, the more so if packed during the rainy season. Where the previous heated state of the jute has been observed, and the fore and after hatches have been opened, and windsails let down while passing through the tropics, the ship has been saved. The liability to spontaneous combustion, arising from being packed green, or imperfectly dried, is stated to be at an end long before the termination of a voyage from Calcutta to the United States. When a portion only of the cargo consists of jute, due regard should be paid to its position in the hold, on account of this dangerous property.

At Calcutta, 5 bales, weighing 15 cwt., and measuring 46 cubic feet, go to a ton; when badly screwed, 50 cubic feet; when shipped by measurement only, 50 cubic feet compressed, in bales, weigh sometimes 17 cwt. Bengal and Madras ton, 50 cubic feet in bales. Calcutta bales loaded at Bombay have measured 12 feet 6 inches each, 62½ feet to the ton. Every removal increases the bulk of a bale.

Lard.—Lard is much injured by salt water, and should not be placed near guano, sugar, cotton, flour, or wheat. In steamers keep well off from the bulk head of the engine room. In computing the freight of kegs of lard at Philadelphia, 200 lbs. net weight are considered equal to a barrel of 5 cubic feet.

Lead.—When pig lead only is taken, dunnage with coal or rubble, until the keelson is completely covered, in order to raise the lead and make the ship easy at sea. Lay plank, and stow in the middle in stacks, by placing the pigs three or four inches apart, and crossing at the same distance. Large billet wood makes good dunnage, stowed between.

Lead Pipe requires great care to prevent its being bruised. Stow on a platform, in sizes, coil on coil, the lesser inside the greater ; the height of the stack will depend on the weight of the pipe per foot,—the heavier the pipe the higher the stack. Coils are sometimes bound with twisted straw, or packed in casks with loose straw. 300 pigs of lead, weighing 22 tons, will occupy a space of 283 cubic feet. A pig of lead is about 3 feet long, and weighs 1¼ to 1½ cwt. Spanish pigs are about 1 cwt.

Leather should be stowed dry, and kept clear of salt water; a damp air alone will greatly injure it.

Liquids should be stowed at a distance from guano, coal, grain, flour, rice, fruit, and other goods liable to generate heat, or leakage will inevitably ensue. Stow beer and porter on the floor; oil and molasses in the wings ; and spirits and wine on the top of that part of the cargo not liable to be damaged by the breaking of the casks; and endeavor to keep all the liquids, of whatever kind, as much in one part of the ship as possible ; to have good cross beds at the quarters, and not trust to hanging beds; to be well chocked with wood, and allowed to stow three heights of pipes or butts, four of puncheons, and six of hogsheads or half puncheons,—all with their bungs up. If not a full cargo, stow the liquids at each end. Water casks should never be painted for use below deck, or they will rot. Wooden casks are said to be better for stowing biscuit than iron tanks, because the wood absorbs the dampness from the bread.

Liquids, such as castor oil, packed in tins, leak occasionally, from the sea-water having acted on the soldering of the cases, and sometimes having corroded the tin plate itself.

Machinery should be placed in the vessel prior to any other part of the cargo, on account of its great weight, and to afford the opportunity of securing the several pieces properly, by beds and chocks made purposely. Such articles as cog-wheels and castings of similar shape should be lashed vertically, or edgewise, to the masts or stanchions, taking care subsequently to chock them on each side with rough cases of goods, well dunnaged. Where a boiler, or any similar article is carried on deck, it should be placed in beds and chocks, as near the centre as circumstances will admit, resting upon the beams, which should be shored to prevent the weight from injuring the deck. If two are shipped they are generally secured on opposite sides, by means of lashings to the ring bolts and by cross lashings to each other. For long voyages, vessels are selected having hatchways purposely constructed for enlarging. If the boilers are to be placed in the main hold, examine the slings, hooks, and rings, and see that the chains used are, by scale, well able to bear the weight. In discharging very heavy machinery, it may be necessary to follow it up as it leaves the hold with pieces of timber or planks, so placed that in the event of the lifting tackle giving way, the fall shall be confined to a few inches. Similar precautions may be necessary when receiving such articles. It is said that the best way to get heavy machinery out is to cant the main yard a little, untruss, and lash it to the mainmast; have a spare spar with a piece of plank under the heel, for a shore from the deck, lashed to the yard, about a foot inside where the foot tackle comes. Over the main hatchway a pair of sheers should be rigged with planks under the heels, which should be on the beam before the main hatchway; the beams require to be well shored in the 'tween decks. According to size of sheers and strength of purchase, almost any weight can be thus lifted; the yard tackle over the hatchway can be used as well as the other, in case of accident; and in lowering over the side, use the tackle on the sheers to lower with, as well as the yard tackle.

Molasses.—No dunnage is necessary for molasses, excepting beds and chocks to keep the bilges of the casks free; care must be taken to avoid a "falling short in the longers." The ground tier should be straight fore and aft, each side the keelson, and the heads separated by about an inch; this is done to save the length in the second and third tiers. In placing the ground tier the "breakage" caused by the masts is omitted and filled with wood; to avoid "crossing the heads" of the casks, each cask should be carefully bedded and chocked.* The first tier of riders is stowed the same way, observing that the casks rest fairly on the ground tier, so as not to have the entire weight on any one point. The third (and fourth if loaded) is placed empty, bedded and chocked and there filled by a hose. So also are the 'tween deck casks. The bungs should be left out to admit of fermentation.

Nitrate of Soda is imported in large quantities from Iquique, a port on the coast of Peru. It requires good dunnage, and to be stowed in a dry position, apart from brimstone, and under sugar, from which it should be well dunnaged. At Valparaiso a quintal is 100 lbs.; some say it is a little over 101 lbs. Many cargoes of nitrate of soda are shipped to the United States. It is used chiefly for the manufacture of sulphuric and nitric acid, and for a top dressing in farming operations. By a chemical process which sets free its soda and throws the nitric acid into combination with potash, it can be converted into saltpetre. A cubic foot well pressed down, weighs about 88 lbs.

Nearly all ships with cargoes of nitrate or ores are too stiff; experienced masters try to make them a little tender, so as to turn their sides up and fall away from a heavy sea. Deals, plank, or wood of any kind, for platform or dunnage purposes, are very expensive all along the west coast of South America. If freights for wool are low, it is desirable, at Peruvian ports, to take as much dead weight, say nitrate of copper ore, as will complete the whole cargo; it generally pays best. It is considered advantageous to take in a dead weight of nitrate, and to fill up with wool; if both are properly stowed, the ship will be easier at sea. Cargoes of nitrate and of copper ore occupy only so much of the hold as will leave ample space for ventilation. Large quantities of borate of lime are shipped at Iquique; if in the same vessel with nitrate, being lighter, it should go on it, and be well dunnaged with mats over all, to prevent injury from vapor. At Pisagua, the mines are about 50 miles from the shore. Water is obtained there, but not in Pisagua, excepting from steam condensers, and as there is no herbage for the mules which bring

the nitrate to the coast, they die in such numbers that strangers
are said to be easily able to trace their route to the mines by the
number of dead bodies lying about. There are no port charges
of any account at Pisagua. Nitrate is also shipped at Mexillones,
Ochata, and several other open bays in Peru, in bags varying
from 150 to 180 lbs. each; at Iquique they usually weigh 280
lbs. gross. Captains should sign bills of lading "not accountable
for condition of bags on delivery." Dunnage as high as possible; casks are sometimes used; they are not so dangerous as
with copper ore, which, when a cask is broken, falls in immediately; whereas if a cask continues whole for five or six days, the
nitre by that time becomes solidified; for this reason, the bags
are sometimes stowed open or hollow below. Nitre has usually
to be dug out of the hold on discharging, and if there is not
more than a loss of five per cent., it is considered satisfactory,
and the master obtains a gratuity. Nitrate shipped at Iquique,
is dug out of the earth in immense plains beyond a range of
mountains, part of the Andes. As it arrives the bags are stacked
in the warehouses. Eight months are sometimes occupied in
storing a cargo, and while that part first stored is dry, the last is
green, and is therefore liable to leak. When stowed in a ship's
hold, it is preferable to receive the green first, and to arrange it
equally over her bottom. If put in one part only, say forward,
and leakage occurs at sea, the trim of the vessel will be altered,
and she will then, of course, become too deep aft. Nitrate is
brought off at Iquique and Pisagua in boats, and delivered to the
ship's boats at a distance of 30 or 40 yards from the beach. The
nitrate is at shipper's risk immediately it is received in the ship's
boats.

Nuts require to be well dunnaged, kept dry, and not put in the
same hold with bone dust, guano, etc. Madras ton, 12 cwt., nuts
ground, in shell, 16 cwt. shelled. A bag of Messina contains
from 1½ to 1¾ cwt.; at Barcelona, 1 cwt. 16 lbs., of which 14
go to a ton.

Oil-cake is the remains of various seeds after they have been
pressed for the extraction of their oil. In bulk, oil-cake should

be placed by itself; in bags or casks, it may be put on dry goods, but they should be well matted when necessary, for if the weather be close and warm the oil will perforate through the sacking. Oil-cake may cause spontaneous combustion if its exhalations reach cotton, hemp, jute, etc. If placed too near the ceiling, although the ship may not leak, the cakes will draw dampness from the wood; at the same time they may leave a dampness in the wood not easily removed. It should not be stowed over grain, even if well dunnaged.

Ores.—It is recommended that the ores of copper, iron, or lead be carried in vessels having a platform built in the hold at about one-fourth of her depth from the bottom; this would make a ship lively in a sea-way, and less liable to strain and carry away spars. In shipping for short voyages, it has been a common practice to load ores through the main hatch without trimming; and small coasting craft of all ages, and of various classes, have gone wonderfully safe; but long vessels should either load partly through the fore and after hatches, or trim the ore fore and aft, to equalize the strain. For want of this precaution, some new vessels fall in the waist several inches when afloat. A proportion of light cargo underneath ore may be found advantageous. It is recommended that all vessels regularly engaged in the foreign copper ore trade have the main keelson raised to the height of about four feet above the skin, on which is laid the platform, which should run as far as possible fore and aft, as many cases have occurred of vessels straining in consequence of the shortness of the platform, and the weight falling too much on one part. Some ships are prepared with two bilge keelsons each side the main keelson, on which a trunk is fitted for the reception of the ore; the platform is blocked off, say two feet from the ceiling; it runs fore and aft from bulkhead to bulkhead; the sides fall in, say three to four feet in all, when they reach the deck. A ship will not conveniently carry more of the Valparaiso ore than will fill one-third of the cubical contents of her hold. The trunk prevents the cargo from pressing against the sides, and generally slopes inwards about three feet. At the top it may be about

15

one-third the breadth of the vessel. Some very narrow vessels dispense altogether with the trunk, and use a platform only; in which case the bilge keelsons are raised considerably higher than the main keelson, so that both sides slope down towards the centre. It constantly happens that ships not fitted with platforms or trunks are compelled to put into intermediate ports leaky.

Copper ores from Chili, and from Bolivian ports, are always shipped in bulk. When loading this ore, it should be run up in three pyramids towards the fore, main, and after hatchways, keeping the greatest weight in the centre of the ship.

Copper ores from Sydney are generally in bags, which must be kept dry, and not placed near the iron hoops of casks of oil or tallow. New Zealand ore, which is a combination of sulphurates of iron and copper, is subject to spontaneous combustion. South Australian ore, being carbonate and oxide of copper, has not that dangerous property. At Adelaide, copper ore is shipped in bulk as well as in bags, at a low freight for ballast, to receive wool. Copper ore lies heavier than a stowed or loose cargo of bar iron, and will therefore test the strength of the ship to a greater extent.

Plumbago, a carburet of iron, known as black lead, called also graphite. An experienced master who traded at Colombo says, that of plumbago one tier is frequently taken as dead weight; this is not sufficient stiffening for a crank-built ship; stone or other heavy ballast should be used with it. Ships built with beams placed for the West India sugar trade, have not sufficient space between for the large-sized coffee casks; therefore, masters of such vessels should look out for this in time by putting aside all the casks suitable for beam fillings; by using this precaution a larger cargo can be stowed. A ship will, if well stowed with a mixed Colombo cargo, carry a little over her dead weight capacity.

Potatoes stowed in bulk require great care; the hold vent-holes should be freed, and, when practicable, either the fore or after hatchways should be kept open; this applies more especially to vessels constantly in the trade, as the vapor is very injurious to the ceiling, timbers and decks. Where potatoes have been carried in the fore hold of a schooner, the vapor has been known, after a few days, to pass through to the main or after holds, although protected by bulkheads, and to damage other goods in a general cargo. Potatoes of different kinds are often separated in the hold by temporary bulkheads. Those have occasionally given way, when the entire contents of one compartment have been first discharged, to the imminent risk of those employed in that compartment. If such a dangerous course is unavoidable, sufficiently strong supports should be fitted against the bulkheads as the unloading progresses. Barrels of potatoes are sometimes perforated with holes to admit air and let out water, in case the barrels should get wet. Many potatoes are shipped to coastwise ports in the U. S. from Canada, generally in bulk, and in small vessels. They lose somewhat in weight on the passage. Potatoes, as ships' stores, can be preserved from rot by putting them into a berth or pen in a room in the house on deck, generally the carpenter's room, so called, in the forward house, next to the galley, the door of the room to be kept open in fine weather. When putting them into the room or pen, one quart of fine air-slacked lime is thrown over every 25 bushels. Pick them over once in the course of a month, and rub off the sprouts. Potatoes thus cared for will keep good five or six months. 17 tons of potatoes in bulk occupy 850 cubic feet.

Provisions.—*Wet* provisions are beef, pork, suet, vinegar, rum, etc.; *Dry* provisions are peas, oatmeal, flour, tea, sugar, raisins, etc. Wet provisions should be always kept together, and, as a rule, are generally stowed nearest amidships, because they are heavier than dry provisions. As *cargo*, barrels of provisions are allowed to stow six heights. Some recommend that beef for *ship's use* should go on the starboard side, and pork on the port, if both are in packages of the same size; while others object to it as involving the necessity of breaking out and re-stowing both sides, instead of one, every time provisions are required. When they are in casks of the same size, and are mixed, it may be convenient to mark each plainly B. or P. on the head, with white

paint or chalk, or on the bilge, close to the bungs, as they are
stowed, it being difficult to make out the brands after they have
been some time in the hold, without removing them. This
marking might be done by the provision dealer prior to shipment, and is more particularly of consequence if the bung is not
turned over, through the liability of the stevedores stowing some
of the homeward-bound stock in the after run, bung downward.
Leakage ensues, and the chances are that the meat is discolored,
if not unfit for use at a time when no further supply can be obtained. For long voyages, dry provisions should be put up in
air-tight casks, and well coopered with iron hoops, and tightened
every three months; the tea in light iron or tin cases. Salted
provisions to be well coopered with an extra iron hoop, put on
each end and bilge before shipment, and stowed carefully away
where there will be no chance of disturbing them, and if moved
to be coopered and filled up with pickle. If the voyage exceeds
twelve or fifteen months, they should be fresh pickled at the middle of this time. The bung is usually between the rivets of any
two opposite hoops. Casks of provisions, flour, rice, sugar,
water, etc., should be noted down in the hold book, and, if
possible, a plan of this part of the hold should be taken. Raisins and currants should never be placed over water. Flour,
suet and raisins should be contiguous to each other. Flour and
bread should never be stowed in the hold, if it can be avoided,
as the steam generated there deteriorates them in a very short
time. Potatoes, onions, etc., are frequently stowed in the tops
when ships are fully laden. All casks are stowed fore-and-aft,
except in broken stowage, when they must be placed with chief
regard to economy of space. Fire-wood is used for dunnage,
mixed among the casks in quantity proportionate to the consumption of provisions. If the salt provisions are buried under
the dry, an additional quantity of the former should be stowed
in the square of the hatchway, to last until broken down to the
foremast longer, when the way can be worked along evenly.
When loading dried beef in the River Platte, it is usual to cover
the entire hold with straw supplied by the merchant or charterer.

Rags.—Rags, particularly when unwashed, should not be stowed near oil, linseed oil especially, or turpentine, as spontaneous combustion may follow; when subjected to heavy pressure, the liability is increased.

Rattans.—There are usually 100 canes in a bundle of rattans. Although shipped at different ports at various rates of freight, according to the requirements for dunnage, ships are chartered with rattans alone for shipment to the United States. Large quantities are shipped at Singapore. Banca tin in quantity is desirable for stiffening, keeping a portion in 'tween decks or elsewhere to stow towards, or at either end of the ship to trim with.

Rice.—In the United States, sowing is generally completed by March 15th; harvest commences August 31st, and extends through the end of September, sometimes later. It is usually shipped in barrels, or tierces of six to seven cwt. each; dunnage, say nine inches in the bottom, 14 in the bilge, and 2½ against the sides; the tierces stowed bilge and contlines, and carefully chocked. The rice shipped from the United States is always clean. East India rice is often mouldy when first shipped, in consequence of the wetness of the seasons. At Moulmein, although in appearance perfectly dry, and quite cool in the heap, yet after being packed in gunny bags, and stowed in a ship's hold, it becomes very hot, and, when the hatches are closed, condenses speedily, and drops on goods below. Cargoes in a hot state injure the ceiling, decks, and timbers of ships. Ventilation is absolutely necessary. In India, two crops of flooded rice are obtained annually. An ordinary ship cannot take a full cargo of clean rice, so ballast is unnecessary; but a good depth of dunnage is required, and may be used without loss of freight; if in bags, say 20 inches to 2 feet on the floor, carried well up, and the sides plentifully supplied with dunnage. Mat over all. The loss on good clean rice is from two to three per cent., but a well-ventilated cargo turns out better weight than one not ventilated. At Calcutta, with general cargo, rice is often injured by black lead, indigo, and turmeric. Sugar should be well covered with mats to receive rice, which should never be stowed under it.

Rice absorbs moisture, generates heat, and consequently creates leakage from all liquids near. At Calcutta, Akyab, Rangoon, Bassien, Moulmein, Madras, Bombay, and Singapore, rice is packed in bags, double and single; the single will burst unless carefully handled. The exports from Bombay and Singapore are not extensive. Bilge water, with a rice cargo, is very offensive; especially if there is a difficulty in getting at the body of the water by the main pumps or bilge pumps; the stench from the dregs is then almost unbearable.

Salt cannot be kept too dry. In small vessels, and vessels engaged in the salt trade between Turk's Island and the United States, dunnage is seldom used. When vessels with 'tween decks are loaded with common salt in bulk, it is usual to leave open the main hatches of the lower deck, and to remove some planks each side, to replenish the lower hold and relieve the beams of the weight as the cargo settles; in this case, the salt in the 'tween decks should be free from the sides and extremities. Old salt shrinks very little. Merchants delivering to the Tyne and Dublin calculate at 2½ per cent. for shrinkage of old salt, and 5 per cent. for that newly manufactured. Being free from lime, Runcorn is preferred for use for curing Newfoundland fish and meat. The component parts of ground rock salt used for agricultural and chemical purposes are—

Chloride of Sodium,	97 per cent.	
" Potassium,		
" Magnesium,		3
Sulphate of Lime,		
Insoluble Matter,		
	—— 100	

And of common salt—

Chloride of Sodium,	.	92
Water,	. . .	8
	——	100

Salt, from its moisture, should be divided by bulkheads from other goods; even crates should not come in contact, for the straw will rot and breakage follow; it will draw liquids out of casks, and it is said, reduce the strength of spirits, tea, &c., and prevent port wine from fining. The evaporation from salt, which settles against the under part of the decks will, when it falls, prove very injurious to some descriptions of perishable goods below, iron and machinery especially. It is well to broom and wash the hold, and dry it with mops before taking in salt. If the vessel is sharp-built, sound and perfectly tight, the risk can be run of stowing the salt without either dunnage or mats, provided also that the ceiling is tight; this would be a saving, for mats are expensive, and the cargo will work out easier when there is nothing to impede the shovel. If there is any fear of leakage, dunnage and mats ought to be used, as there will be plenty of room. Keep the cargo up high under the main hatch that the vessel may not be too stiff, and so labor heavily in a sea-way. Should the salt be old and dry it may be better to sprinkle the top sparingly with salt water; this will crust it, and in a great measure prevent the cargo from shifting in heavy weather. When landing the salt, if the vessel is likely to be tender, and it is necessary to retain 10 or 15 tons to keep her on her legs, trim it all out under the main hatch, where it will be handy for delivery. If the hold is dunnaged it can then be broomed down and washed. Should fresh water be convenient, use it, for the hold will dry quicker and keep dry better than if with salt water. Coarse well-made salt from Liverpool, will generally turn out the quantity shipped. Large quantities of salt are carried to the River Platte for the purpose of pickling beef and hides. Of this a considerable portion comes from Cadiz, where it is sold by the last, 5000 lbs. Sp. nominal, but which is said to weigh occasionally little over 4000 lbs. Sp. Dunnage is seldom used when the ship is perfectly dry, clean, and in good condition. The discharge of salt at River Platte is very slow. More salt is required there in December, January, February and March, than during the other part of the year. The customary time allowed for discharging salt at Philadelphia is at the rate of 1000 bushels per day, but vessels ordinarily discharge much faster.

A ship well salted is given a better classification at Lloyds. Some ships, especially those built in the United States and

Canada, are supplied between the skins with rock salt, or waste pickling salt from beef, pork, hides, &c., which is thrown into the air holes in the hold and 'tween decks, and under the covering-boards, until the entire space is filled, in order to preserve the timber. Ships thus supplied require particular attention with dry cargoes, as a certain degree of dampness always pervades the sides and bottom in wet weather. The skin should be caulked tight enough to keep the salt from the hold when it dissolves. Some large ships take upwards of 100 tons. It is a well known ' fact that iron bolts embedded in salt, back out as fresh in appearance and as clean as the day they were driven; the want of air prevents oxidation.

Soda.—For the crystals of soda, dunnage 9 inches, sides 2½. Soda, soda ash, or alkali, is very absorbent of moisture, and is therefore subject to increase of weight, or by access of water to be dissolved and destroyed; having a most powerful action on most animal and vegetable substances, it should be stowed clear of them. When loose soda gets into the bilge water, the effluvia has tarnished plates of copper stowed near. A part of the ship should be selected for the stowage of soda. The packages should be sufficiently safe to hold them, and every precaution should be taken to prevent water reaching them in any manner. 16 tons soda in casks, or 21 in bulk, occupy 850 cubic feet. Soda is packed in casks of 2 to 6 cwt.

Spirits and *Wines* in casks should be stowed bung up; to have good *cross beds* at the quarters, and not to trust to hanging beds; to be well chocked with wood, and allowed to stow three heights of pipes or butts, four of puncheons, and six of hogsheads or half-puncheons. The bilges of casks should be not only free below, but what is termed " finger-free " from each other. They may be stowed close until the longer is completed, and then wedged off by driving quoins on each upper quarter. If the casks are not exactly a fore and aft line, the chimes will lock and get broken in breaking them out of their places. The space between casks should be filled up just high enough for the beds to rest upon, that the strain from the upper heights may not fall

entirely on the lower casks. One experienced master says—
"In flooring a ship, I recommend that all casks of liquids have
four beds ; if spirits or wine, you *must* have four. If a cask is
laid upon two beds, it bends between them, and the bilge settles
down on the skin when under pressure, and thus breaks ; or if
the beds are high, the bilge staves break outwards. But when
four beds are put properly under hogsheads or puncheons, and
six under pipes or butts of wine, bung up and bilge free, well
quoined on the beds and quarters, they cannot start, and will bear
almost any weight ; when a cask is bilge free, it must not only
be free of pressure from beds laid under it, but must also be free
from pressure on the bilge on each side and on the top. It must
be bung up, for then the pieces of the head are perpendicular,
and will bear a great strain ; but if the cask slues only half a
stave, there is danger of the head shifting with very little pressure,—an oil cask might do it by its own weight. To stow bilge
and bilge, with hanging beds and quoins, half a cargo of wood
would be wanted, and consequently there must be great waste of
space. Stowing wine and spirits in the second tier, care must be
taken to have the bilge of the casks protected from the stanchions,
as, if they are not blocked off and quoined, there is danger of
leakage from undue pressure. Also, in stowing bales and cases
on the top of casks, the weight must be kept off the bilge by
pieces of wood athwart the quarters of the casks. By doing this
you will land your casks in good order ; if not, there may be
leakage."

Spirits lose in quantity by being stowed in a very dry place,
and gain in a damp locality, but suffer loss of strength ; the extreme is said to be two gallons in a puncheon ; the strength de-
creases in a high temperature.

All spirits, whether for ship's use or for freight, should be
received and struck down below with as little delay as possible,
to avoid the inquisitiveness of the boy with the gimlet. Whenever wines or spirits are stowed with general cargo, a bulkhead
of other goods should, if practicable, be built against them, that
there may be no temptation to plunder. Keep at a distance from

salt, which will reduce the strength, and from grain, flour, oil-cake, sugar, or any other heat producing goods, which will cause the casks to leak. Spirits for ship's use should, if possible, be drawn by daylight. Many lives have been sacrificed through accidental fire when drawing spirits by candle light in the lazarette ; it is suggested as preferable to have a small place, even a sleeping berth in the cabin, appropriated specially for the purpose.

17 tuns of wine, brandy, or any other spirit, reckoning the full gauges of the casks, 4,284 gallons, weigh 20 tons, and occupy a space of 850 cubic feet.

Stone Cargoes being heavy, should be kept well up from the ship's floor, by which she can be loaded and discharged readily, and will obtain a better equilibrium at sea.

Marble in blocks should be stowed on the flat of the floor, in the middle of the vessel, taking care to have good dunnage so as to prevent other portions of the cargo from damaging it. Some merchants consider that slabs of marble are more safely carried when stuck together by plaster of Paris. At Leghorn, wrought marbles and statuary are measured by the palmas, and the rough parts (like granite) make the tonnage for freight very heavy, but as the exports there consist usually of light goods, the shipment of a few additional tons of marble may be convenient for trimming. All packages and cases should be stowed with the right side up, or breakage may take place. No goods of a greasy nature or in any way likely to leak, should be placed over or near marbles ; two drops of oil will spoil a fine slab ; great attention is required to this fact, especially when loading at Leghorn and Genoa, where marbles and oils are frequently stowed in the same hold. Bark should not be stowed on marble. Sugar, also, is injurious to marble, and the expectoration of those who use tobacco is detrimental ; its use should be prohibited while receiving or discharging marble. Water, especially salt-water, will create stains, and if water enters packages, the nails will rust, the straw become rotten, and the contents rendered valueless ; oak and mahogany shavings when wet, greatly discolor marbles.

Many cargoes of marble and rags only, are shipped from Genoa, Leghorn, and other Italian ports for the United States. 13 cubic feet to the ton is usually allowed for freight, a cubic foot of white marble weighing 169 lbs.

Sugar.—Sugar shipped from the West Indies is packed in hogsheads, tierces, barrels, boxes and bags. Hogsheads, 15 to 22 cwt.; tierces, 10 to 12 cwt. The hogsheads from Porto Rico are the smallest, those from Trinidad and Barbadoes the largest. A Cuba bocoy is a cask containing 50 to 54 arrobas. Havana boxes are frapped with strips of hide; they measure, on an average, 3½ feet long, 2 broad, and 1 foot 8 inches deep—say 11 cubic feet; and five of them generally make a ton, gross weight; a hogshead usually weighs 1,300 lbs.; the average loss on Havana cargoes is 2 to 2½ per cent. West India cargoes should have at least 6 inches dunnage on the flat bottom, and 9 on the bilges, three beds under each sugar hogshead, and two under each tierce. Ballast is unnecessary if the ship be tight, excepting with sugar in boxes and bags, which stow more compactly in the 'tween decks than on the skin, and are liable to make the ship crank. Dunnage not less than six inches on the floor and nine in the bilges, carried well up; it should be covered with mats for bags, to prevent the loose sugar from being wasted among the dunnage. To get two or three heights of hogsheads in low-decked vessels, the dunnage is sometimes diminished, but this is at the ship's risk. When the entire cargo consists of sugar, the hogsheads of the ground tier are placed close together, fore and aft, with strips of board up and down the ceiling; after which every hogshead is duly bedded and chocked with billets of wood, and the riding tiers stowed in the same manner. Where a third height cannot be had, it is usual to finish loading with bags, barrels, or boxes; this, however, depends upon the manner in which the sugar is shipped from the port of loading.

Natal sugars are in bags, 1½ to 2 cwt.

Sandwich Island sugars in bags and barrels, 2 to 4 cwt., are sent chiefly to California and British Columbia.

South America sugars are packed in chests, 15 to 23 cwt., cases, 8 to 10 cwt., and bags, 1½ cwt. Brazil chest, about 10 cwt.;

also in hogsheads, tierces, and barrels; and quantities are shipped in December at Calcutta in bags of 160 lbs. each, 20 cwt. estimated to occupy 39 cubic feet.

Tallow in casks is allowed to stow six heights; it should be stowed low for the sake of coolness; the casks should always be treated as if they contained wet goods, and never stowed near oats or other heat-producing goods. In the River Platte, tallow in pipes is ordinarily stowed as a ground tier, and receives a layer of bones or horns, on which hides are placed; for England it is usually packed in wine pipes and half pipes, and sometimes in boxes containing 2¼ cwt. each. Tallow casks readily absorb salt water, which will soon rot the wooden hoops used in St. Petersburg; they are sometimes not strong enough to hold together until the ship is discharged, and, when striking out cargo, will fly off and leave the tallow unsupported; the crowbar should be used with caution.

17 tons tallow occupy 850 cubic feet. Philadelphia and New York, six barrels to the ton. Russian tallows are in casks, 8 feet by 6, containing 12½ to 13 cwt., and 6 feet by 4, 9¼ cwt., gross.

Tar.—A full cargo does not require ballast except the ship be large, when about 30 to every 500 tons burthen will be necessary. Some stevedores recommend the skin and ceiling to be covered with saw-dust, sprinkled with water to prevent leakage from running into the pumps, which require special attention with this description of cargo. From the United States to Europe, it is usual to have some turpentine to throw down the pumps when choked, as being the only available substance by which tar can be dissolved. Pumps fitted with long, loose, wood toggles, instead of leather clappers, will raise tar. When tar and turpentine go together, the former should be stowed in the extremities, to avoid pressure, and to keep it off from the pumps. Place the barrels each side the keelson, bilge and contline with each other, with small billets of wood between, to prevent working at sea. Tar, turpentine, rosin, etc., should have flat beds of wood under the quarters, an inch thick, and allowed to stow six heights. 136 barrels American tar and rosin, 17 tons, 100 barrels Archangel tar, 16 tons, 100 barrels Stockholm tar, 16 tons, will occupy 850 cubic feet.

Tea.—The principal ports in China are Canton, Amoy, Foochow-foo, Ningpo, and Shanghai. Souchong is a corruption of "Siau-chung," meaning "little plant." Hyson is derived from "Yu-tsien," meaning "before the rains;" some say from "Hi-chun," meaning "flourishing spring." Pekoe, the name applied to the coarse leaves gathered earliest, is a corruption of "Pee-co," meaning "white hairs," the very young leaves having a white down upon them. Most commonly there are three periods of gathering tea in China; the first commences about 15th April, the second at midsummer, and the last in August and September. Another authority says there are four distinct tea harvests. The first is in April, when the young leaves furnish the very finest kinds. The second in May, is the principal one as regards quantity; from the earlier portion of this harvest is supplied the "new season's tea," which dealers advertise in August and September, and which is so eagerly awaited that it is the custom for the merchant who receives the first cargo, to reward the celerity of the vessel bringing it by presenting a handsome premium to her owner and master. The third harvest is in July, and the fourth in August, when the "stripping" affords only large, coarse leaves, consumed chiefly by the poorer classes of Chinese laborers. The names given to the different teas refer more to the time at which they were gathered than to their quality, of which, in each kind, there is every grade.

The hold should be well ventilated with windsails several days before receiving cargo. To do this when full, some American vessels have large ventilators fitted forward and aft, which are much approved; shippers prefer a vessel supplied with them, if she is in good order, and well painted. Sometimes for the reception of tea the hold is whitewashed, which makes them light and sweet, but it causes the ironwork to rust. It is contended that the iron should be painted red and the woodwork scraped clean. American ships are rarely whitewashed; their 'tween decks are always painted white, which makes them light and easily scrubbed. The heavier the ballast the better; it is generally metal, or granite built in ; these are covered with shingle, which is much approved, and about three-fourths of the whole are leveled over the keel-son, even with it or below it, as the case may be—the depth being regulated by a gauge to receive so many heights of chests be-tween the beams and the ballast, which is first covered with half-inch fir. The Chinese stevedores are not surpassed for good stowage in any part of the world, and the course usually observed by them at Canton, with, say a vessel of 500 tons register, has thus been described. Tiers of chests are laid fore and aft, say five from side to side, amidships eight tiers. Take a set between the 'midship tiers and the end tiers, and set them up square and tight ; then three or five tiers more, both amidships and aft, and set them up perfectly square from one wing to the other ; if the tiers come in regularly up to the meeting of the chests of tea, they are dropped in in pairs, or what is termed " married ;" but if they require setting, the whole tiers are set upon and the last dropped in. This tier, when completed, is gauged in like manner as the ballast from underneath the beams, to see they are perfectly level. Slips of wood are put on should there be the least hol-low ; and if any chest stands high it is lifted, and the ballast robbed to make the tier level, but should the deviation not exceed one-eighth of an inch, the mere jumping on the chest will do. The gauge is then lessened one tier, and it is carefully tried fore and aft, to see there is no discrepancy. This method is pursued up to underneath the beams, and when that is completed, if no convenient chests can be had to suit the height of the beams, the beam-fillings are five and ten catty boxes, placed so as to make a level as near as possible, and all deficiencies filled in with China fir. Great care is taken with this tier, the height being measured from the upper beams, and the stowing goes on as it did below. When the deck beams are reached, caution is necessary in order to make the stowage of the vessel advantageous to the owner, as it is not always that chests are to be had to suit the filling close up to the upper deck—five catty boxes being the least to fill up a space often 12 by 14 inches. On rising from the ballast in the lower hold, close to the skin, from the fore shoulder to abreast the mainmast, it is necessary to keep the tea at least nine inches from the sides.

When stowing the last chest in an early tier, a Chinaman, rather than strike it with any hard instrument, walks off to a distance, and running back, jumps into the air and falls in a sitting posture on the chest, which is thus sent uninjured into its place. Formerly, when a tier was "commanded" and the screws used to gain an inch, the whole tier was sometimes crushed; Now, if screws are used, a plank is so placed as to take a whole tier and prevent injury to any chest. Experienced stevedores are too correct in their measurements to require the frequent use of screws. Sometimes strips of bamboo are nailed up and down the side lining, and over the deck, to preserve the tea boxes from the influence of chafe and from damage by leakage; by its silicious exterior bamboo resists wet and carries it off; the throats of the beams are muffled with canvas, or sennet nailed across the upper part, and led down so as to train any leakage towards the sides, and thus prevent water from running along the beams to the stanchions, where it will edge off and fall into the centre of the cargo. It is particularly necessary to muffle the beams in the wake of the fore top-mast backstay bolts; it would be prudent also to do so immediately below all scuppers. Damage from causes mentioned here seldom amounts to *an average*; and the insurer, being freed, the loss falls on the merchant, who would have some difficulty to establish a claim for bad stowage, or insufficient dunnage, but he would afterwards prefer chartering some other vessel, on board which more caution is observed. The lower tier should be on their bottoms, because the soldering is more perfect; but the chests are sometimes stowed on their sides for the sake of getting in heights; the other tiers, on their sides or edges, as they will come in for heights. In the wings are occasionally stowed the remaining fourth of the ballast, or (in American ships), mats of cassia; for it sometimes happens that this portion of the ballast is required to trim the ship, either forward or aft, in which case the wings of most tea-laden ships are liable to make them roll; in the ends it makes them twist at sea. Some contend that its best position for sailing is in a trunkway on the keelson; this involves much loss of stowage for the tea, but the gain in sailing may more than compensate. For a ship constantly in the trade, iron kentlige is best; granite is dear in the north of China, but reasonable at Canton. The heat of tea, like many other dry cargoes, will draw dampness from any porous stone previously in contact with water. Some ballast from Australia is very unsuitable ; many cargoes have been delivered out of condition and flat, in consequence of being stowed on Sydney ballast, which is a porous sandstone. It is better to leave out the wing chests, for, if wetted one inch, it will run through the whole chest ; sometimes half chests are stowed here, but they must be well ballasted off from the skin. In order to assist in protecting from injury by leakages, chests of tea are sized and stopped with a composition of blood, etc.; they are then covered with plain paper and afterwards with transparent paper having figures on it. Both these papers are pasted on. The boxes are afterwards ranged in stacks, and one side being oiled, the sides are changed until the boxes are oiled over completely. When applied, the oil emits a very obnoxious stench, which is said not to be injurious to the contents. Every chest and catty is carefully lined with a loose leaden case, and that again with paper. The leaden case is very strongly soldered with a bright metal, which is said to contain quite an appreciable quantity of silver.

Catty boxes are shipped in bundles of four tied together, and if so delivered, full freight is paid ; if the rattan is cut, and the boxes used for small stowage, half freight only is paid. Tea ships will stow 50 to 60 per cent. over their register tonnage, and so much as 75 if supplied with an assortment of catty or other small boxes. American ships for the United States will fill every crevice with cassia in mats ; fire-crackers in small boxes, and 10 catty boxes, and half chests of green tea, for the bulk shipped at Shanghai for the United States is green, which is seldom packed in anything larger than half-chests and boxes ; occasionally a few hundred chests are put in, and sometimes a few hundred chests and half-chests of black tea. At Foo Choo, a large quantity of half chests of black tea (Oolong and Ning Yong) and some thousands of boxes of black, are shipped for the United States, which in proportion, takes more fine teas than any other country. They form the staple of American shipments and are generally

matted, and are, therefore, more liable to damage if only partially
wetted; large quantities of matting in rolls are also shipped as
cargo, with teas. On an average, tea from Shanghai weighs
heavier than that from Canton. The cassia shipped in American
vessels is in mats containing 1 lb. and 2 lbs. each, and they are
stowed under the beams, &c., and where nothing else will go.
Tea must be kept apart from any article likely to create strong
fumes; from ship chandlery of every description, ropes, cordage,
and sails, the latter having much tar in the roping and seaming;
these stores should be all stowed on the upper deck, the seams
of which require to be examined frequently on the voyage
home, for the damage done to one chest will often destroy
many others near. Tight ships in the China trade are more
liable to injure their cargoes than ships which leak a little, as the
effluvia from the bilge water of tight ships will be more injurious,
especially where there are 'tween decks. Bilge water naturally
affects tea; and where a ship is tight, clean water should be let
down and pumped up again, at least once every week. A pint
of chloride of lime in each bucket of water, will be very efficacious.
Some contend that no ship which has carried grain, sugar, coal,
or any similar cargo, should take in tea before her hold has been
washed with lime-water, and every particle of the old cargo extracted from the ballast and bilges. Ships built of American pine
or other resinous woods, do not generate bilge-water so injurious
as others, and their cargoes consequently suffer less. An experienced tea taster can quickly discover that a chest of tea has
been brought in an iron ship. Ships with a broad beam are best
adapted for carrying tea: what is lost in speed is more than
gained in stowage. Long, narrow ships carry more dead-weight
and measurement, but require more ballast with tea. Tea averages rather more than nine cwt. to a ton of 50 cubic feet.
Taking the weight of tea (cargo with cargo), 50 feet will average
1,200 lbs., which is 10½ cwt. At Hankow the chests are so
large that eight will measure 50 cubic feet. Green teas are
heavier than black; hence cargoes for America weigh more per
100 measurement tons than those for England, but as American
ships take other and light goods, there is no available scale of

16

estimate.   Tea is computed to lose four per cent. in weight during the voyage to the United States.   It will lose weight in a
very dry store, and gain in a damp store ; the difference of ex-
tremes is said to be about two pounds per chest.   Fine teas
weigh heavier than common.

Timber.—Ships of ordinary capacity will carry of the usual
cargoes from American colonial ports, about 45 per cent. beyond
the builder's tonnage, allowing for deck loads which would be
generally equal to 7½ per cent. ; from Savannah, Brunswick,
Pensacola, and Mobile, about 25 per cent. above builder's tonnage ; from Leghorn and Ancona, and the West Indies, with
greenheart, it is rarely that ships turn out equal to the builder's
tonnage. perhaps from 5 to 10 per cent. less.   Timber merchants
calculate that for Quebec and Baltic cargoes (not hard wood) a
ship will carry one-third in loads more than her register tonnage ;
this includes the usual deck loads ; thus, a ship registering 500
tons will probably carry 670 loads of timber.   Ships having
wooden vertical knees are ill adapted for stowing a full cargo of
timber ; iron knees are of course preferable.

Squared Timber is in most countries freighted by the load of
50 cubic feet ; rough, 40 cubic feet.

Mahogany, Lignum Vitæ, and *Cedar*, are usually estimated by
ton weight.

Hackmatack, a hard wood, for sleepers, &c., at per piece.

Sawn Plank and *Deals* are calculated at 55 feet cube, or at a
rate per Petersburg standard hundred equivalent to three times
the *rate* per load of 50 cubic feet, and for 165 feet cube.

Round or *Unhewn Oak, Elm, Ash*, and *Beech*, are taken by
string measurement of 40 cubic feet.

Deal Ends are usually carried for two-thirds freight ; the quantity as a general rule, is restricted to what is required by the
ship for broken stowage ; deal ends are eight feet and under.

Battens.—An entire cargo is much against the ship compared
with deals at the same proportionate rate of freight.

Lathwood, Plank, Deals, Staves, &c., are computed according
to length and thickness, but the computations vary at different
ports ; and as they often tell against the ship, special attention

must be given to prevent an undue proportion of sorts or sizes which do not stow well.

Logwood is imported in large billets or logs, 4 feet in length, 18 inches in diameter, and of very irregular shape; the larger they are the more valuable. It should be kept from getting wet, as dampness causes the wood to turn black, and the dye is thereby reduced, especially when in the leakage in the ship's lee bilge. Large quantities of yellow pine lumber is shipped from the South Atlantic and Gulf ports of the United States for coastwise ports, Cuba and Europe. The forms of charter-parties used may be found elsewhere in this work. Vessel average from 70 M to 75 M feet for every 100 tons register.

Wool.—A ship with a cargo of wool requires about two-thirds the quantity of ballast necessary when in ballast only; it should be as dry as possible and levelled fore and aft. Some experienced masters contend that cargoes of wool, like cotton, require for dead weight, if the ship is tolerably stiff, not less than one-third her register tonnage; tender ships require more. Pig iron is the most economical, as by its use a height of bales of wool may be saved; this cannot be done with lighter ballast. The dunnage for the ground tiers should be laid as the bales are being stowed, the depth, if the ballast be perfectly dry, need not exceed three inches; this will keep the wrappers of the bales clear. Should the ballast be the least damp, as great a depth of dunnage must be laid as the heights will allow, without loss of stowage, for wool will draw moisture from any damp substance near; although the bale may not touch the ballast, yet the wrapper will become damp, heated and rotten; this of itself constitutes damage, and the wool shares the same fate to a greater or lesser extent. The ballast should be levelled so as to be equi-distant from all parts of the beams above,—in other words, so as to meet their sweep or bevel, or great loss of stowage space must occur on reaching the upper tier under the beams. The method of stowing is by commencing each tier at both ends, and by heaving off every longer with quarter trunks, excepting the ground tier, as it is more liable to rise in the wings than the tiers over it. To make good stowage it is necessary, as each tier is being stowed, to use

screws of different lengths, from six inches up to four feet, together with sampson posts and trunk planks, etc. Merchants
contend that bales should not be pressed in any other direction
than that in which the wool was packed into them. In stowing
wool near the water tanks, great care is necessary to prevent
their becoming leaky by over-pressure, or the water will be lost
and the wool damaged.

Wool should, if possible, be shipped dry ; when wet is is liable
to spontaneous combustion. A wet package should not be received by the vessel under any circumstances. All of the cargo
should be perfectly secured from rain and off the ground. Wool
should also be cleansed from grease. Vessels loading Sydney
wool generally obtain dead weight of hides, tallow, etc. Hides
are sometimes spread out flat and salted in the hold, but generally ashore ; they are levelled off with treenails a sufficient depth
to keep the wool apart ; hides form an excellent dead weight, are
sometimes stowed in blocks, and are very useful for trimming
the ship. When casks of tallow are used, they are always well
coopered before shipment, and common bones or hoofs are stowed
in the cantlines. On this surface is placed treenails, spokes, rattans, ox horns, bones, or any other cargo that will not damage,
and the whole is covered to prevent contact with the outsides of
the wool bales ; horns must be kept clear of tallow, which may
injure them. Wool should never be stowed on oil, as the casks
are then likely to become very dry, and leakage will follow.
Three average bales of Sydney wool, if properly pressed, will
occupy about forty cubic feet. Sometimes ships with a dead-
weight cargo of nitrate, say at Iquique, proceed to Arica (and or)
Islay, to fill up with alpaca wool. Vessels filled up with this
wool should be supplied with ventilators, either on the hatches
or screwed to the deck, fitted to keep open in any weather ; they
are made of circular iron tubing, about one foot in diameter, and
stand five feet high, with a revolving bonnet over all. Deck
ventilators are the best ; two are sufficient. Alpaca wool (like
saltpetre) is brought to the port of Pisagua in small bundles,
which are sometimes opened, re-packed in larger bales, and
hydraulically pressed for stowage.

THE

AMERICAN FIRE

INSURANCE COMPANY.

INCORPORATED 1810.   CHARTER PERPETUAL.

OFFICE, COMPANY'S BUILDINGS,

308 & 310 WALNUT ST.

PHILADELPHIA.

CASH CAPITAL, ... **$400,000 00**
Reserve for Re-insurance and all other claims, ... **1,070,610 92**
Surplus over all Liabilities, ... **447,821 13**
TOTAL ASSETS, January 1, 1886, ... **1,918,432 05**

TERM AND PERPETUAL INSURANCES.

DIRECTORS.

T. H. MONTGOMERY,	ISRAEL MORRIS,	PEMBERTON S. HUTCHINSON,
JOHN WELSH,	WILLIAM W. PAUL,	CHARLES P. PEROT,
JOHN T. LEWIS,	ALEXANDER BIDDLE,	JOSEPH E. GILLINGHAM.

THOMAS H. MONTGOMERY, President.

ALBERT C. L. CRAWFORD,   RICHARD MARIS,
          Secretary.   Assistant Secretary.

INSURANCE COMPANIES.

The Marine and Fire Insurance Companies of Philadelphia are as sound and reliable as any similar institutions in the United States. The Insurance Company of North America was organized at a meeting of merchants and others held in Independence Hall, Dec. 10, 1792, and this was the first successful effort to create an incorporated company for the taking of marine risks. The first board met the following day at the City Tavern, on Second Street, now the site of the Appraisers' stores. Two days later the company began business in a leased office at No. 213 South Front Street, for which they paid one hundred pounds per annum. Front and Walnut streets were then the centre of business, and the merchants lived over their stores. The Custom House was next door south of the insurance office, the president lived opposite and several of the directors in the neighborhood. The secretary opened the books and wrote the first policies, and in a short time was given the aid of a clerk at $500 salary, and a porter for "six pounds per month and an hint of a douceur at Christmas." The first marine policy was issued on the ship America, bound from Philadelphia to Londonderry, for $5,333.33 at $2\frac{1}{4}$ per cent., and the second on her cargo for $3,200. The United States Bank took policy No. 10, on $20,000 cash brought from Charleston, at 1 per cent. The first six months showed $62,114. premiums received, and the first loss was on the ship Industry, $4,000, paid June 10, 1793. The second six months showed $151,350 premiums. Fire insurance was added to the business in 1794. Fire insurance on goods was at that time unknown, and the first fire policy was issued Dec. 10, 1794, on dry goods, at 21 High Street (now Market Street), for $8,000, at 30 cents per $100 per annum. Life insurance, out of a project for which the company had its origin, was only made to a limited amount, and was abandoned before the company had become 10 years old. The first life policy was issued Feb. 11th, 1794, on Capt. John Collet, "on his person against Algerines or other Barbary Corsairs, in a voyage from Philadelphia to London, in the ship George Barclay, himself master, valuing himself at $5,000." This risk was taken for two per cent.

The company secured a charter from the Pennsylvania Legislature April 14, 1794, a few days only before the charter granted to the Insurance Company of the State of Pennsylvania, which company still exists and occupies an office directly opposite that of the Insurance Company of North America. It was originated in opposition, but always maintained the most . friendly and harmonious relations with its neighbor.

The original authorized capital was $600,000, and upon this the company thrived, but subsequently passed through long periods of adversity, including the fierce wars between England and France, in Napoleon's time, when both nations mercilessly plundered the commerce of the United States. England settled all claims against her, but the celebrated French spoliation claims remain ; but after a persistent energy lasting nearly ninety years, the perseverance of this company has at last been rewarded by an act of the last Congress, sending these claims to the Court of Claims for adjudication. The policy of dividing all of its surplus funds was a great mistake ; the yellow fever almost obliterated its business ; dividends were suspended, and the company found itself compelled to sustain the price of its stock by buying it in the market. In 1842 the stock was reduced to $5 per share, and the capital to $300,000, and on Jan. 1, 1843, the assets had diminished to $385,060. In 1850 they had increased to $911,667. In 1851 the capital was increased to $500,000. In 1858 the assets were $1,007,825, and ten years later were $1,962,836, while $900,000 dividends had been paid during the decade. Then continued a career of almost unexampled prosperity, until in 1885 the capital has reached $3,000,000, the assets $9,079,481, and the company, besides its immense surplus, was paying annual dividends of twenty per cent., amounting to $600,000 a year, and the shares of ten dollars par, are quoted at 36⅛. In 1883-4 the two years premiums were $7,525,601, and the losses paid $4,781,172. During the first half of the present century all the premiums the company received did not amount to $6,000,000, while the losses paid exceeded $5,000,000, so that it now compresses into a single year as much business as was then spread over twenty-five years. Its agencies cover now almost every part of the globe.

The Delaware Mutual Safety Insurance Company is another Philadelphia institution, with assets approximating $1,750,000. Incorporated in 1835, it has steadily expanded its business, and is everywhere noted for its carefulness, solidity, and promptness. This company is largely indebted to its president, Mr. Thomas C. Hand, for its success. His instinctive foresight, and trained knowledge of marine matters, together with great financial abilities, have been largely instrumental in placing the company in its present popular and strong position. It has agencies established in the principal ports, and enjoys a reputation honestly earned. It has paid millions of dollars for marine losses, and has a line of business extended over the entire country.

There are other sound and reliable marine companies which do a steady and profitable business and are safe in every way, and in which the shipping public have great confidence, notably the Insurance Co. of the State of Pennsylvania, and the Union Insurance Co. of Philadelphia. The former is only a few days younger than the Insurance Co. of North America, which is the oldest insurance company in the United States. By good management and prudent expenditures the Insurance Co. of the State of Pennsylvania has accumulated a net surplus exceeding $200,000, which is the amount of its capital stock, while its assets foot up about $700,000. Henry D. Sherrerd, its president, is one of the oldest insurance officers in the city, and is known far and near for his keen judgment and excellent business qualities. Mr. Sherrerd speaking at the semi-centennial celebration of the Franklin Fire Insurance Company, of the peculiarities of the insurance business in Philadelphia, said, " I have stated elsewhere that insurance was without music or poetry, a proposition to-

which I have no doubt you will agree with me.   Nevertheless, I
am in possession of a bill of lading, with an old Dutch galiot for
a vignette, which reads, 'Shipped by the Grace of God, by
George Fox and James Thomas, of Philadelphia, on board the
good ship "Marmaid" (it is to be presumed that she was a sloop)
four boxes of soape bound to Barbadoes,' terminating with the
pious hope, 'and so God send the good ship to her desired port
in safety, bearing date ye 9th mo., 9th, 1696,' one hundred and
eighty-two years ago.   A peculiarity of this bill of lading is that
it is signed by 'Robert Grymes,' the master.   The fame of this
good old man has been celebrated in song and story as long back
as the memory of man runneth ; and it is satisfactory to know
that he pursued the respectable though perilous calling of an
ancient mariner.   So you will perceive that there is some connection between marine insurance and both music and poetry."
It is very evident that Mr. Sherrerd possesses a humorous appreciation of the "eternal fitness of things."   The connection of
"old Grymes" with the insurance business and its hidden music
and poetry, shows the penetrating eye of the "relic of the last
century."

The Union Insurance Company of Philadelphia was incorporated in 1804, and is, therefore, ranked among the grandfathers
of the business.   Its assets are creeping up to a million.   It does
quite a large marine business, and pays losses, if required, in
London, and in the principal seaboard cities on the Continent.
This feature is a desirable one for the assured.

The American Fire Insurance Company was the first company
in this State chartered for a general fire insurance business.   Its
charter bears the date of 1810.   It passed through all of the
financial troubles which wrecked so many incorporated companies
and private business enterprises, and withstood the consequent
monetary depressions of the war with Great Britain, to come out
of it all in a stronger condition than ever.   It started business
with a paid up capital of $200,000, on the 15th of March, 1810,
in the office of the secretary, who resided at No. 73 Chestnut
Street, now 229.   It was shortly afterward removed to No. 111

Chestnut Street, now 311 and 313. The building had been the mansion of Moses Levy, who resided in it when he was City Recorder. The property was purchased for the use of the company. This building is in the device of the company's seal.

Edward Fox and his friends were the active persons in organizing the association, and he was its secretary until the time of his death, which occurred in 1822. Mr. Fox was an uncle of John Sergeant, who some years later became a leading lawyer and politician of this city. He was sent on that mission to Panama which caused so much controversy during the administration of John Quincy Adams, and he subsequently represented the "old city" in Congress. Mr. Sergeant was a director of this company until his death in 1850. While Mr. Fox was secretary, he resided in the dwelling part of the house, as did his successors, until 1840, when this convenient arrangement was abandoned when the office was removed to Walnut Street.

The office of president in those days was considered entirely honorary, and the duties almost exclusively devolved upon the secretary, who was the only salaried officer. The first president, Capt. William Jones, distinguished himself in the war of the Revolution, first in the army and subsequently in the Continental navy, under Commodore Truxton. He was afterwards a member of Congress, was president of the Bank of the United States, and secretary of the U. S. Navy, which office he left to assume the duties of secretary of this company. He was then appointed Naval Officer of this port in 1824 by President Monroe, and died in 1831, at the age of 71.

After occupying its office on Chestnut Street for thirty years, the company removed to Nos. 70 and 72 Walnut Street. This was on a lot adjoining the "old Junkers' Almshouse," whose unsightly wall was so long a detriment to the business of that part of the street. The property was bought in 1838, and the present building was erected at a large expense. The front of the edifice contained two offices, the company occupied the western one, and the second floor subsequently became the first office of the Pennsylvania Railroad Co. Recently the whole front has been converted into one office, which the "American" now occupies.

The "American" was the first Fire Insurance Co. which did an agency business. It did not, however, await the appointment of an agent to write risks in distant cities, and its first loss resulted from the burning of Dr. Burgoyne's dwelling, in Charleston, S. C., in Sept., 1810, before an agent had been appointed for that city.

By an amendment to the charter made in 1812, it was made perpetual, and at once the issuing of perpetual policies was commenced. In 1827 the surplus capital was $83,953, which was gradually increased until 1836, when it amounted to $102,312. In the immediate subsequent years the company was less fortunate, and in the year ending April, 1840, the surplus was reduced to $2,538. In 1847 the Legislature gave permission to the stockholders to reduce the capital to $277,500. The great fire of July 9th, 1850, at Vine and Water Streets, caused a loss to the company of $103,942, which was promptly paid. This was the most serious loss incurred until the fire in Boston, in November, 1872, when the company suffered to the extent of $457,801.

Another amendment of the charter was procured in 1863, which permitted an addition of new stock to the amount of $500,000; and at a meeting of the stockholders, held in May of that year, the existing capital of the company was augmented so as to make it $400,000, at which figure it yet remains.

For the past twenty-five years, the condition of the company has been improving. The last official statement of its finances shows a surplus fund of $640,940.63, and the total assets, $1,545,887.17. There have been nine presidents; and but one vice-president. The latter was Thomas H. Montgomery, the present president, who succeeded Thomas Ross Maris, who resigned April 12, 1882. Mr. Montgomery was elected vice-president in 1880, which office he held until elected president in 1882. The management of this company has always been in good hands. Its present officers are well booked in insurance lore; and the recognition of their ability and activity is daily shown in its increasing business and the steady accumulation of its surplus funds.

The Franklin Fire Insurance Company of Philadelphia occupies an honored place for reliability and fair dealing.

After the old Contributionship, the Mutual Assurance of 1784, the Insurance Co. of North America, 1794, the State of Pennsylvania, 1794, the Union, 1804, the American Fire, 1810, the Fire Association, 1820, the Pennsylvania Fire, 1825, comes the Franklin, 1829, with its wonderful show of continued prosperity and able management. Its history has been one of constant success, and its present elevated position is due to the untiring energy and wise judgment of its officers. None of the original twelve commissioners are living. The first meeting of the stockholders was held June 8th, 1829, when Richard Willing and Charles Dutilh were selected as president and secretary respectively. The company has since had eight presidents, five vice-presidents, eight secretaries and three assistant secretaries, including the present incumbents. It began business June 25, 1829, at No. 163½ Chestnut street, under a lease from Stephen Girard, duly signed by himself. In October, 1844, from the demands of an increasing business, an adjoining property was rented also. These buildings subsequently were numbered 435 and 437. The rental in 1849 was $2,400 per annum, which was gradually increased to $6,000 in 1870. The company moved to its present capacious quarters upon May 1, 1873, the directors having purchased the building to meet the growing wants of the company. The first perpetual policy was issued July 20, 1829, to Alexander Henry, covering a three-story brick building, situate No. 65 North Second street, for the sum of $2,000, at 3 per cent. deposit. The first temporary insurance was placed July 21, for four months, on seven unfinished four-story brick houses, on the S. W. corner of Fourth and Walnut streets, for $5,000, at 30 cts. per $100. Numbers two and three were issued to the firm of Carey, Lea & Carey, the orders being signed in the handwriting of Henry C. Carey, Esq.; Isaac Lea, Esq., a member of that firm, and one of the present directors of this company; is still living at the age of 95 years.

The "Franklin" has paid many large claims for losses by fire in Philadelphia, among which may be named the great fire in

Water street, near Callowhill, in 1850, which cost the company $94,123.96; fire at Strawberry and Bank streets in 1852, $78,453.94; Sixth and Chestnut in 1856, $60,480.09; Fifth and Chestnut in 1854, $53,699.45.

It has always been the aim of the company to carry on the business with safety to both the policy-holders and the share-holders. The latter have become accustomed to the twenty per cent. dividends, and continue to receive it with commendable forbearance and graceful dignity.

The total assets of the "Franklin," January 1, 1886, were $3,130,255.97.

There are many agents in this city representing a large number of foreign companies, both marine and fire. The Liverpool, London and Globe Insurance Co. is well established in its elegant new building on Walnut Street, below Fourth, and enjoys the confidence and patronage of a large portion of the mercantile community and manufacturers.

The Penn Mutual Life Insurance Co., of Philadelphia, was chartered by the Legislature of Pennsylvania on Feb'y 24, 1847. It began operations on the 25th of May following. The company is purely mutual, and its charter provides that all persons who insure in it, and continue to be insured, thereby become members of the corporation, and entitled to elect the trustees, who manage its business. The profits are annually divided among the policy-holders in equitable proportion. The first division of surplus was made in 1849, and annual divisions have since been made.

The transactions of this company were restricted for many years to the States of Pennsylvania, Delaware and Maryland. Its business has been more limited in amount than that of other companies of its age and standing, the operations of which were extended in many cases over every portion of our country. The aim of the officers and trustees has been not to do a large busi-ness, but rather a moderate and safe one, and their course has been strictly conservative as regards the investment of their funds, and the acceptance of risks offered them, as well as the region of country in which they have transacted business. The number of policies issued by the company from its organization to the 31st day of December, 1885, was 41,788, insuring over $90,000,000, of which 19,834, covering insurance to the amount of $47,989,223 were in force at that date. Its last annual statement shows that over 69 per cent. of the entire premium receipts of the company has been returned to members or their families, in death losses, endowments, returned premiums, or surplus, and surrendered policies; that but 13 per cent. has been expended for commissions, office and other expenses, rents, etc., and that nearly 33 per cent. of the gross receipts is yet in possession of the company as a reserve for future losses, and as surplus to be returned to members to reduce the payment of their future premiums.

The gross assets of the Company on the first day of January, 1886, amounted to $10,392,531.21. In order to afford ample security to the members, the Company's reserve for re-insurance is based upon interest at the rate of four per cent. only, and by this standard the Company has a surplus of $1,432,234.38. Based upon the requirements of the Insurance Departments of Pennsylvania and New York, it has a surplus of nearly $1,969,283, being more than $123 of invested funds for every $100 of liabilities, present or contingent. This evidence of stability and ample security, united with the fact that the returns of surplus have averaged nearly 26 per cent. of the premiums received since its organization, is a source of gratification to the management, which has maintained so high a degree of security while furnishing insurance at low cost.

Although the Guarantee Company of North America is neither a Marine nor Fire Company, it is, strictly speaking, an Insurance Company, and the statement of its business may be placed under this head with just a modicum of squeezing. The Company represents a Corporate Suretyship, and made its first contract with corporations of the United States in 1873. It was organized in 1872, but having afterwards absorbed two companies dating back to 1863, it may be said to possess the experience of its predecessors, which failed of success through associating other branches of insurance with its suretyship. This Company has a

Canadian charter, although the bulk of its capital and business is in the United States, which renders it virtually an American Company. It guarantees the honesty of cashiers, tellers, collectors, clerks, and, in fact, all persons holding positions of trust; and as the defaulter's eye is generally cast towards Canada as the haven of security against interference, the Company, by having a Canadian charter, is in a desirable position to successfully interview the nocturnal excursionist. The Guarantee transacts the business of guarantee pure and simple upon a sound and legitimate basis, such as that of the original Guarantee Society of London, which has successfully transacted this business for 42 years.

The company, and the two it absorbed, have paid no less than $750,000 in recouping employers for the defaults of dishonest employes. In addition to its having two-thirds of its capital in the United States, it has branch offices, with regular working boards, secretaries, and inspectors in nearly all of the great financial centres, and ample balances appear to the credit of each branch for local purposes. The boards of directors are composed of men at the head of some of the most important and influential institutions of the country. Its list of patrons comprises the majority of the railroad, express, and telegraph corporations, together with an array of many of the leading banks in the Continent, numbering in all over 600 corporations. It has paid in the United States alone several hundreds of claims made by these corporations for losses sustained by unfaithful employes, and has not in a single instance had recourse to law to evade payment.

The capital and resources of the Guarantee Company of North America are ample, footing up some $800,000. Its business is strictly confined to the bonding of officers and employes of financial and commercial corporations. It does not go beyond this. It does not venture on the risks of bonds for guardians, trustees, State officers, or contractors. It has a revenue of over $160,000 per annum, and is second only to the old Guarantee Society of London, the largest company of the kind in the world.

The board in Montreal has among its members Sir Alexander T. Galt, president; the Hon. James Ferrier, chairman of the Grand Trunk Railway, vice-president; and Mr. W. J. Buchanan, general manager of the Bank of Montreal, with Mr. Edward Rawlings, managing director, names which carry the assurance of conservatism and business integrity. The Philadelphia directors are Benjamin B. Comegys, Pres't. Philadelphia National Bank; J. Livingston Erringer, Pres't. Philadelphia Trust and Safe Deposit Co.; Alfred M. Collins, of A. M. Collins, Sons & Co.; Henry Lewis, director Philadelphia and Reading R. R. Co.; John C. Sims, Jr., Sec'y. Pennsylvania R. R. Co., etc. The Philadelphia Branch Office is located at 506 Walnut Street, with A. F. Sabine, Esq., as agent and attorney.

The total business in force Jan. 1st, 1886, was 18,402 bonds covering $25,207,650; the gross annual premiums on which are $195,877.70. Its net assets were $457,168.46, and the capital subscribed and subject to call, $368,600; making the total resources, $825,768.46.

FINANCIAL AND COMMERCIAL NOTICES.

The banking facilities of Philadelphia are fully adequate to meet the requirements of business. New capital is added as business enterprises increase. Elegant bank edifices are erected with all the modern improvements and ancient styles of architecture, ornamental to an extreme, and as safe against fire and burglars as could possibly be devised, while many of the old banks are sprucing up to suit the tastes of their patrons, and add to the comfort and convenience of the officers. The new building of the National Bank of the Republic, next door to its solid neighbor the First National, and the ancient and wealthy North America, is one of the finest and most ornamental structures in this city. A full description of this building may be found herein, on a page especially reserved for it, and opposite a fine phototype picture taken by Gutekunst, representing the exterior of the bank. The business of this bank has greatly increased during the past few months, and with a continuance of the present Board of Directors, whose management is characterized by good judgment and liberality, nothing can prevent the National Bank of the Republic from always enjoying the confidence of its many friends and making many new ones.

The Columbian Bank was incorporated in 1871 with an authorized capital of one million dollars. It has branches and agencies in all the principal cities in the world. It transacts a general banking and agency business, both domestic and foreign, and is able to offer facilities which meet every requirement of financial business. Its business is divided into several departments, viz.: —Banking Department, Saving Fund Department, Foreign Exchange Department, Stock Department, and Commercial Department. It receives accounts of individuals, corporations, etc.;

makes collections on every point, and in all currencies; discounts sound commercial paper; makes loans upon collateral security; gives particular attention to savings fund accounts; acts as treasurer and fiscal agent of building societies, etc.; issues circular notes, which are received as cash in all countries of the world; buys and sells bills of exchange on all parts of Europe and the East, China, Japan, Mexico, Canada, South America, West Indies, etc.; procures passports; buys and sells, strictly on commission, bonds, stocks, and other securities; issues commercial credits available in all parts of the world; executes orders for merchandise in foreign countries, merely charging a small commission upon the original invoice; attends to all custom-house business; and, in fact, gives special care and attention to all the details of the regular business coming under the several heads indicated by the names of the several departments. Its Philadelphia office is at 433 Chestnut street, and its Baltimore agency at 8 South street.

The Guarantee Trust and Safe Deposit Co., which occupies its new and commodious building on Chestnut Street, above Third, has a capital of one million dollars, and the most complete facilities of any similar corporation in the city. Its fire and burglar proof vaults are as complete and protective as the ingenuity of man could devise. This company collects interest on incomes, allows interest on deposits, executes trusts, acts as Registrar or transfer agent of mining, railroad, and other corporation stocks, receives valuables of every description, under guarantee, and transacts other business of that character and in that line which the title of the company suggests. The directors are some of the most solid and sagacious business men of Philadelphia, and its officers are men of large experience and marked ability.

The Chalmers-Spence Co., of this city, are manufacturers of non-conducting coverings, asbestos products, and fire-proof materials, and they have established a trade in these articles which is continually expanding. The merits of their Asbestos materials are as follows:—

17

As a non-conductor of heat.—The practice of applying non-conducting coverings on steam and other heated surfaces to prevent the radiation of heat is now universal. No enlightened engineer questions the desirability of such practice or doubts the saving of fuel as a result. On the contrary, he endeavors to procure for his use the best covering he can obtain and that his employer will pay for. On examining the many kinds of non-conducting materials in the market, we find that coverings may be divided into two classes; the composition or plastic coverings and the felt or fabric coverings. Which, of the many offered, may be the best, is a matter of great diversity of opinion. It involves the question of cheapness, durability and efficiency. We dispose of the question of cheapness by the assertion that, within a reasonable limit of cost, a cheap covering is one that possesses durability and efficiency in a high degree. The durability of *asbestos* under the most intense radiated heat, is a matter of fact and not opinion. Its long mineral fibres remain quite unaffected by intense heat and chemical or mechanical action. No other known fibre, useful in the manufacture of coverings, possesses these qualities. Any covering, then, having a large proportion of pure *asbestos fibre* must, if properly constructed, have a high degree of durability. All the higher grades of covering made by this company contain from 25 to 100 per cent. of pure *asbestos*, and are the most durable goods of the kind known. In the matter of durability, therefore, *asbestos* stands unrivalled. In the matter of efficiency, there are various and conflicting opinions. This is chiefly because many people have been misled by so-called experts, who decide upon the merits of various coverings after a few weeks' trial, praising the most efficient regardless of durability. Manifestly a covering that shows a high degree of efficiency but burns out or goes to pieces in a year or so is not a desirable covering. Leaving out of the question then, all materials containing organic or perishable substances, we find on examining composition coverings that those constructed of infusorial earths show less radiation of heat than any other plastic materials; but they have very little structural strength. Of the felt coverings it is also known that fibres felted so as to hold air in the interstices form better non-conductors of heat than any other fabrics. Hair felt, for instance, is a superior non-conductor; but it perishes under a moderate heat. With these facts in view, this company is manufacturing a composition in which infusorial earth, giving high non-conducting powers, is combined with *asbestos fibre*, giving great structural strength and durability. They call it Patent Infusorial Silicate Composition. For a felt or fabric covering, they manufacture a patent removable covering, in which pure *asbestos fibre* in felted form is placed between confining walls of the same material. In this they obtain the air-confining and heat-resisting structure of hair felt in the lasting and heat-enduring form of *asbestos*.

Asbestos as a Steam Packing.—The Chalmers-Spence Co.'s steam packing made from this mineral appeals at once to the judgment of engineers. The long fibres are braided into the various forms of cotton or hemp piston and valve packings, and the same elasticity and compactness is obtained, but with greater durability. The millboard and sheathing for flat joints is cheaper and more lasting than rubber or any other composition that is used. *Asbestos* does not burn or char under the heat of superheated steam, and is not affected by acids.

Asbestos as a Fire-proof Material.—The uninflammable qualities of *asbestos* render it a useful lining for any fire-exposed portions of buildings or vessels. It is cheaper than iron, and just as serviceable.

Asbestos in the Mechanical Arts.—It is impossible to enumerate the many uses to which *asbestos* is put. Metal-workers, glassmakers, chemists and others find it useful in moulding, soldering and handling their goods, and an improvement over old methods.

The curtain now in use in the American Academy of Music is made of *asbestos* cloth, furnished by this Company, and is believed to be the only complete barrier of protection to an audience in case of fire, *in the world*.

Being miners and manufacturers, this Company has the advantage of being first hands, and can therefore sell at the lowest possible figures.

It has many prominent customers in all parts of the country, among which may be named, Ocean Steamship Co., N. Y., and Cuba Mail Steamship Co., Pacific Mail Steamship Co., Clyde Coastwise Lines, East River Bridge, U. S. Custom House and Post Office, Quintard Iron Works, Pennsylvania Steel Works, The E. & G. Brooke Iron Co., Bethlehem Iron Co., Cambria Iron Co., Carnegie Bros., Continental Sugar Refinery, J. A. Roebling's Sons Co. The company has offices at New York, Chicago, Providence, and Pittsburgh.

Among the ship yards alluded to on page 14, should be specially named that of Morris & Mathis, Ship Builders and Contractors, at Cooper's Point, Camden. They occupy a most eligible location which is well adapted for their business. Their yard embraces about three acres of ground, and is well supplied with all the paraphernalia for building and repairing vessels. They usually employ from seventy-five to one hundred skilled workmen, and as nothing but the very best material is used, the work is always satisfactory and of the highest degree of merit. They have turned out some of the very best wooden vessels afloat. Being practical ship builders and fully posted regarding the wants of the different trades, both foreign and domestic, they are able to supply what is needed. Considerable experience in this special branch of business, and a thorough knowledge of maritime matters are absolutely necessary to insure success. It is well known that this firm is possessed of every requisite, which explains the reason for the reputation which they enjoy, and the large line of work which they have on hand when the shipping business is in any way active. The fact that they give almost as much study and personal care to the repairing of vessels as is required on new work, and are fully as careful, is another reason for their popularity among vessel owners.

The old-established Steam Engine and Boiler Works, at Beach and Marlborough streets, of which A. L. Archambault is proprietor, continue to furnish all descriptions of high pressure, jet and surface condensing, single or compound engines, with boilers to suit, for steam-tugs or yachts of any length or power, and also propeller wheels from 2 to 8 feet, cast to order. Mr. Archambault is the builder of the celebrated portable engine which bears his name, with or without hoisting drum, from 8 to 30 horse-power. The vertical engines built at these works are everywhere noted for their durability and power. They are in constant use at iron mills, machine works, paint works, etc., and cost so little to keep in repair, and require such a small quantity of coal to run them, that they are classed among the most economical engines in use. Many of the tug-boats owned in Philadelphia are supplied with engines from these works, and the severe strain to which they are often subjected, and the labor they are made to perform are good evidences of their superiority.

Want of space prevents further mention of special business enterprises. An attempt to enumerate them in detail would astonish even the compiler himself. They are multitudinous in number and varied in character, and comprise every feature of commercial importance as well as of industry and skill, and show the immense resources which Philadelphia possesses which could be easily further developed to its honor and profit.

In closing this volume, the editor assures his many friends and patrons, of his proper appreciation of their kind co-operation and assistance in imparting to him much of the desired information on many of the leading subjects of this work, and would as heartily respond to any inquiries that may be made from any source regarding the maritime interests of Philadelphia, and its commercial relations with the world.

NATIONAL BANK OF THE REPUBLIC,
OF PHILADELPHIA.

AMONG recent specimens of bank architecture is the new banking house of the National Bank of the Republic, of Philadelphia. An illustration of the front of this beautiful and unique building is shown on the opposite page. It is of English red-stone and Philadelphia red pressed brick, surmounted by red tile and slate roof. The building covers a lot of thirty feet front and one hundred and eighty feet in depth. The main banking room is twenty-nine feet wide, one hundred and twenty feet long and thirty-four feet high, and is lighted from sky and ceiling lights throughout its length. The interior finish is of cherry; the counters and desks are of mahogany and beveled plate glass; the walls, where not of tile and richly carved Caen stone, are painted in warm colors, a rich dark red predominating, the effect of which is novel and pleasing; and the main floor throughout is covered with red and small black tiles laid upon brick arches. The main room is divided by the mahogany partitions into apartments for officers, tellers and clerks, back of which is the directors' room. The vaults are of massive granite work with steel lining, within which are steel safes. The bank occupies the entire building, giving ample room in all the apartments and abundant space outside of counters. The building is heated by steam and from open fire-places, and is admirably ventilated.

On December 5, 1885, the National Bank of the Republic completed the first twenty years of its existence, and was duly authorized to continue for another twenty years under a renewal of its charter until Dec. 5, 1905.

The officers are William H. Rhawn, President, and Joseph P. Mumford, Cashier, both of whom received their training in the old Philadelphia Bank, and have been together nearly twenty years in their respective positions.

During the year that the Bank has occupied its new banking house it has received a gratifying increase of business, as shown in the statement below, reported to the Comptroller of the Currency on March 1st, 1886.

RESOURCES.		LIABILITIES.	
Loans and Discounts .	$2,215,336 01	Capital Stock	$500,000 00
Real Estate, Furniture		Surplus and Net Pro-	
and Safes , . . .	115,287 10	fits	290,719 73
Due from Banks . . .	174,864 40	Circulation	450,000 00
Cash and Reserve . .	1,337,419 86	Deposits	2,602,187 64
Total	$3,842,907 37	Total	$3,842,907 37

The policy of the Bank has always dictated the selection of active business men for its Directors, and the names of those now serving are:

WILLIAM H. RHAWN,

FREDERIC A. HOYT,	CHARLES T. PARRY,	HENRY W. SHARPLESS,
CHARLES RICHARDSON,	JAMES M. EARLE,	EDWIN J. HOWLETT,
WILLIAM HACKER,	JOHN F. SMITH,	EDWARD K. BISPHAM,
WILLIAM B. BEMENT,	HOWARD HINCHMAN,	HENRY T. MASON.

F. GUTEKUNST. Front 30 Feet. Depth 180 Feet. PHOTOTYPE

NATIONAL BANK OF THE REPUBLIC,

No. 313 CHESTNUT STREET,

PHILADELPHIA.

JOSEPH P. MUMFORD, 1884. WILLIAM H. RHAWN,
CASHIER. PRESIDENT.

◁INDEX TO ADVERTISERS▷

www.ingramcontent.com/pod-product-compliance
Lightning Source LLC
Chambersburg PA
CBHW030339270326
41926CB00009B/885